Justice

and Economic Distribution

Edited by

JOHN ARTHUR

WILLIAM H. SHAW

University of Tennessee-Nashville

Justice

and Economic Distribution

PRENTICE-HALL, INC., *Englewood Cliffs, New Jersey* 07632

Library of Congress Cataloging in Publication Data

Main entry under title:

Justice and economic distribution.

    Includes bibliographical references.
    1. Distributive justice—Addresses, essays,
lectures. I. Arthur, John, 1946-
II. Shaw, William H., 1948-
HB771.J87   330   77-27951
ISBN 0-13-514166-4

Printed in the United States of America

10 9 8 7

PRENTICE-HALL INTERNATIONAL, INC., *London*
PRENTICE-HALL OF AUSTRALIA PTY. LIMITED, *Sydney*
PRENTICE-HALL OF CANADA, LTD., *Toronto*
PRENTICE-HALL OF INDIA PRIVATE LIMITED, *New Delhi*
PRENTICE-HALL OF JAPAN, INC., *Tokyo*
PRENTICE-HALL OF SOUTHEAST ASIA PTE. LTD., *Singapore*
WHITEHALL BOOKS LIMITED, *Wellington, New Zealand*

For Beth and Jim and Mary

contents

Part II   Criticisms and Alternatives   133

preface

The vast disparities in wealth and styles of life between virtual neighbors in the same society often seem incredible. How, it is natural to ask, can it be just or fair that some persons are barely able to meet even their minimum nutritional needs, while others spend hundreds of dollars a month heating their private swimming pools? Perhaps even more striking than this is the fact that so many take this state of affairs to be normal, never questioning its legitimacy. Yet, in other contexts, the fairness of society's economic arrangements is an issue about which people feel strongly. Individuals argue, agitate, campaign, organize, lobby, and fight over the justice of the allocation of economic goods and bads. Are taxes fair? Is welfare a rip-off? What about farm subsidies? Do corporations deserve their huge profits, or their executives and owners such large salaries and other benefits? Lying behind political disputes, frequently, are rival claims and assumptions about economic justice, and examining these leads one to philosophy. Today, certainly, the problem of what constitutes a just economic distribution is central to social and political philosophy.

This anthology is an attempt to bring together in a single volume the ideas of some of the most perceptive and interesting contemporary writers on this subject. The book itself was inspired by an undergraduate seminar taught by the editors in which we utilized the well-known work of John Rawls and Robert Nozick to introduce students to this much debated topic. While the controversy between Rawls and Nozick provides a springboard for many of the authors, the book is not just a collection of secondary criticisms. The articles include both analyses of the normative and methodological issues raised by these and other familiar positions and original, positive contributions to the debate by philosophers of the left and right.

Throughout the process of working with contributors and organizing this volume, we have endeavored to strike a balance between philosophical sophistication on the one hand and the needs of philosophy students on the other. With this goal in mind, our contributors have made a special effort to avoid needless technicality and recondite issues. Our introductory essay and the shorter introductions to each of the sections are designed to provide sufficient background for introductory students to follow, at least in broad outline, the major argument.

Finally, we wish to thank our contributors for their enthusiasm and cooperation in this project. Professors Rawls and Nozick also deserve our gratitude for allowing the republication of selections from *A Theory of Justice* and *Anarchy, State, and Utopia*. We have, of course, been able to present only an overview of their positions on justice and economic distribution. While this serves well enough for many purposes, readers must be referred to the complete books if they are to appreciate the full richness of these theories.

John Arthur
William H. Shaw

on the problem of
economic justice

The problem of economic justice can be expressed with remarkable simplicity: On what basis should economic goods and services be distributed? Answers to this question, however, are as numerous as those to any important philosophical issue. Some (libertarians) believe that the operation of a free market guarantees justice. Others (utilitarians) hold that the needs or interests of people should be of primary concern. Still others look to how much is deserved, as measured by labor time, effort, or contribution, as the basis for distribution. Equal distribution, since it seems to reflect the common humanity shared by all, is also viewed by many to be the core of economic justice. The philosophical problem is to decide which among these and other positions is in fact superior, and to give reasons for one's conclusion which will convince others.

This volume is an attempt to help us resolve the issue of economic justice. The very existence of such an anthology, however, reflects an important fact about recent events in the philosophical world: Issues of social justice have been close to center stage for nearly a decade. That this is so will not seem surprising to nonphilosophers, but it was not so many years ago that political philosophy was declared by its former practitioners to be dead. The announcement of its passing, however, startled no one because its illness had been widely acknowledged to be terminal, and philosophers had already turned their attentions elsewhere.

The disease with which political philosophy was presumed to have been stricken had been diagnosed much earlier as a congenital ailment

1

of all moral theory. Logical positivism classified as meaningless any prop-
osition which was neither verifiable by empirical evidence nor true by
definition and so relegated ethical and political theory to the realm of
nonsense, along with poetry, metaphysics, and other emotional ejacu-
lations. No serious philosopher, so it was thought, need waste his or
her time on social or moral philosophy. This advice was not entirely
heeded, and philosophers, under the influence of so-called ordinary language philosophy, began to turn their attention to the analysis of the
key terms of ethical discourse. Philosophy could have something to say
about morality, but still one should not expect too much. In particular,
it was said, one should not expect philosophy to provide any substantive
answers to the hard questions of ethics and social policy. There is a
logic to moral and social discourse, but the truth of these matters cannot
be known; indeed there is no real truth to know because in the end it is
all a matter of individual emotional preference.

A rejection of the narrow horizons of logical positivism and a close
attention to actual linguistic practice—both products of ordinary language philosophy—did, however, guide some away from this dead end.
Philosophers looked more carefully at the nature of ethical discourse
and were forced to abandon their noncognitivism (that is, the belief that
ethical claims can be neither correct nor incorrect) for an appreciation
of the real and legitimate role which reasoning and argument play in
moral and political philosophy and of the possibility of reaching philosophical answers to the pressing questions of those topics.

Gradually in the late 1950s and then throughout the 1960s, articles,
anthologies, and books appeared as interest was restored in substantive
political philosophy. John Rawls' *A Theory of Justice,* published in
1971, marked a watershed, as growing attention to social philosophy
evolved into a major concern of the discipline. While philosophers now
explore confidently such topics as preferential hiring, health care de-
livery, and civil disobedience, among many others, a central concern of
social and political philosophy has been, and remains, that of economic
justice. This is not surprising, since it is an issue which lies at the heart
of all philosophizing about society: What constitutes a just distribution
of the benefits and burdens of economic life?

THE CONCEPT OF JUSTICE

Justice is an old concept with a rich history, a concept which is fundamental to any discussion of how society ought to be organized. Philosophical concern with it goes back at least to ancient Greece. For Plato
and some of his contemporaries, justice seems to have been the para-
mount virtue or, more precisely, the sum of virtue with regard to our
relations with others. "Justice" had the ring of "righteousness," and to
know an act was just was to know it was right. Although there is still a
sense in which to do what is just is to do what is right, philosophers
today generally distinguish justice from the whole of morality.

To claim something is "unjust" is a more specific complaint than to say it is "bad" or "immoral." I may be rude to you, behave selfishly, sleep with your spouse, and engage in a variety of other naughty or immoral behavior without—it seems—being unjust to you. On the other hand, an act which is unjust might be morally justified on the whole, as when the necessities of war require denial of legal due process to a traitor. We can make sense of the thought that the act is unjust but, on balance, still should be done. This suggests that in speaking of justice or injustice we are discussing only one sphere of the moral picture. In general, however, an injustice is acceptable only if it can be shown that the consequence of not committing it would be very bad indeed, and to know something is unjust is to have a good reason to think it is wrong overall.

If justice is a part of morality, what sorts of facts make an act unjust rather than simply wrong in general? Consider someone who is locked up for criticizing the government; here liberty has been violated and an injustice done. Similarly, if someone else is punished for a crime he did not commit or is singled out from his philosophy class and required to write twice as many papers as the others, then we naturally speak of injustice.

What seems to be going on is that talk of justice or injustice focuses on at least one of several related ideas. First, a claim that one is treated unjustly often suggests that one's moral rights have been violated—in particular, that one has been made to suffer some burden one had a right to avoid or has been denied some benefit one had a right to possess. If we agree to go into business together and you back out without justification, costing me time and money, then you have violated a right of mine and I may well claim that you have treated me unjustly.

Second, the term *injustice* is often used to mean *unfairness*. Justice frequently concerns the treatment of members of groups of people or else looks backwards to the compensating of prior injuries, demanding fairness in our handling of such situations. Exactly what fairness requires is hard to say, and different standards may well be applied to the same case. If Nixon committed high crimes and misdemeanors, he is justly impeached under the Constitution. If Presidents Kennedy and Johnson committed equally heinous acts, then Nixon suffers a comparative injustice since he was singled out. On the other hand, our treatment of Nixon and other white-collar lawbreakers is unjust, although this time for the opposite reason, when compared to the stiffer sentences meted out to "common" criminals for less grave offenses.

Injustice in one sense of unfairness occurs when like cases are not treated in the same fashion. Following Aristotle, many philosophers believe that we are required, as a formal principle of justice, to treat similar cases alike except where there is some relevant difference. This principle emphasizes the role of impartiality and consistency in justice, but it is purely formal because we are not told which differences are relevant and which are not. Satisfying this formal requirement, furthermore, does not guarantee that justice is done; for example, by treating like cases similarly a judge can administer non-arbitrarily a law (like an apartheid regulation in South Africa) which is in fact unjust. (Similarly it may be noted that a fair procedure can lead to unjust results, as when a guilty man is mistakenly acquitted by an honest jury, or vice versa, as when the police unscrupulously trick a person who turns out to be guilty into confessing.)

Related to Aristotle's fairness requirement is a third idea commonly bound up with the concept of justice, namely, that of equality. "All persons are morally equal," it is said, and so justice is frequently held to require that our treatment of them reflect this fact. While Aristotle's formal principle of justice does not say whether we are to assume equality of treatment until some difference between cases is shown or to assume the opposite until some relevant similarities are demonstrated, a claim of injustice based on *equality* is meant to place the burden of proof on those who would endorse unequal treatment.

The demand that equality be respected, though still abstract, does have more content than the two previously mentioned aspects of justice. Even so, to claim simply that all persons are equal is not to establish a relationship between justice and economic distribution. We all believe that *some* differences in the treatment of persons are consistent with equality (punishment, for example), and neither respect for equality nor the requirement of equal treatment implies by itself an egalitarian distribution of economic goods.

Despite equality, then, individual circumstances—in particular, what a person has done—do make a difference. We think it is unfair, for example, when a guilty person goes free or an innocent person hangs, regardless of how others have been treated, because the first fails to get his or her due and the second suffers an undeserved fate. This suggests that justice sometimes involves, as a fourth aspect, something beyond equal or even impartial treatment: justice requires that individuals get what they deserve. But what do people deserve? A substantive theory of justice is needed to answer this as well as to explain when a failure to get what one deserves is a failure of justice. (For example, if I study hard for the exam, while Roger with his photographic memory goofs off all term, it may seem that I deserve to pass more than he. But when Roger breezes through the test and I fail, have I been done an injustice?) Nonetheless, the idea of desert, however it is fleshed out, is frequently tied up with discourse about justice.

Social and Economic Justice

Justice, then, is an important subclass of morality in general, a subclass which generally involves appeals to the overlapping notions of rights, fairness, equality, or desert. Justice is not the only virtue an individual or a social institution can pursue, and many of the most difficult moral dilemmas arise when the requirements of justice conflict with other goods or obligations.

Within the general category of justice, however, further distinctions must be drawn. In particular, many cases of injustice are not instances of *social* injustice. Consider, for example, parents who permit only their favorite daughter to attend college, when it is within their means to send all their children. They behave unfairly, but the injustice in question is not a social injustice. While justice is in a sense a social virtue, since it is a characteristic of our relations with others, the concept of social justice is not used to capture this simple fact. Rather, social justice refers to the *structure* and *policies* of a society, to its political, legal, economic, and social institutions. (Are they fair? Do they violate rights? Do they reflect the equality of citizens?) Thus a constitutional structure which gives undue influence to one group is unjust, as is a policy requiring the registration of Jews. Both cases involve the shared institutions of a society; they are failures of social justice. A corrupt judge who abuses the legal system by throwing an innocent into jail perpetrates a grievous injustice, but such an individual transgression is not a matter of social injustice unless the social system in question tolerates or encourages such corruption.

Justice in general and social justice in particular involve the distribution of benefits and burdens, but distributive justice has come to be synonymous with economic justice, that is, with the distribution of *economic* benefits and burdens. Social justice includes but is not identical to economic justice, although both are concerned in part with how to distribute things that people care about. Political powers and liberties may be distributed unjustly, yet this is not a problem of economic justice as such (unless, perhaps, the political injustice in question results from a particular economic distribution).

Distinguishing the distribution of economic from other social goods goes only part of the way toward defining our subject. Worldwide poverty and starvation, for example, raise serious moral problems involving the distribution of economic goods, yet these problems are not obviously ones of economic *justice* at all. How can this be if, as some philosophers maintain, there is no relevant moral difference between aiding a person in your own town and helping someone overseas?

Some, of course, think that for one person to have more than another is intrinsically unjust, but disparity of wealth itself cannot be the source of the injustice. (Only in a cosmic or poetic sense is it unjust for me to thrive on my Iowa farm while you barely eke out an existence in the Yukon.) If we are to speak of justice at all, there must be some relation between the parties by virtue of which a right is violated or an unfairness done. And furthermore, if we are to speak of hunger overseas as being a matter of social or, more specifically, economic justice for us, the situation must reflect upon the policies or structure of our society as a whole. (Other moral considerations, of course, may oblige us to assist those in need outside our own country, if justice does not.)

However, even if foreign poverty were a matter of economic justice for some wealthy country (perhaps because it enjoys an economically exploitative relation with the countries in question or because its hoarding of resources violates some right of theirs), there would still be the issue of the justice of its own economic institutions as this affects its citizens. The joint enterprises and shared institutions of a society, the economic interrelatedness and mutual dependence of its citizens, and the fact that its members often view themselves as a community of persons who share certain aims and ideals suggest that the question of intra-societal economic distribution is different from moral problems concerning relations between persons in separate societies. In addition, it may be, as some philosophers think, that resolving the former issue will shed light on the latter, just as, in general, determining the requirements of justice will take us some way toward understanding our overall moral obligation. In any case, intra-societal economic distribution is the topic of the writers in this volume.

Finally, it is worth noting that the philosophical problem of economic justice is distinct from the numerous empirical problems discussed by economists. The latter are largely concerned to predict outcomes of various economic policies. Important examples are the effect of monetary and fiscal policy on prices and employment, and of tax schedules on capital investment, spending, and saving. Now obviously any philosopher should consider such factors in arguing for a particular conception of economic justice, at least to the extent of ensuring that implementation of a certain philosophy will not have a disastrous economic impact. Still, the point to emphasize here is that the two questions (economic justice and the impact of policies) are distinct. Just as a theory of economic justice must take economics into account, so also it is important that economists should consider philosophy. What use is predicting the effect of policies until it is known what end ought to be sought or what justice requires?

DIFFERENT APPROACHES

How, then, ought economic costs and benefits to be distributed? Although some answers, like "according to race or sex," can surely be ruled out, there is still a wide range of principles which have been offered in answer to this question. Distribution has been recommended in accordance with equality, need, and effort, to name only a few.

Strict equality of income may appear superficially attractive. Yet distribution of society's product according to this criterion would ignore what seem to be morally relevant differences: for example, some people have dependents to feed or large medical bills to pay. A satisfactory principle of equality will surely require that individual circumstances and needs be respected, not denied.

Distribution according to need, however, ignores the question of how much is deserved. A lazy student may need a passing grade more than a diligent one, but his need hardly seems a just basis for his passing. Similarly, that Jones worked hard and Smith did not would seem to be important in determining a just distribution of income. In addition, since no society could hope to satisfy every whim of every person, notorious problems are posed by trying to compare needs between individuals or by trying to discriminate between basic needs and secondary ones (or "true" needs and "false" ones).

Questions of merit and desert are discussed further in Part II, but it is clear that while effort, ability, contribution, or moral merit may seem plausible as a basis of distribution in some circumstances, each faces problems when elevated to *the* principle of economic justice. This has led some philosophers to deny that any single principle of distribution will suffice. Combining two or more criteria, however, into a more complicated principle seems almost as arbitrary—which criteria should one choose and which are to be weighed more heavily? As a result, other philosophers have denied that there is a solution to the issue of distributive justice. The problem is so complicated, they seem to say, that we had best leave things alone.

This skeptical conclusion is inescapable if we continue only to juxtapose or combine simple principles of distribution. The answer will come only if one has recourse to a more general normative theory which provides a theoretical reason to justify a particular economic distribution.

Utilitarianism is one such theory. According to it, the rightness of an action or social policy is determined by its total consequences for all concerned, measured in terms of happiness (or satisfied desires). Justice is not a consideration which is independent of this general principle, and utilitarians would demur to the categorization of justice as a specific realm within morality as a whole. For them there is only one moral issue: Which course of action promotes the greatest sum of happiness for all concerned? Accordingly, the best distribution of economic goods is that which produces more happiness than any other. Which system actually provides this optimal distribution is an empirical question for social scientists to resolve.

Although utilitarianism in its various guises has been popular for over a century, it has been thought by many to be seriously flawed. Utilitarianism, some philosophers charge, does not take seriously enough the differences between persons. The happiness of each person should not count equally in the total, without regard to his or her past behavior. Further, an increase in total happiness might be unfairly purchased at the price of the pain of some innocent individual.

John Rawls is among those contemporary philosophers unhappy with utilitarianism, and his social contract approach is an effort to find an alternative theoretical basis for determining social and economic justice. We are to imagine ourselves in a hypothetical situation, choosing the principles of distribution which will then serve to govern all members of society. In Rawls' view, such a choice should be made without knowledge of one's own race, religion, or social position in order to insure the fairness of the result. It is a hypothetical thought experiment which, he argues, guarantees that whatever principles are chosen are just. Rawls gives the term "difference principle" to the choice which, he contends, would be made by his social contractors—namely, that economic goods should be distributed equally unless an unequal distribution would

work to the benefit of all, especially the worst off. Justice for Rawls is
not the only focal point of morality, but it is the first virtue of social
institutions.

Even philosophers who are dissatisfied with Rawls' approach, his
principles of justice, or both acknowledge that he has raised the level of
discourse in political philosophy to a new height. Robert Nozick is one
of those philosophers, and his disagreements with Rawls set the stage
for the discussion of economic justice in this volume. Agreeing only with
Rawls' repudiation of utilitarianism, Nozick's libertarian philosophy operates with a radically different conception of the relation of the individual to society. Liberty is the cardinal political virtue. Justice ensures
the right of individuals not to be coerced, a right which cannot be overridden by other moral obligations. Beyond this, justice insists upon little.
Whatever economic arrangements individuals freely consent to are just,
and Nozick's entitlement theory holds simply that a distribution is just
if it results, via gifts or voluntary exchanges, from a prior just distribution. The type of economic system which justice requires is a laissez-
faire, free-market system.

This conclusion is rejected by both J. J. C. Smart and R. M. Hare,
who present the case for utilitarianism. Although they argue from vastly
different theoretical perspectives, they unite in defending utilitarian theory in the face of the rival approaches of Rawls and Nozick. Part I of
this book thus presents the three major approaches to economic justice
which dominate contemporary political philosophy. Part II proceeds to
explore various issues raised by this clash of perspectives, probe short-
comings in the leading theories, and suggest alternative positions. First,
however, it will be useful to offer some further, more general reflections
on the debate.

Remarks on Methodology

There are three general questions that may be asked about a theory
which tries to resolve a moral dispute of this sort. The first is, of course,
What answer does the theory offer—what principle of distribution does
it recommend? The governing criterion could be one which looks to
the past behavior of individuals (effort), their present situation (need),
their choices (market distribution), or their structural relations (the difference principle or equality), among other possibilities. Justice might
be thought to require a certain distributive result or only a particular
process or method of distribution.

There is more than one way, it should be noted, to defend a particular principle or organization of distribution. For example, contemporary
libertarians argue for an unregulated, capitalistic market society in terms
of rights or liberty, while nineteenth-century friends of laissez faire appealed more to utilitarian considerations. Similarly, Rawls concedes that
one might affirm his contract approach but eschew the difference principle, or vice versa.

In evaluating a particular theory one must examine, secondly, how it approaches the problem of choosing a criterion of distribution. For instance, does the theory recommend that one decide how goods ought to be distributed according to the consequences of the distribution, or does it take the acknowledgment of rights or the following of certain moral rules as essential? The former view (called "consequentialism") would contend that the right or just principle is to be chosen on the basis of its having the best consequences. Of course, any such theory, if it is ever to get off the ground, also needs to specify which consequences are good and so should be aimed at. Utilitarianism is the best known and most widely accepted consequentialist theory; it holds, as we said before, that maximization of happiness is the goal that should be pursued. Other consequentialists might wish to promote some other end—for example, religious faithfulness or human excellence—and would argue for criteria of distribution which realize that good.

The other type of approach which a theory might adopt is a "deontological" one. Here, rather than justifying a distribution pattern by appealing to its consequences, the theory claims that rules (or alternatively, rights of persons) ought to be respected in distributing economic goods. As with the dispute among consequentialists over what good to promote, deontologists disagree widely over which rights or rules are to count and how much. Some may value greatly the right to inherit property, for example, while others discount it in favor of principles that emphasize the importance of work as a means to acquire income justly.

Depending on whether the theory one accepts is consequentialist (looking to realize the best outcome) or deontological (protecting rights or following moral rules) in its approach, one will perceive economic justice very differently. Of the major approaches included here, only utilitarianism is fully consequentialist, while libertarianism and Rawls' social contract are deontological theories.

The third question which it is useful to keep in mind when considering a particular theory of justice is the basis on which it defends its answer. Philosophers have argued in favor of their theories, and thus the specific principles of distribution which those theories endorse, in very different ways.

One approach, as we have seen, is that of Rawls' hypothetical social contract. But why should principles chosen by imaginary persons in a hypothetical original position carry any weight with real persons in a real society? Rawls' basic answer is that the initial position, as he describes it, represents a situation of fairness; upon philosophical reflection we will come to agree, he believes, that what rational self-interested persons decide under these conditions *does* illuminate the nature of justice. Furthermore, the principles chosen accord well with our considered intuitions about justice. The theoretical construction which generates Rawls' principles is thus anchored in our existing judgments of what constitutes justice.

Nozick, it seems, has rather different intuitions about justice and a contrasting vision of the purpose and role of society. The right not to have others interfere in one's life is taken as fundamental. Whatever persons consent to is just, and any coercion is illegitimate. The relevant standard of comparison for evaluating social institutions is an imaginary state of nature, a prepolitical world of autonomous individuals. Persons are seen as having certain natural rights, including the right to property, which are logically prior to society and which must be respected if we are to treat individuals as ends in themselves and not means in the projects of others. While Rawls' social contract emphasizes the fairness of the society established in contract, Nozick and other libertarians see as just those arrangements which result from the uncoerced choices and agreements of actual individuals. Such a theory begins with a strong intuition about the primacy of liberty and then paints an attractive picture of the world in which the right of noncoercion is treated as the basic good. On the strength of this, libertarians hope to persuade us to revise some of our previous ideas about what justice requires in the economic realm.

Both Rawls and Nozick rely on moral intuitions to some extent, and Smart defends utilitarianism solely by appeal to our natural feelings of benevolence, which should, in his view, lead us to adopt the utilitarian principle. But what is "intuition"? Intuitions, as contemporary moral philosophers use the term, are essentially moral attitudes or judgments which we feel fairly sure are correct. These may be of two types: intuitions about particular cases (taking your neighbor's car without consent in order to go to the January sales is wrong) or regarding general moral rules (theft is usually wrong). Intuitions are used to arrive at answers to disputed problems like economic justice by showing that a certain principle is more consistent with our intuitions about particular cases than any alternative, and then employing that principle in turn to resolve moral issues about which our intuitions are uncertain. In this way our given moral beliefs are extended to cover more difficult cases. On the other hand, very firm intuitions about individual cases may be used to jettison a generally plausible moral principle when it is discovered to conflict with these particular judgments.

Many moral philosophers today see ethical theory as a matter of working back and forth between our moral intuitions about particular cases and the general principles which account for those particular judgments or are themselves intuitively attractive, in order to weave our moral thinking into a coherent and consistent web. R. M. Hare, however, rejects this approach, taking an essentially skeptical view of moral intuition as a basis for moral theory. Such attitudes, learned at society's knee, as it were, are subject to all the prejudices and inconsistencies ever held by a mother.

Hare argues that by paying close attention to the uses and logical implications of ethical language, we can go a long way toward resolving moral issues like that of economic justice. An understanding of the functioning of moral language and of the requirements of logical consistency supports a utilitarian approach which can, when supplemented by certain factual claims, lead us to affirm egalitarian conclusions concerning economic distribution.

We have, then, several very different approaches to distributive justice, and choosing between rival methods and theories is not easy. At various points in each essay, the writer provides some justification for the claim that conclusions reached by his theoretical method are for that reason worthy of belief. These arguments are all-important in evaluating each alternative. Furthermore, considerations are advanced against competing theories and rival approaches. Thus Hare argues against reliance on intuition, Nozick against social contract theory, and both Rawls and Nozick against utilitarianism.

We can see now that each theory is a complex blend of specific normative conclusions about economic justice, more general normative principles, and rather abstract metaethical considerations. So in our effort to determine what is a just distribution of economic benefits and burdens—and to justify our conclusion—we are led back to very serious and profound philosophical issues. The place to begin answering for ourselves the problem of economic justice is with a study of the major contemporary approaches to the issue, presented in Part I.

part

1

the major approaches

the social contract

Social Contract

Social contract is the name given to an important tradition in political philosophy, one with roots in medieval and ancient Greek thought but which blossomed in the seventeenth and eighteenth centuries. Hobbes, Locke, Rousseau, Kant, and others, all in rather different ways, used the notion of a social contract. It was also an important part of the political view of the writers of the Declaration of Independence.

Traditionally, social contract theorists have hypothesized the existence of a presocial, prepolitical stage of human existence, a "state of nature" prior to the uniting of individuals in society. These antonomous persons are then seen as coming together to determine the principles and organizational form of their social union—that is, to agree on a social contract. Individuals with certain rights and interests are, in this view, logically prior to society, and society is in turn the result of the covenant of these individuals. The legitimacy of government derives, thus, from the consent of the governed, and the social contract approach provides a vehicle for attempting to specify the proper role of government, its purpose and limits.

John Rawls, as we have mentioned, returns to the social contract tradition in an effort to develop a conception of justice, and indeed a basis for political philosophy, which does not rest solely on intuition, yet is distinct from utilitarianism. For him, the contract is only a *hypothetical* construction. Neither a prehistorical state of nature nor an actual contract situation is suggested. He is concerned, rather, with what principles free and rational persons would choose to govern their basic social and political institutions if they were brought together in an imaginary "original position" for this purpose.

In Rawls' view, society is to be seen as a "cooperative venture for mutual advantage," and one should imagine the individuals in the hypothetical original position as choosing, in an initial situation of equality and fairness, those principles most in accord with their rational self-interest. These people do not choose the principles they do because they believe them to be just. They are concerned with their share of the primary social goods (including wealth, power, self-respect, and liberty) and seek to look after their own interests. The principles chosen are principles of justice because they would be chosen by such persons under the (fair) conditions of the original position.

These conditions are elaborated by Rawls in the selections below. One crucial feature of the original position is that its participants are ignorant of their personal characteristics and endowments, their social position, and their historical period. If the procedure is to be fair, none of these things, argues Rawls, should be known. This "veil of ignorance" makes the decision impartial and thus makes unanimity possible. Since the conditions and constraints on the original position are, in Rawls' view, fair, the principles chosen have a certain justification. In addition, the principles are thought by Rawls to conform with our considered convictions or intuitions about justice.

Under conditions of ignorance, a rational person in the original position would reason conservatively. Not knowing his or her particular situation, one would wish to reduce one's losses in the event of the worst possible outcome. Thus, Rawls contends, a person in the original position would choose the general principle that all social values—including liberty, income, and opportunity—be distributed equally unless an unequal distribution of these goods is to everyone's advantage. Under appropriate conditions of material well-being, the general conception yields to the "special conception" of justice, composed of two principles. The first, which has priority over the second, calls for as extensive a system of equal liberty as possible. The second guarantees equality of opportunity and requires that any social and economic inequalities benefit the least advantaged. Contrary to utilitarianism, it is not enough that inequalities increase the total social good; they must work to the favor of the least advantaged members of society.

A virtue of the two principles, according to Rawls, is their acceptability once the veil of ignorance is lifted. In contrast again to utilitarianism, they are thought by him to be principles to which the participants could remain committed no mattter what their situation in society. Their implementation would result in both a stable society and one which promotes the self-respect of its citizens. The type of economic system which would be best in this society is, Rawls says, for social scientists to determine; but he does believe that a regime of either welfare capitalism or democratic socialism could realize his two principles of justice.

In the addendum to this section, taken from a recent article, Rawls defends his assumption that "the basic structure of society is the primary subject of justice." In this way, he responds to criticisms by libertarians, like Robert Nozick, who approach economic justice solely in terms of market transactions between individuals who possess natural rights.

JOHN RAWLS

Harvard University

A Theory of Justice

I. An Overview of the Theory

THE MAIN IDEA OF THE THEORY OF JUSTICE

My aim is to present a conception of justice which generalizes and carries to a higher level of abstraction the familiar theory of the social contract as found, say, in Locke, Rousseau, and Kant.[1] In order to do this we are not to think of the original contract as one to enter a particular society or to set up a particular form of government. Rather, the guiding idea is that the principles of justice for the basic structure of society are the object of the original agreement. They are the principles that free and rational persons concerned to further their own interests would accept in an initial position of equality as defining the fundamental terms of their association. These principles are to regulate all further agreements: they specify the kinds of social cooperation that can be entered into and the forms of government that can be established. This way of regarding the principles of justice I shall call justice as fairness.

Thus we are to imagine that those who engage in social cooperation

Reprinted by permission of the publishers from *A Theory of Justice* by John Rawls, Cambridge, Mass.: The Belknap Press of Harvard University Press, Copyright © 1971 by the President and Fellows of Harvard College.

choose together, in one joint act, the principles which are to assign basic rights and duties and to determine the division of social benefits. Men are to decide in advance how they are to regulate their claims against one another and what is to be the foundation charter of their society. Just as each person must decide by rational reflection what constitutes his good, that is, the system of ends which it is rational for him to pursue, so a group of persons must decide once and for all what is to count among them as just and unjust. The choice which rational men would make in this hypothetical situation of equal liberty, assuming for the present that this choice problem has a solution, determines the principles of justice.

In justice as fairness the original position of equality corresponds to the state of nature in the traditional theory of the social contract. This original position is not, of course, thought of as an actual historical state of affairs, much less as a primitive condition of culture. It is understood as a purely hypothetical situation characterized so as to lead to a certain conception of justice.[2] Among the essential features of this situation is that no one knows his place in society, his class position or social status, nor does any one know his fortune in the distribution of natural assets and abilities, his intelligence, strength, and the like. I shall even assume that the parties do not know their conceptions of the good or their special psychological propensities. The principles of justice are chosen behind a veil of ignorance. This ensures that no one is advantaged or disadvantaged in the choice of principles by the outcome of natural chance or the contingency of social circumstances. Since all are similarly situated and no one is able to design principles to favor his particular condition, the principles of justice are the result of a fair agreement or bargain. For given the circumstances of the original position, the symmetry of everyone's relations to each other, this initial situation is fair between individuals as moral persons, that is, as rational beings with their own ends and capable, I shall assume, of a sense of justice. The original position is, one might say, the appropriate initial status quo, and thus the fundamental agreements reached in it are fair. This explains the propriety of the name "justice as fairness": it conveys the idea that the principles of justice are agreed to in an initial situation that is fair. The name does not mean that the concepts of justice and fairness are the same, any more than the phrase "poetry as metaphor" means that the concepts of poetry and metaphor are the same.

Justice as fairness begins, as I have said, with one of the most general of all choices which persons might make together, namely, with the choice of the first principles of a conception of justice which is to regulate all subsequent criticism and reform of institutions. Then, having chosen a conception of justice, we can suppose that they are to choose a constitution and a legislature to enact laws, and so on, all in accordance with the principles of justice initially agreed upon. Our social situation is just if it is such that by this sequence of hypothetical agreements we would have contracted into the general system of rules which defines it. Moreover, assuming that the original position does determine a set of principles (that is, that a particular conception of justice would be chosen), it will then be true that whenever social institutions satisfy these principles those engaged in them can say to one another that they are cooperating on terms to which they would agree if they were free and equal persons whose relations with respect to one another were fair. They could all view their arrangements as meeting the stipulations which they would acknowledge in an initial situation that embodies widely accepted and reasonable constraints on the choice of principles. The general recognition of this fact would provide the basis for a public acceptance of the corresponding principles of justice. No society can, of course, be a scheme of cooperation which men enter voluntarily in a literal sense; each person finds himself placed at birth in some particular position in some particular society, and the nature of this position materially affects his life prospects. Yet a society satisfying the principles of justice as fairness comes as close as a society can to being a voluntary scheme, for it meets the principles which free and equal persons would assent to under circumstances that are fair. In this sense its members are autonomous and the obligations they recognize self-imposed.

One feature of justice as fairness is to think of the parties in the initial situation as rational and mutually disinterested. This does not mean that the parties are egoists, that is, individuals with only certain kinds of interests, say in wealth, prestige, and domination. But they are conceived as not taking an interest in one another's interests. They are to presume that even their spiritual aims may be opposed, in the way that the aims of those of different religions may be opposed. Moreover, the concept of rationality must be interpreted as far as possible in the narrow sense, standard in economic theory, of taking the most effective means to given ends. I shall modify this concept to some extent, as explained later, but one must try to avoid introducing into it any controversial ethical elements. The initial situation must be characterized by stipulations that are widely accepted.

In working out the conception of justice as fairness one main task clearly is to determine which principles of justice would be chosen in the original position. To do this we must describe this situation in some detail and formulate with care the problem of choice which it presents. These matters I shall take up in the immediately succeeding chapters. It may be observed, however, that once the principles of justice are thought of as arising from an original agreement in a situation of equality, it is an open question whether the principle of utility would be acknowledged. Offhand it hardly seems likely that persons who view themselves as equals, entitled to press their claims upon one another, would agree to a principle which may require lesser life prospects for some simply for the sake of a greater sum of advantages enjoyed by others. Since each desires to protect his interests, his capacity to advance his conception of the good, no one has a reason to acquiesce in an enduring loss for himself in order to bring about a greater net balance of satisfaction. In the absence of strong and lasting benevolent impulses, a rational man would not accept a basic structure merely because it maximized the algebraic sum of advantages irrespective of its permanent effects on his own basic rights and interests.

Thus it seems that the principle of utility is incompatible with the conception of social cooperation among equals for mutual advantage. It appears to be inconsistent with the idea of reciprocity implicit in the notion of a well-ordered society. Or, at any rate, so I shall argue.

I shall maintain instead that the persons in the initial situation would choose two rather different principles: the first requires equality in the assignment of basic rights and duties, while the second holds that social and economic inequalities, for example inequalities of wealth and authority, are just only if they result in compensating benefits for everyone, and in particular for the least advantaged members of society. These principles rule out justifying institutions on the grounds that the hardships of some are offset by a greater good in the aggregate. It may be expedient but it is not just that some should have less in order that others may prosper. But there is no injustice in the greater benefits earned by a few provided that the situation of persons not so fortunate is thereby improved. The intuitive idea is that since everyone's well-being depends upon a scheme of cooperation without which no one could have a satisfactory life, the division of advantages should be such as to draw forth the willing cooperation of everyone taking part in it, including those less well situated. Yet this can be expected only if reasonable terms are proposed. The two principles mentioned seem to be a fair agreement on the basis of which those better endowed, or more fortunate in their social position, neither of which we can be said to deserve, could expect the willing cooperation of others when some workable scheme is a necessary condition of the welfare of all.[3] Once we decide to look for a conception of justice that nullifies the accidents of natural endowment and the contingencies of social circumstance as counters in quest for political and economic advantage, we are led to these principles. They express the result of leaving aside those aspects of the social world that seem arbitrary from a moral point of view.

The problem of the choice of principles, however, is extremely difficult. I do not expect the answer I shall suggest to be convincing to everyone. It is, therefore, worth noting from the outset that justice as fairness, like other contract views, consists of two parts: (1) an interpretation of the initial situation and of the problem of choice posed there, and (2) a set of principles which, it is argued, would be agreed to. One may accept the first part of the theory (or some variant thereof), but not the other, and conversely. The concept of the initial contractual situation may seem reasonable although the particular principles proposed are rejected. To be sure, I want to maintain that the most appropriate conception of this situation does lead to principles of justice contrary to utilitarianism and perfectionism, and therefore that the contract doctrine provides an alternative to these views. Still, one may dispute this contention even though one grants that the contractarian method is a useful way of studying ethical theories and of setting forth their underlying assumptions.

Justice as fairness is an example of what I have called a contract theory. Now there may be an objection to the term "contract" and related expressions, but I think it will serve reasonably well. Many words have misleading connotations which at first are likely to confuse. The terms "utility" and "utilitarianism" are surely no exception. They too have unfortunate suggestions which hostile critics have been willing to exploit; yet they are clear enough for those prepared to study utilitarian doctrine. The same should be true of the term "contract" applied to moral theories. As I have mentioned, to understand it one has to keep in mind that it implies a certain level of abstraction. In particular, the content of the relevant agreement is not to enter a given society or to adopt a given form of government, but to accept certain moral principles. Moreover, the undertakings referred to are purely hypothetical: a contract view holds that certain principles would be accepted in a well-defined initial situation.

The merit of the contract terminology is that it conveys the idea that principles of justice may be conceived as principles that would be chosen by rational persons, and that in this way conceptions of justice may be explained and justified. The theory of justice is a part, perhaps the most significant part, of the theory of rational choice. Furthermore, principles of justice deal with conflicting claims upon the advantages won by social cooperation; they apply to the relations among several persons or groups. The word "contract" suggests this plurality as well as the condition that the appropriate division of advantages must be in accordance with principles acceptable to all parties. The condition of publicity for principles of justice is also connoted by the contract phraseology. Thus, if these principles are the outcome of an agreement, citizens have a knowledge of the principles that others follow. It is characteristic of contract theories to stress the public nature of political principles. Finally there is the long tradition of the contract doctrine. Expressing the tie with this line of thought helps to define ideas and accords with natural piety. There are then several advantages in the use of the term "contract." With due precautions taken, it should not be misleading.

A final remark. Justice as fairness is not a complete contract theory. For it is clear that the contractarian idea can be extended to the choice of more or less an entire ethical system, that is, to a system including principles for all the virtues and not only for justice. Now for the most part I shall consider only principles of justice and others closely related to them; I make no attempt to discuss the virtues in a systematic way. Obviously if justice as fairness succeeds reasonably well, a next step would be to study the more general view suggested by the name "rightness as fairness." But even this wider theory fails to embrace all moral relationships, since it would seem to include only our relations with other persons and to leave out of account how we are to conduct ourselves toward animals and the rest of nature. I do not contend that the contract notion offers a way to approach these questions which are certainly of the first importance; and I shall have to put them aside. We must recognize the limited scope of justice as fairness and of the general type of view that it exemplifies. How far its conclusions must be revised once these other matters are understood cannot be decided in advance.

The Original Position and Justification

I have said that the original position is the appropriate initial status quo which insures that the fundamental agreements reached in it are fair. This fact yields the name "justice as fairness." It is clear, then, that I want to say that one conception of justice is more reasonable than another, or justifiable with respect to it, if rational persons in the initial situation would choose its principles over those of the other for the role of justice. Conceptions of justice are to be ranked by their acceptability to persons so circumstanced. Understood in this way the question of justification is settled by working out a problem of deliberation: we have to ascertain which principles it would be rational to adopt given the contractual situation. This connects the theory of justice with the theory of rational choice.

If this view of the problem of justification is to succeed, we must, of course, describe in some detail the nature of this choice problem. A problem of rational decision has a definite answer only if we know the beliefs and interests of the parties, their relations with respect to one another, the alternatives between which they are to choose, the procedure whereby they make up their minds, and so on. As the circumstances are presented in different ways, correspondingly different principles are accepted. The concept of the original position, as I shall refer to it, is that of the most philosophically favored interpretation of this initial choice situation for the purposes of a theory of justice.

But how are we to decide what is the most favored interpretation? I assume, for one thing, that there is a broad measure of agreement that principles of justice should be chosen under certain conditions. To justify a particular description of the initial situation one shows that it incorporates these commonly shared presumptions. One argues from widely accepted but weak premises to more specific conclusions. Each of the presumptions should by itself be natural and plausible; some of them may seem innocuous or even trivial. The aim of the contract approach is to establish that taken together they impose significant bounds on acceptable principles of justice. The ideal outcome would be that these conditions determine a unique set of principles; but I shall be satisfied if they suffice to rank the main traditional conceptions of social justice.

One should not be misled, then, by the somewhat unusual conditions which characterize the original position. The idea here is simply to make vivid to ourselves the restrictions that it seems reasonable to impose on arguments for principles of justice, and therefore on these principles themselves. Thus it seems reasonable and generally acceptable that no one should be advantaged or disadvantaged by natural fortune or social circumstances in the choice of principles. It also seems widely agreed that it should be impossible to tailor principles to the circumstances of one's own case. We should insure further that particular inclinations and aspirations, and persons' conceptions of their good do not affect the principles adopted. The aim is to rule out those principles that it would be rational to propose for acceptance, however little the chance of success, only if one knew certain things that are irrelevant from the standpoint of justice. For example, if a man knew that he was wealthy, he might find it rational to advance the principle that various taxes for welfare measures be counted unjust; if he knew that he was poor, he would most likely propose the contrary principle. To represent the desired restrictions one imagines a situation in which everyone is deprived of this sort of information. One excludes the knowledge of those contingencies which sets men at odds and allows them to be guided by their prejudices. In this manner the veil of ignorance is arrived at in a natural way. This concept should cause no difficulty if we keep in mind the constraints on arguments that it is meant to express. At any time we can enter the original position, so to speak, simply by following a certain procedure, namely, by arguing for principles of justice in accordance with these restrictions.

It seems reasonable to suppose that the parties in the original position are equal. That is, all have the same rights in the procedure for choosing principles; each can make proposals, submit reasons for their acceptance, and so on. Obviously the purpose of these conditions is to represent equality between human beings as moral persons, as creatures having a conception of their good and capable of a sense of justice. The basis of equality is taken to be similarity in these two respects. Systems of ends are not ranked in value; and each man is presumed to have the requisite ability to understand and to act upon whatever principles are adopted. Together with the veil of ignorance, these conditions define the principles of justice as those which rational persons concerned to advance their interests would consent to as equals when none are known to be advantaged or disadvantaged by social and natural contingencies.

There is, however, another side to justifying a particular description of the original position. This is to see if the principles which would be chosen match our considered convictions of justice or extend them in an acceptable way. We can note whether applying these principles would lead us to make the same judgments about the basic structure of society which we now make intuitively and in which we have the greatest confidence; or whether, in cases where our present judgments are in doubt and given with hesitation, these principles offer a resolution which we can affirm on reflection. There are questions which we feel sure must be answered in a certain way. For example, we are confident that religious intolerance and racial discrimination are unjust. We think that we have examined these things with care and have reached what we believe is an impartial judgment not likely to be distorted by an excessive attention to our own interests. These convictions are provisional fixed points which we presume any conception of justice must fit. But we have much less assurance as to what is the correct distribution of wealth and authority. Here we may be looking for a way to remove our doubts. We can check an interpretation of the initial situation, then, by the capacity of its principles to accommodate our firmest convictions and to provide guidance where guidance is needed.

In searching for the most favored description of this situation we work from both ends. We begin by describing it so that it represents generally shared and preferably weak conditions. We then see if these conditions are strong enough to yield a significant set of principles. If not, we look for further premises equally reasonable. But if so, and these principles match our considered convictions of justice, then so far well and good. But presumably there will be discrepancies. In this case we have a choice. We can either modify the account of the initial situation or we can revise our existing judgments, for even the judgments we take provisionally as fixed points are liable to revision. By going back and forth, sometimes altering the conditions of the contractual circumstances, at others withdrawing our judgments and conforming them to principle, I assume that eventually we shall find a description of the initial situation that both expresses reasonable conditions and yields principles which match our considered judgments duly pruned and adjusted. This state of affairs I refer to as reflective equilibrium.[4] It is an equilibrium because at last our principles and judgments coincide; and it is reflective since we know to what principles our judgments conform and the premises of their derivation. At the moment everything is in order. But this equilibrium is not necessarily stable. It is liable to be upset by further examination of the conditions which should be imposed on the contractual situation and by particular cases which may lead us to revise our judgments. Yet for the time being we have done what we can to render coherent and to justify our convictions of social justice. We have reached a conception of the original position.

I shall not, of course, actually work through this process. Still, we may think of the interpretation of the original position that I shall present as the result of such a hypothetical course of reflection. It represents the attempt to accommodate within one scheme both reasonable philosophical conditions on principles as well as our considered judgments of justice. In arriving at the favored interpretation of the initial situation there is no point at which an appeal is made to self-evidence in the traditional sense either of general conceptions or particular convictions. I do not claim for the principles of justice proposed that they are necessary truths or derivable from such truths. A conception of justice cannot be deduced from self-evident premises or conditions on principles; instead, its justification is a matter of the mutual support of many considerations, of everything fitting together into one coherent view.

A final comment. We shall want to say that certain principles of justice are justified because they would be agreed to in an initial situation of equality. I have emphasized that this original position is purely hypothetical. It is natural to ask why, if this agreement is never actually entered into, we should take any interest in these principles, moral or otherwise. The answer is that the conditions embodied in the description of the original position are ones that we do in fact accept. Or if we do

not, then perhaps we can be persuaded to do so by philosophical reflection. Each aspect of the contractual situation can be given supporting
grounds. Thus what we shall do is to collect together into one conception
a number of conditions on principles that we are ready upon due consideration to recognize as reasonable. These constraints express what we
are prepared to regard as limits on fair terms of social cooperation. One
way to look at the idea of the original position, therefore, is to see it as
an expository device which sums up the meaning of these conditions and
helps us to extract their consequences. On the other hand, this conception is also an intuitive notion that suggests its own elaboration, so that
led on by it we are drawn to define more clearly the standpoint from
which we can best interpret moral relationships. We need a conception
that enables us to envision our objective from afar: the intuitive notion
of the original position is to do this for us. . . .[5]

THE VEIL OF IGNORANCE

The idea of the original position is to set up a fair procedure so that
any principles agreed to will be just. The aim is to use the notion of
pure procedural justice as a basis of theory. Somehow we must nullify
the effects of specific contingencies which put men at odds and tempt
them to exploit social and natural circumstances to their own advantage.
Now in order to do this I assume that the parties are situated behind a
veil of ignorance. They do not know how the various alternatives will
affect their own particular case and they are obliged to evaluate principles solely on the basis of general considerations.[6]

It is assumed, then, that the parties do not know certain kinds of
particular facts. First of all, no one knows his place in society, his class
position or social status; nor does he know his fortune in the distribution
of natural assets and abilities, his intelligence and strength, and the like.
Nor, again, does anyone know his conception of the good, the particulars
of his rational plan of life, or even the special features of his psychology
such as his aversion to risk or liability to optimism or pessimism. More
than this, I assume that the parties do not know the particular circumstances of their own society. That is, they do not know its economic or
political situation, or the level of civilization and culture it has been
able to achieve. The persons in the original position have no information
as to which generation they belong. These broader restrictions on
knowledge are appropriate in part because questions of social justice
arise between generations as well as within them, for example, the
question of the appropriate rate of capital saving and of the conservation
of natural resources and the environment of nature. There is also,
theoretically anyway, the question of a reasonable genetic policy. In
these cases too, in order to carry through the idea of the original position,
the parties must not know the contingencies that set them in opposition.
They must choose principles the consequences of which they are prepared
to live with whatever generation they turn out to belong to.

As far as possible, then, the only particular facts which the parties know is that their society is subject to the circumstances of justice and whatever this implies. It is taken for granted, however, that they know the general facts about human society. They understand political affairs and the principles of economic theory; they know the basis of social organization and the laws of human psychology. Indeed, the parties are presumed to know whatever general facts affect the choice of the principles of justice. There are no limitations on general information, that is, on general laws and theories, since conceptions of justice must be adjusted to the characteristics of the systems of social cooperation which they are to regulate, and there is no reason to rule out these facts. It is, for example, a consideration against a conception of justice that in view of the laws of moral psychology, men would not acquire a desire to act upon it even when the institutions of their society satisfied it. For in this case there would be difficulty in securing the stability of social co-operation. It is an important feature of a conception of justice that it should generate its own support. That is, its principles should be such that when they are embodied in the basic structure of society men tend to acquire the corresponding sense of justice. Given the principles of moral learning, men develop a desire to act in accordance with its principles. In this case a conception of justice is stable. This kind of general information is admissible in the original position.

The notion of the veil of ignorance raises several difficulties. Some may object that the exclusion of nearly all particular information makes it difficult to grasp what is meant by the original position. Thus it may be helpful to observe that one or more persons can at any time enter this position, or perhaps, better, simulate the deliberations of this hypothetical situation, simply by reasoning in accordance with the appropriate restrictions. In arguing for a conception of justice we must be sure that it is among the permitted alternatives and satisfies the stipulated formal constraints. No considerations can be advanced in its favor unless they would be rational ones for us to urge were we to lack the kind of knowledge that is excluded. The evaluation of principles must proceed in terms of the general consequences of their public recognition and universal application, it being assumed that they will be complied with by everyone. To say that a certain conception of justice would be chosen in the original position is equivalent to saying that rational deliberation satisfying certain conditions and restrictions would reach a certain conclusion. If necessary, the argument to this result could be set out more formally. I shall, however, speak throughout in terms of the notion of the original position. It is more economical and suggestive, and brings out certain essential features that otherwise one might easily overlook. . . .

Thus there follows the very important consequence that the parties have no basis for bargaining in the usual sense. No one knows his situation in society nor his natural assets, and therefore no one is in a position to tailor principles to his advantage. We might imagine that one of the contractees threatens to hold out unless the others agree to principles favorable to him. But how does he know which principles are especially in his interests? The same holds for the formation of coalitions: if a group were to decide to band together to the disadvantage of the others, they would not know how to favor themselves in the choice of principles. Even if they could get everyone to agree to their proposal, they would have no assurance that it was to their advantage, since they cannot identify themselves either by name or description. . . .

The restrictions on particular information in the original position are, then, of fundamental importance. Without them we would not be able to work out any definite theory of justice at all. We would have to be content with a vague formula stating that justice is what would be agreed to without being able to say much, if anything, about the substance of the agreement itself. The formal constraints of the concept of right, those applying to principles directly, are not sufficient for our purpose. The veil of ignorance makes possible a unanimous choice of a particular conception of justice. Without these limitations on knowledge the bargaining problem of the original position would be hopelessly complicated. Even if theoretically a solution were to exist, we would not, at present anyway, be able to determine it. . . .

The Rationality of the Parties

I have assumed throughout that the persons in the original position are rational. In choosing between principles each tries as best he can to advance his interests. But I have also assumed that the parties do not know their conception of the good. This means that while they know that they have some rational plan of life, they do not know the details of this plan, the particular ends and interests which it is calculated to promote. How, then, can they decide which conceptions of justice are most to their advantage? Or must we suppose that they are reduced to mere guessing? To meet this difficulty, I postulate that they would prefer more primary social goods rather than less. . . . (i.e., rights and liberties, powers and opportunities, income and wealth and self-respect). Of course, it may turn out, once the veil of ignorance is removed, that some of them for religious or other reasons may not, in fact, want more of these goods. But from the standpoint of the original position, it is rational for the parties to suppose that they do want a larger share, since in any case they are not compelled to accept more if they do not wish to nor does a person suffer from a greater liberty. Thus even though the parties are deprived of information about their particular ends, they have enough knowledge to rank the alternatives. They know that in general they must try to protect their liberties, widen their opportunities, and enlarge their means for promoting their aims whatever these are. Guided by the theory of the good and the general facts of moral psychology, their deliberations are no longer guesswork. They can make a rational decision in the ordinary sense. . . .

The assumption of mutually disinterested rationality, then, comes to this: the persons in the original position try to acknowledge principles which advance their system of ends as far as possible. They do this by attempting to win for themselves the highest index of primary social goods, since this enables them to promote their conception of the good most effectively whatever it turns out to be. The parties do not seek to confer benefits or to impose injuries on one another; they are not moved by affection or rancor. Nor do they try to gain relative to each other; they are not envious or vain. Put in terms of a game, we might say: they strive for as high an absolute score as possible. They do not wish a high or a low score for their opponents, nor do they seek to maximize or minimize the difference between their successes and those of others. The idea of a game does not really apply, since the parties are not concerned to win but to get as many points as possible judged by their own system of ends. . . .

. . . Once we consider the idea of a contract theory it is tempting to think that it will not yield the principles we want unless the parties are to some degree at least moved by benevolence, or an interest in one another's interests. Perry, as I mentioned before, thinks of the right standards and decisions as those promoting the ends reached by reflective agreement under circumstances making for impartiality and good will. Now the combination of mutual disinterest and the veil of ignorance achieves the same purpose as benevolence. For this combination of conditions forces each person in the original position to take the good of others into account. In justice as fairness, then, the effects of good will are brought about by several conditions working jointly. The feeling that this conception of justice is egoistic is an illusion fostered by looking at but one of the elements of the original position. Furthermore, this pair of assumptions has enormous advantages over that of benevolence plus knowledge. As I have noted, the latter is so complex that no definite theory at all can be worked out. Not only are the complications caused by so much information insurmountable, but the motivational assumption requires clarification. For example, what is the relative strength of benevolent desires? In brief, the combination of mutual disinterestness plus the veil of ignorance has the merits of simplicity and clarity while at the same time insuring the effects of what are at first sight morally more attractive assumptions. And if it is asked why one should not postulate benevolence with the veil of ignorance, the answer is that there is no need for so strong a condition. Moreover, it would defeat the purpose of grounding the theory of justice on weak stipulations, as well as being incongruous with the circumstances of justice. . . .

II. The Two Principles of Justice

Two Principles of Justice

I shall now state in a provisional form the two principles of justice that I believe would be chosen in the original position. In this section I wish to make only the most general comments, and therefore the first formulation of these principles is tentative. As we go on I shall run through several formulations and approximate step by step the final statement to be given much later. I believe that doing this allows the exposition to proceed in a natural way.

The first statement of the two principles reads as follows.

> First: each person is to have an equal right to the most extensive basic liberty compatible with a similar liberty for others.
> Second: social and economic inequalities are to be arranged so that they are both (a) reasonably expected to be to everyone's advantage, and (b) attached to positions and offices open to all.

There are two ambiguous phrases in the second principle, namely "everyone's advantage" and "equally open to all." Determining their sense more exactly will lead to a second formulation of the principle. . . .

By way of general comment, these principles primarily apply, as I have said, to the basic structure of society. They are to govern the assignment of rights and duties and to regulate the distribution of social and economic advantages. As their formulation suggests, these principles presuppose that the social structure can be divided into two more or less distinct parts, the first principle applying to the one, the second to the other. They distinguish between those aspects of the social system that define and secure the equal liberties of citizenship and those that specify and establish social and economic inequalities. The basic liberties of citizens are, roughly speaking, political liberty (the right to vote and to be eligible for public office) together with freedom of speech and assembly; liberty of conscience and freedom of thought; freedom of the person along with the right to hold (personal) property; and freedom from arbitrary arrest and seizure as defined by the concept of the rule of law. These liberties are all required to be equal by the first principle, since citizens of a just society are to have the same basic rights.

The second principle applies, in the first approximation, to the distribution of income and wealth and to the design of organizations that make use of differences in authority and responsibility, or chains of command. While the distribution of wealth and income need not be equal, it must be to everyone's advantage, and at the same time, positions of authority and offices of command must be accessible to all. One applies the second principle by holding positions open, and then, subject to this constraint, arranges social and economic inequalities so that everyone benefits.

These principles are to be arranged in a serial order with the first principle prior to the second. This ordering means that a departure from the institutions of equal liberty required by the first principle cannot be justified by, or compensated for, by greater social and economic advantages. The distribution of wealth and income, and the hierarchies of authority, must be consistent with both the liberties of equal citizenship and equality of opportunity.

It is clear that these principles are rather specific in their content, and their acceptance rests on certain assumptions that I must eventually try to explain and justify. A theory of justice depends upon a theory of society in ways that will become evident as we proceed. For the present, it should be observed that the two principles (and this holds for all formulations) are a special case of a more general conception of justice that can be expressed as follows.

> All social values—liberty and opportunity, income and wealth, and the bases of self-respect—are to be distributed equally unless an unequal distribution of any, or all, of these values is to everyone's advantage.

Injustice, then, is simply inequalities that are not to the benefit of all. Of course, this conception is extremely vague and requires interpretation.

As a first step, suppose that the basic structure of society distributes certain primary goods, that is, things that every rational man is presumed to want. These goods normally have a use whatever a person's rational plan of life. For simplicity, assume that the chief primary goods at the disposition of society are rights and liberties, powers and opportunities, income and wealth. (Later on in Part Three the primary good of self-respect has a central place.) These are the social primary goods. Other primary goods such as health and vigor, intelligence and imagination, are natural goods; although their possession is influenced by the basic structure, they are not so directly under its control. Imagine, then, a hypothetical initial arrangement in which all the social primary goods are equally distributed: everyone has similar rights and duties, and income and wealth are evenly shared. This state of affairs provides a benchmark for judging improvements. If certain inequalities of wealth and organizational powers would make everyone better off than in this hypothetical starting situation, then they accord with the general conception.

Now it is possible, at least theoretically, that by giving up some of their fundamental liberties men are sufficiently compensated by the resulting social and economic gains. The general conception of justice imposes no restrictions on what sort of inequalities are permissible; it only requires that everyone's position be improved. We need not suppose anything so drastic as consenting to a condition of slavery. Imagine instead that men forego certain political rights when the economic returns are significant and their capacity to influence the course of policy by the exercise of these rights would be marginal in any case. It is this kind of exchange which the two principles as stated rule out; being arranged in serial order they do not permit exchanges between basic liberties and economic and social gains. The serial ordering of principles expresses an underlying preference among primary social goods. When this preference is rational so likewise is the choice of these principles in this order. . . .

The fact that the two principles apply to institutions has certain consequences. Several points illustrate this. First of all, the rights and liberties referred to by these principles are those which are defined by the public rules of the basic structure. Whether men are free is determined by the rights and duties established by the major institutions of society.

Liberty is a certain pattern of social forms. The first principle simply requires that certain sorts of rules, those defining basic liberties, apply to everyone equally and that they allow the most extensive liberty compatible with a like liberty for all. The only reason for circumscribing the rights defining liberty and making men's freedom less extensive than it might otherwise be is that these equal rights as institutionally defined would interfere with one another.

Another thing to bear in mind is that when principles mention persons, or require that everyone gain from an inequality, the reference is to representative persons holding the various social positions, or offices, or whatever, established by the basic structure. Thus in applying the second principle I assume that it is possible to assign an expectation of well-being to representative individuals holding these positions. This expectation indicates their life prospects as viewed from their social station. In general, the expectations of representative persons depend upon the distribution of rights and duties throughout the basic structure. When this changes, expectations change. I assume, then, that expectations are connected: by raising the prospects of the representative man in one position we presumably increase or decrease the prospects of representative men in other positions. Since it applies to institutional forms, the second principle (or rather the first part of it) refers to the expectations of representative individuals. As I shall discuss below, neither principle applies to distributions of particular goods to particular individuals who may be identified by their proper names. The situation where someone is considering how to allocate certain commodities to needy persons who are known to him is not within the scope of the principles. They are meant to regulate basic institutional arrangements. We must not assume that there is much similarity from the standpoint of justice between an administrative allotment of goods to specific persons and the appropriate design of society.

Now the second principle insists that each person benefit from permissible inequalities in the basic structure. This means that it must be reasonable for each relevant representative man defined by this structure, when he views it as a going concern, to prefer his prospects with the inequality to his prospects without it. One is not allowed to justify differences in income or organizational powers on the ground that the disadvantages of those in one position are outweighed by the greater advantages of those in another. Much less can infringements of liberty be counterbalanced in this way. Applied to the basic structure, the principle of utility would have us maximize the sum of expectations of representative men (weighted by the number of persons they represent, on the classical view); and this would permit us to compensate for the losses of some by the gains of others. Instead, the two principles require that everyone benefit from economic and social inequalities. It is obvious, however, that there are indefinitely many ways in which all may be advantaged when the initial arrangement of equality is taken as a benchmark. How then are we to choose among these possibilities? The principles must be specified so that they yield a determinate conclusion. I now turn to this problem.

INTERPRETATIONS OF THE SECOND PRINCIPLE

I have already mentioned that since the phrases "everyone's advantage" and "equally open to all" are ambiguous, both parts of the second principle have two natural senses. Because these senses are independent of one another, the principle has four possible meanings. Assuming that the first principle of equal liberty has the same sense throughout, we then have four interpretations of the two principles. These are indicated in the table below.

"Equally open"	"Everyone's advantage"	
	Principle of efficiency	Difference principle
Equality as careers open to talents	System of Natural Liberty	Natural Aristocracy
Equality as equality of fair opportunity	Liberal Equality	Democratic Equality

I shall sketch in turn these three interpretations: the system of natural liberty, liberal equality, and democratic equality. In some respects this sequence is the more intuitive one, but the sequence via the interpretation of natural aristocracy is not without interest and I shall comment on it briefly. In working out justice as fairness, we must decide which interpretation is to be preferred. I shall adopt that of democratic equality, explaining in this chapter what this notion means. The argument for its acceptance in the original position does not begin until the next chapter.

The first interpretation (in either sequence) I shall refer to as the system of natural liberty. In this rendering the first part of the second principle is understood as the principle of efficiency adjusted so as to apply to institutions or, in this case, to the basic structure of society; and the second part is understood as an open social system in which, to use the traditional phrase, careers are open to talents. I assume in all interpretations that the first principle of equal liberty is satisfied and that the economy is roughly a free market system, although the means of production may or may not be privately owned. The system of natural liberty asserts, then, that a basic structure satisfying the principle of efficiency and in which positions are open to those able and willing to strive for them will lead to a just distribution. Assigning rights and duties in this way is thought to give a scheme which allocates wealth and income, authority and responsibility, in a fair way whatever this allocation turns out to be. The doctrine includes an important element of pure procedural justice which is carried over to the other interpretations.

At this point it is necessary to make a brief digression to explain the principle of efficiency. . . . The principle holds that a configuration is efficient whenever it is impossible to change it so as to make some persons (at least one) better off without at the same time making other persons (at least one) worse off. Thus a distribution of a stock of commodities among certain individuals is efficient if there exists no redistribution of these goods that improves the circumstances of at least one of these individuals without another being disadvantaged. The organization of production is efficient if there is no way to alter inputs so as to produce more of some commodity without producing less of another. For if we could produce more of one good without having to give up some of another, the larger stock of goods could be used to better the circumstances of some persons without making that of others any worse. These applications of the principle show that it is, indeed, a principle of efficiency. A distribution of goods or a scheme of production is inefficient when there are ways of doing still better for some individuals without doing any worse for others. I shall assume that the parties in the original position accept this principle to judge the efficiency of economic and social arrangements. . . .

Now these reflections show only what we knew all along, that is, that the principle of efficiency cannot serve alone as a conception of justice.[7] Therefore it must be supplemented in some way. Now in the system of natural liberty the principle of efficiency is constrained by certain background institutions: when these constraints are satisfied, any resulting efficient distribution is accepted as just. The system of natural liberty selects an efficient distribution roughly as follows. Let us suppose that we know from economic theory that under the standard assumptions defining a competitive market economy, income and wealth will be distributed in an efficient way, and that the particular efficient distribution which results in any period of time is determined by the initial distribution of assets, that is, by the initial distribution of income and wealth, and of natural talents and abilities. With each initial distribution, a definite efficient outcome is arrived at. Thus it turns out that if we are to accept the outcome as just, and not merely as efficient, we must accept the basis upon which over time the initial distribution of assets is determined.

In the system of natural liberty the initial distribution is regulated by the arrangements implicit in the conception of careers open to talents (as earlier defined). These arrangements presuppose a background of equal liberty (as specified by the first principle) and a free market economy. They require a formal equality of opportunity in that all have at least the same legal rights of access to all advantaged social positions. But since there is no effort to preserve an equality, or similarity, of social conditions, except insofar as this is necessary to preserve the requisite background institutions, the initial distribution of assets for any period of time is strongly influenced by natural and social contingencies. The existing distribution of income and wealth, say, is the cumulative effect of prior distributions of natural assets—that is, natural talents and abilities—as these have been developed or left unrealized, and their use favored or disfavored over time by social circumstances and such chance contingencies as accident and good fortune. Intuitively, the most obvious injustice of the system of natural liberty is that it permits distributive shares to be improperly influenced by these factors so arbitrary from a moral point of view.

The liberal interpretation, as I shall refer to it, tries to correct for this by adding to the requirement of careers open to talents the further condition of the principle of fair equality of opportunity. The thought here is that positions are to be not only open in a formal sense, but that all should have a fair chance to attain them. Offhand it is not clear what is meant, but we might say that those with similar abilities and skills should have similar life chances. More specifically, assuming that there is a distribution of natural assets, those who are at the same level of talent and ability, and have the same willingness to use them, should have the same prospects of success regardless of their initial place in the social system, that is, irrespective of the income class into which they are born. In all sectors of society there should be roughly equal prospects of culture and achievement for everyone similarly motivated and endowed. The expectations of those with the same abilities and aspirations should not be affected by their social class.[8]

The liberal interpretation of the two principles seeks, then, to mitigate the influence of social contingencies and natural fortune on distributive shares. To accomplish this end it is necessary to impose further basic structural conditions on the social system. Free market arrangements must be set within a framework of political and legal institutions which regulates the overall trends of economic events and preserves the social conditions necessary for fair equality of opportunity. The elements of this framework are familiar enough, though it may be worthwhile to recall the importance of preventing extensive accumulations of property and wealth and of maintaining equal opportunities of education for all. Chances to acquire cultural knowledge and skills should not depend upon one's class position, and so the school system, whether public or private, should be designed to even out class barriers.

While the liberal conception seems clearly preferable to the system of natural liberty, intuitively it still appears defective. For one thing, even if it works to perfection in eliminating the influence of social contingencies, it still permits the distribution of wealth and income to be determined by the natural distribution of abilities and talents. Within the limits allowed by the background arrangements, distributive shares are decided by the outcome of the natural lottery; and this outcome is arbitrary from a moral perspective. There is no more reason to permit the distribution of income and wealth to be settled by the distribution of natural assets than by historical and social fortune. Furthermore, the principle of fair opportunity can be only imperfectly carried out, at least as long as the institution of the family exists. The extent to which natural capacities develop and reach fruition is affected by all kinds of social conditions and class attitudes. Even the willingness to make an effort, to try, and so to be deserving in the ordinary sense is itself dependent upon happy family and social circumstances. It is impossible in practice to secure equal chances of achievement and culture for those similarly endowed, and therefore we may want to adopt a principle which recognizes this fact and also mitigates the arbitrary effects of the natural lottery itself. That the liberal conception fails to do this encourages one to look for another interpretation of the two principles of justice.

Before turning to the conception of democratic equality, we should note that of natural aristocracy. On this view no attempt is made to regulate social contingencies beyond what is required by formal equality of opportunity, but the advantages of persons with greater natural endowments are to be limited to those that further the good of the poorer sectors of society. The aristocratic ideal is applied to a system that is open, at least from a legal point of view, and the better situation of those favored by it is regarded as just only when less would be had by those below, if less were given to those above.[9] In this way the idea of *noblesse oblige* is carried over to the conception of natural aristocracy.

Now both the liberal conception and that of natural aristocracy are unstable. For once we are troubled by the influence of either social contingencies or natural chance on the determination of distributive shares, we are bound, on reflection, to be bothered by the influence of the other. From a moral standpoint the two seem equally arbitrary. So however we move away from the system of natural liberty, we cannot be satisfied short of the democratic conception. This conception I have yet to explain. And, moreover, none of the preceding remarks are an argument for this conception, since in a contract theory all arguments, strictly speaking, are to be made in terms of what it would be rational to choose in the original position. But I am concerned here to prepare the way for the favored interpretation of the two principles so that these criteria, especially the second one, will not strike the reader as too eccentric or bizarre. I have tried to show that once we try to find a rendering of them which treats everyone equally as a moral person, and which does not weight men's share in the benefits and burdens of social cooperation according to their social fortune or their luck in the natural lottery, it is clear that the democratic interpretation is the best choice among the four alternatives. With these comments as a preface, I now turn to this conception.

DEMOCRATIC EQUALITY AND THE DIFFERENCE PRINCIPLE

The democratic interpretation, as the table suggests, is arrived at by combining the principle of fair equality of opportunity with the difference principle. This principle removes the indeterminateness of the principle of efficiency by singling out a particular position from which the social and economic inequalities of the basic structure are to be judged. Assuming the framework of institutions required by equal liberty and fair equality of opportunity, the higher expectations of those better situated are just if and only if they work as part of a scheme which improves the expectations of the least advantaged members of society. The intuitive idea is that the social order is not to establish and secure the more attractive prospects of those better off unless doing so is to the advantage of those less fortunate. . . .

To illustrate the difference principle, consider the distribution of income among social classes. Let us suppose that the various income groups correlate with representative individuals by reference to whose expectations we can judge the distribution. Now those starting out as members of the entrepreneurial class in property-owning democracy, say, have a better prospect than those who begin in the class of unskilled laborers. It seems likely that this will be true even when the social injustices which now exist are removed. What, then, can possibly justify this kind of initial inequality in life prospects? According to the difference principle, it is justifiable only if the difference in expectation is to the advantage of the representative man who is worse off, in this case the representative unskilled worker. The inequality in expectation is permissible only if lowering it would make the working class even more worse off. Supposedly, given the rider in the second principle concerning open positions, and the principle of liberty generally, the greater expectations allowed to entrepreneurs encourages them to do things which raise the long-term prospects of the laboring class. Their better prospects act as incentives so that the economic process is more efficient, innovation proceeds at a faster pace, and so on. Eventually the resulting material benefits spread throughout the system and to the least advantaged. I shall not consider how far these things are true. The point is that something of this kind must be argued if these inequalities are to be just by the difference principle.

I shall now make a few remarks about this principle. First of all, in applying it, one should distinguish between two cases. The first case is that in which the expectations of the least advantaged are indeed maximized (subject, of course, to the mentioned constraints). No changes in the expectations of those better off can improve the situation of those worst off. The best arrangement obtains, what I shall call a perfectly just scheme. The second case is that in which the expectations of all those better off at least contribute to the welfare of the more unfortunate. That is, if their expectations were decreased, the prospects of the least advantaged would likewise fall. Yet the maximum is not yet achieved. Even higher expectations for the more advantaged would raise the expectations of those in the lowest position. Such a scheme is, I shall say, just throughout, but not the best just arrangement. A scheme is unjust when the higher expectations, one or more of them, are excessive. If these expectations were decreased, the situation of the least favored would be improved. How unjust an arrangement is depends on how excessive the higher expectations are and to what extent they depend upon the violation of the other principles of justice, for example, fair equality of opportunity; but I shall not attempt to measure in any exact way the degrees of injustice. The point to note here is that while the difference principle is, strictly speaking, a maximizing principle, there is a significant distinction between the cases that fall short of the best arrangement. A society should try to avoid the region where the marginal contributions of those better off are negative, since, other things equal, this seems a greater fault than falling short of the best scheme when these contributions are positive.

The even larger difference between rich and poor makes the latter even worse off, and this violates the principle of mutual advantage as well as democratic equality. . . .

. . . And therefore, as the outcome of the last several sections, the second principle is to read as follows.

> Social and economic inequalities are to be arranged so that they are both (a) to the greatest benefit of the least advantaged and (b) attached to offices and positions open to all under conditions of fair equality of opportunity.

Finally, it should be observed that the difference principle, or the idea expressed by it, can easily be accommodated to the general conception of justice. In fact, the general conception is simply the difference principle applied to all primary goods including liberty and opportunity and so no longer constrained by other parts of the special conception. This is evident from the earlier brief discussion of the principles of justice. These principles in serial order are, as I shall indicate from time to time, the form that the general conception finally assumes as social conditions improve. This question ties up with that of the priority of liberty which I shall discuss later. For the moment it suffices to remark that in one form or another the difference principle is basic throughout. . . .

THE TENDENCY TO EQUALITY

I wish to conclude this discussion of the two principles by explaining the sense in which they express an egalitarian conception of justice. Also I should like to forestall the objection to the principle of fair opportunity that it leads to a callous meritocratic society. In order to prepare the way for doing this, I note several aspects of the conception of justice that I have set out.

First we may observe that the difference principle gives some weight to the considerations singled out by the principle of redress. This is the principle that undeserved inequalities call for redress; and since inequalities of birth and natural endowment are undeserved, these inequalities are to be somehow compensated for.[10] Thus the principle holds that in order to treat all persons equally, to provide genuine equality of opportunity, society must give more attention to those with fewer native assets and to those born into the less favorable social positions. The idea is to redress the bias of contingencies in the direction of equality. In pursuit of this principle greater resources might be spent on the education of the less rather than the more intelligent, at least over a certain time of life, say the earlier years of school.

Now the principle of redress has not to my knowledge been proposed as the sole criterion of justice, as the single aim of the social order. It is plausible as most such principles are only as a prima facie principle, one that is to be weighed in the balance with others. For example, we are to weigh it against the principle to improve the average standard of life, or to advance the common good.[11] But whatever other principles we hold, the claims of redress are to be taken into account. It is thought to represent one of the elements in our conception of justice. Now the difference principle is not of course the principle of redress. It does not require society to try to even out handicaps as if all were expected to compete on a fair basis in the same race. But the difference principle would allocate resources in education, say, so as to improve the long-term expectation of the least favored. If this end is attained by giving more attention to the better endowed, it is permissible; otherwise not. And in making this decision, the value of education should not be assessed only in terms of economic efficiency and social welfare. Equally if not more important is the role of education in enabling a person to enjoy the culture of his society and to take part in its affairs, and in this way to provide for each individual a secure sense of his own worth.

Thus although the difference principle is not the same as that of redress, it does achieve some of the intent of the latter principle. It transforms the aims of the basic structure so that the total scheme of institutions no longer emphasizes social efficiency and technocratic values. We see then that the difference principle represents, in effect, an agreement to regard the distribution of natural talents as a common asset and to share in the benefits of this distribution whatever it turns out to be. Those who have been favored by nature, whoever they are, may gain from their good fortune only on terms that improve the situation of those who have lost out. The naturally advantaged are not to gain merely because they are more gifted, but only to cover the costs of training and education and for using their endowments in ways that help the less fortunate as well. No one deserves his greater natural capacity nor merits a more favorable starting place in society. But it does not follow that one should eliminate these distinctions. There is another way to deal with them. The basic structure can be arranged so that these contingencies work for the good of the least fortunate. Thus we are led to the difference principle if we wish to set up the social system so that no one gains or loses from his arbitrary place in the distribution of natural assets or his initial position in society without giving or receiving compensating advantages in return.

In view of these remarks we may reject the contention that the injustice of institutions is always imperfect because the distribution of natural talents and the contingencies of social circumstance are unjust, and this injustice must inevitably carry over to human arrangements. Occasionally this reflection is offered as an excuse for ignoring injustice, as if the refusal to acquiesce in injustice is on a par with being unable to accept death. The natural distribution is neither just nor unjust; nor is it unjust that men are born into society at some particular position. These are simply natural facts. What is just and unjust is the way that institutions deal with these facts. Aristocratic and caste societies are unjust because they make these contingencies the ascriptive basis for belonging to more or less enclosed and privileged social classes. The basic structure of these societies incorporates the arbitrariness found in nature. But there is no necessity for men to resign themselves to these contingencies. The social system is not an unchangeable order beyond human control but a pattern of human action. In justice as fairness men agree to share one another's fate. In designing institutions they undertake to avail themselves of the accidents of nature and social circumstance only when doing so is for the common benefit. The two principles are a fair way of meeting the arbitrariness of fortune; and while no doubt imperfect in other ways, the institutions which satisfy these principles are just.

A further point is that the difference principle expresses a conception of reciprocity. It is a principle of mutual benefit. We have seen that, at least when chain connection holds, each representative man can accept the basic structure as designed to advance his interests. The social order can be justified to everyone, and in particular to those who are least favored; and in this sense it is egalitarian. But it seems necessary to consider in an intuitive way how the condition of mutual benefit is satisfied. Consider any two representative men A and B, and let B be the one who is less favored. Actually, since we are most interested in the comparison with the least favored man, let us assume that B is this individual. Now B can accept A's being better off since A's advantages have been gained in ways that improve B's prospects. If A were not allowed his better position, B would be even worse off than he is. The difficulty is to show that A has no grounds for complaint. Perhaps he is required to have less than he might since his having more would result in some loss to B. Now what can be said to the more favored man? To begin with, it is clear that the well-being of each depends on a scheme of social cooperation without which no one could have a satisfactory life. Secondly, we can ask for the willing cooperation of everyone only if the terms of the scheme are reasonable. The difference principle, then, seems to be a fair basis on which those better endowed, or more fortunate in their social circumstances, could expect others to collaborate with them when some workable arrangement is a necessary condition of the good of all.

There is a natural inclination to object that those better situated deserve their greater advantages whether or not they are to the benefit of others. At this point it is necessary to be clear about the notion of desert. It is perfectly true that given a just system of cooperation as a scheme of public rules and the expectations set up by it, those who, with the prospect of improving their condition, have done what the system announces that it will reward are entitled to their advantages. In this sense the more fortunate have a claim to their better situation; their claims are legitimate expectations established by social institutions, and the community is obligated to meet them. But this sense of desert presupposes the existence of the cooperative scheme; it is irrelevant to the question whether in the first place the scheme is to be designed in accordance with the difference principle or some other criterion.

Perhaps some will think that the person with greater natural endowments deserves those assets and the superior character that made their development possible. Because he is more worthy in this sense, he deserves the greater advantages that he could achieve with them. This view, however, is surely incorrect. It seems to be one of the fixed points of our considered judgments that no one deserves his place in the distribution of native endowments, any more than one deserves one's initial starting place in society. The assertion that a man deserves the superior character that enables him to make the effort to cultivate his abilities is equally problematic; for his character depends in large part upon fortunate family and social circumstances for which he can claim no credit. The notion of desert seems not to apply to these cases. Thus the more advantaged representative man cannot say that he deserves and therefore has a right to a scheme of cooperation in which he is permitted to acquire benefits in ways that do not contribute to the welfare of others. There is no basis for his making this claim. From the standpoint of common sense, then, the difference principle appears to be acceptable both to the more advantaged and to the less advantaged individual. Of course, none of this is strictly speaking an argument for the principle, since in a contract theory arguments are made from the point of view of the original position. But these intuitive considerations help to clarify the nature of the principle and the sense in which it is egalitarian. . . .

III. The Reasoning for the Two Principles

It seems clear from these remarks that the two principles are at least a plausible conception of justice. The question, though, is how one is to argue for them more systematically. Now there are several things to do. One can work out their consequences for institutions and note their implications for fundamental social policy. In this way they are tested by a comparison with our considered judgments of justice. . . . But one can also try to find arguments in their favor that are decisive from the standpoint of the original position. In order to see how this might be done, it is useful as a heuristic device to think of the two principles as the maximin solution to the problem of social justice. There is an analogy between the two principles and the maximin rule for choice under uncertainty.[12] This is evident from the fact that the two principles are those a person would choose for the design of a society in which his enemy is to assign him his place. The maximin rule tells us to rank alternatives by their worst possible outcomes: we are to adopt the alternative the worst outcome of which is superior to the worst outcomes of the others. The persons in the original position do not, of course, assume that their initial place in society is decided by a malevolent opponent. As I note below, they should not reason from false premises. The veil of ignorance does not violate this idea, since an absence of information is not misinformation. But that the two principles of justice would be chosen if the parties were forced to protect themselves against such a contingency explains the sense in which this conception is the maximin solution. And this analogy suggests that if the original position has been described so that it is rational for the parties to adopt the conservative attitude expressed by this rule, a conclusive argument can indeed be constructed for these principles. Clearly the maximin rule is not, in general, a suitable guide for choices under uncertainty. But it is attractive in situations marked by certain special features. My aim, then, is to show that a good case can be made for the two principles based on the fact that the original position manifests these features to the fullest possible degree, carrying them to the limit, so to speak.

Consider the gain-and-loss table below. It represents the gains and losses for a situation which is not a game of strategy. There is no one playing against the person making the decision; instead he is faced with several possible circumstances which may or may not obtain. Which circumstances happen to exist does not depend upon what the person choosing decides or whether he announces his moves in advance. The numbers in the table are monetary values (in hundreds of dollars) in comparison with some initial situation. The gain (g) depends upon the individual's decision (d) and the circumstances (c). Thus $g = f(d, c)$. Assuming that there are three possible decisions and three possible circumstances, we might have this gain-and-loss table.

Decisions	Circumstances		
	C_1	C_2	C_3
d_1	−7	8	12
d_2	−8	7	14
d_3	5	6	8

The maximin rule requires that we make the third decision. For in this case the worst that can happen is that one gains five hundred dollars, which is better than the worst for the other actions. If we adopt one of these we may lose either eight or seven hundred dollars. Thus, the choice of d_3 maximizes $f(d,c)$ for that value of c, which for a given d, minimizes f. The term "maximin" means the *maximum minimorum*; and the rule directs our attention to the worst that can happen under any proposed course of action, and to decide in the light of that.

Now there appear to be three chief features of situations that give plausibility to this unusual rule.[13] First, since the rule takes no account of the likelihoods of the possible circumstances, there must be some reason for sharply discounting estimates of these probabilities. Offhand, the most natural rule of choice would seem to be to compute the expectation of monetary gain for each decision and then to adopt the course of action with the highest prospect. . . . Thus it must be, for example, that the situation is one in which a knowledge of likelihoods is impossible, or at best extremely insecure. In this case it is unreasonable not to be skeptical of probabilistic calculations unless there is no other way out, particularly if the decision is a fundamental one that needs to be justified to others.

The second feature that suggests the maximin rule is the following: the person choosing has a conception of the good such that he cares very little, if anything, for what he might gain above the minimum stipend that he can, in fact, be sure of by following the maximin rule. It is not worthwhile for him to take a chance for the sake of a further advantage, especially when it may turn out that he loses much that is important to him. This last provision brings in the third feature, namely, that the rejected alternatives have outcomes that one can hardly accept. The situation involves grave risks. Of course these features work most effectively in combination. The paradigm situation for following the maximin rule is when all three features are realized to the highest degree. This rule does not, then, generally apply, nor of course is it self-evident. Rather, it is a maxim, a rule of thumb, that comes into its own in special circumstances. Its application depends upon the qualitative structure of the possible gains and losses in relation to one's conception of the good, all this against a background in which it is reasonable to discount conjectural estimates of likelihoods.

It should be noted, as the comments on the gain-and-loss table say, that the entries in the table represent monetary values and not utilities. This difference is significant since for one thing computing expectations on the basis of such objective values is not the same thing as computing expected utility and may lead to different results. The essential point though is that in justice as fairness the parties do not know their conception of the good and cannot estimate their utility in the ordinary sense. In any case, we want to go behind de facto preferences generated by given conditions. Therefore expectations are based upon an index of primary goods and the parties make their choice accordingly. The entries in the example are in terms of money and not utility to indicate this aspect of the contract doctrine.

Now, as I have suggested, the original position has been defined so that it is a situation in which the maximin rule applies. In order to see this, let us review briefly the nature of this situation with these three special features in mind. To begin with, the veil of ignorance excludes all but the vaguest knowledge of likelihoods. The parties have no basis for determining the probable nature of their society, or their place in it. Thus they have strong reasons for being wary of probability calculations if any other course is open to them. They must also take in account the fact that their choice of principles should seem reasonable to others, in particular their descendants, whose rights will be deeply affected by it. There are further grounds for discounting that I shall mention as we go along. For the present it suffices to note that these considerations are strengthened by the fact that the parties know very little about the gain-and-loss table. Not only are they unable to conjecture the likelihoods of the various possible circumstances, they cannot say much about what the possible circumstances are, much less enumerate them and foresee the outcome of each alternative available. Those deciding are much more in the dark than the illustration by a numerical table suggests. It is for this reason that I have spoken of an analogy with the maximin rule.

Several kinds of arguments for the two principles of justice illustrate the second feature. Thus, if we can maintain that these principles provide a workable theory of social justice, and that they are compatible with reasonable demands of efficiency, then this conception guarantees a satisfactory minimum. There may be, on reflection, little reason for trying to do better. Thus much of the argument . . . is to show, by their application to the main questions of social justice, that the two principles are a satisfactory conception. These details have a philosophical purpose. Moreover, this line of thought is practically decisive if we can establish the priority of liberty, the lexical ordering of the two principles. For this priority implies that the persons in the original position have no desire to try for greater gains at the expense of the equal liberties. The minimum assured by the two principles in lexical order is not one that the parties wish to jeopardize for the sake of greater economic and social advantages. . . . I present the case for this ordering [elsewhere].

Finally, the third feature holds if we can assume that other conceptions of justice may lead to institutions that the parties would find intolerable. For example, it has sometimes been held that under some conditions the utility principle (in either form) justifies, if not slavery or serfdom, at any rate serious infractions of liberty for the sake of greater social benefits. We need not consider here the truth of this claim, or the likelihood that the requisite conditions obtain. For the moment, this contention is only to illustrate the way in which conceptions of justice may allow for outcomes which the parties may not be able to accept. And having the ready alternative of the two principles of justice which secure a satisfactory minimum, it seems unwise, if not irrational, for them to take a chance that these outcomes are not realized.

So much, then, for a brief sketch of the features of situations in which the maximin rule comes into its own and of the way in which the arguments for the two principles of justice can be subsumed under them. . . . These principles would be selected by the rule. The original position clearly exhibits these special features to a very high degree in view of the fundamental character of the choice of a conception of justice. These remarks about the maximin rule are intended only to clarify the structure of the choice problem in the original position. They depict its qualitative anatomy. The arguments for the two principles will be presented more fully as we proceed. . . .

THE MAIN GROUNDS FOR THE TWO PRINCIPLES OF JUSTICE

In this section my aim is to use the conditions of publicity and finality to give some of the main arguments for the two principles of justice. I shall rely upon the fact that for an agreement to be valid, the parties must be able to honor it under all relevant and foreseeable circumstances. There must be a rational assurance that one can carry through. The arguments I shall adduce fit under the heuristic schema suggested by the reasons for following the maximin rule. That is, they help to show that the two principles are an adequate minimum conception of justice in a situation of great uncertainty. Any further advantages that might be won by the principle of utility, or whatever, are highly problematical, whereas the hardships if things turn out badly are intolerable. It is at this point that the concept of a contract has a definite role: it suggests the condition of publicity and sets limits upon what can be agreed to. Thus justice as fairness uses the concept of contract to a greater extent than the discussion so far might suggest.

The first confirming ground for the two principles can be explained in terms of what I earlier referred to as the strains of commitment. I said that the parties have a capacity for justice in the sense that they can be assured that their undertaking is not in vain. Assuming that they have taken everything into account, including the general facts of moral psychology, they can rely on one another to adhere to the principles adopted. Thus they consider the strains of commitment. They cannot enter into agreements that may have consequences they cannot accept. They will avoid those that they can adhere to only with great difficulty. Since the original agreement is final and made in perpetuity, there is no second chance. In view of the serious nature of the possible consequences, the question of the burden of commitment is especially acute. A person is choosing once and for all the standards which are to govern his life prospects. Moreover, when we enter an agreement we must be able to honor it even should the worst possibilities prove to be the case. Otherwise we have not acted in good faith. Thus the parties must weigh with care whether they will be able to stick by their commitment in all circumstances. Of course, in answering this question they have only a general knowledge of human psychology to go on. But this information is enough to tell which conception of justice involves the greater stress.

In this respect the two principles of justice have a definite advantage. Not only do the parties protect their basic rights but they insure themselves against the worst eventualities. They run no chance of having to acquiesce in a loss of freedom over the course of their life for the sake of a greater good enjoyed by others, an undertaking that in actual circumstances they might not be able to keep. Indeed, we might wonder whether such an agreement can be made in good faith at all. Compacts of this sort exceed the capacity of human nature. How can the parties possibly know, or be sufficiently sure, that they can keep such an agreement? Certainly they cannot base their confidence on a general knowledge of moral psychology. To be sure, any principle chosen in the original position may require a large sacrifice for some. The beneficiaries of clearly unjust institutions (those founded on principles which have no claim to acceptance) may find it hard to reconcile themselves to the changes that will have to be made. But in this case they will know that they could not have maintained their position anyway. Yet should a person gamble with his liberties and substantive interests hoping that the application of the principle of utility might secure him a greater well-being, he may have difficulty abiding by his undertaking. He is bound to remind himself that he had the two principles of justice as an alternative. If the only possible candidates all involved similar risks, the problem of the strains of commitment would have to be waived. This is not the case, and judged in this light the two principles seem distinctly superior.

A second consideration invokes the condition of publicity as well as that of the constraints on agreements. I shall present the argument in terms of the question of psychological stability. Earlier I stated that a strong point in favor of a conception of justice is that it generates its own support. When the basic structure of society is publicly known to satisfy its principles for an extended period of time, those subject to these arrangements tend to develop a desire to act in accordance with these principles and to do their part in institutions which exemplify them. A conception of justice is stable when the public recognition of its realization by the social system tends to bring about the corresponding sense of justice. Now whether this happens depends, of course, on the laws of moral psychology and the availability of human motives. I shall discuss these matters later on. At the moment we may observe that the principle of utility seems to require a greater identification with the interests of others than the two principles of justice. Thus the latter will be a more stable conception to the extent that this identification is difficult to achieve. When the two principles are satisfied, each person's liberties are secured and there is a sense defined by the difference principle in which everyone is benefited by social cooperation. Therefore we can explain the acceptance of the social system and the principles it satisfies by the psychological law that persons tend to love, cherish, and support whatever affirms their own good. Since everyone's good is affirmed, all acquire inclinations to uphold the scheme.

When the principle of utility is satisfied, however, there is no such assurance that everyone benefits. Allegiance to the social system may demand that some should forgo advantages for the sake of the greater good of the whole. Thus the scheme will not be stable unless those who must make sacrifices strongly identify with interests broader than their own. But this is not easy to bring about. The sacrifices in question are not those asked in times of social emergency when all or some must pitch in for the common good. The principles of justice apply to the basic structure of the social system and to the determination of life prospects. What the principle of utility asks is precisely a sacrifice of these prospects. We are to accept the greater advantages of others as a sufficient reason for lower expectations over the whole course of our life. This is surely an extreme demand. In fact, when society is conceived as a system of cooperation designed to advance the good of its members, it seems quite incredible that some citizens should be expected, on the basis of political principles, to accept lower prospects of life for the sake of others. It is evident then why utilitarians should stress the role of sympathy in moral learning and the central place of benevolence among the moral virtues. Their conception of justice is threatened with instability unless sympathy and benevolence can be widely and intensely cultivated. Looking at the question from the standpoint of the original position, the parties recognize that it would be highly unwise if not irrational to choose principles which may have consequences so extreme that they could not accept them in practice. They would reject the principle of utility and adopt the more realistic idea of designing the social order on a principle of reciprocal advantage. We need not suppose, of course, that persons never make substantial sacrifices for one another, since moved by affection and ties of sentiment they often do. But such actions are not demanded as a matter of justice by the basic structure of society.

Furthermore, the public recognition of the two principles gives greater support to men's self-respect and this in turn increases the effectiveness of social cooperation. Both effects are reasons for choosing these principles. It is clearly rational for men to secure their self-respect. A sense of their own worth is necessary if they are to pursue their conception of the good with zest and to delight in its fulfillment. Self-respect is not so much a part of any rational plan of life as the sense that one's plan is worth carrying out. Now our self-respect normally depends upon the respect of others. Unless we feel that our endeavors are honored by them, it is difficult if not impossible for us to maintain the conviction that our ends are worth advancing. Hence for this reason the parties would accept the natural duty of mutual respect which asks them to treat one another civilly and to be willing to explain the grounds of their actions, especially when the claims of others are overruled. Moreover, one may assume that those who respect themselves are more likely to respect each other and conversely. Self-contempt leads to contempt of others and threatens their good as much as envy does. Self-respect is reciprocally self-supporting.

Thus a desirable feature of a conception of justice is that it should publicly express men's respect for one another. In this way they insure a sense of their own value. Now the two principles achieve this end. For when society follows these principles, everyone's good is included in a scheme of mutual benefit and this public affirmation in institutions of each man's endeavors supports men's self-esteem. The establishment of equal liberty and the operation of the difference principle are bound to have this effect. The two principles are equivalent, as I have remarked, to an undertaking to regard the distribution of natural abilities as a collective asset so that the more fortunate are to benefit only in ways that help those who have lost out. I do not say that the parties are moved by the ethical propriety of this idea. But there are reasons for them to accept this principle. For by arranging inequalities for reciprocal advantage and by abstaining from the exploitation of the contingencies of nature and social circumstance within a framework of equal liberty, persons express their respect for one another in the very constitution of their society. In this way they insure their self-esteem as it is rational for them to do.

Another way of putting this is to say that the principles of justice manifest in the basic structure of society men's desire to treat one another not as means only but as ends in themselves. I cannot examine Kant's view here.[14] Instead I shall freely interpret it in the light of the contract doctrine. The notion of treating men as ends in themselves and never as only a means obviously needs an explanation. There is even a question whether it is possible to realize. How can we always treat everyone as an end and never as a means only? Certainly we cannot say that it comes to treating everyone by the same general principles, since this interpretation makes the concept equivalent to formal justice. On the contract interpretation treating men as ends in themselves implies at the very least treating them in accordance with the principles to which they would consent in an original position of equality. For in this situation men have equal representation as moral persons who regard themselves as ends and the principles they accept will be rationally designed to protect the claims of their person. The contract view as such defines a sense in which men are to be treated as ends and not as means only. . . .

Addendum: The Basic Structure as Subject *

I

An important assumption of my book *A Theory of Justice* is that the basic structure of society is the primary subject of justice. By the basic structure is meant the way in which the major social institutions fit together into one system, and how they assign fundamental rights and duties and shape the division of advantages that arises through social cooperation. Thus the political constitution, the legally recognized forms of property, and the organization of the economy, all belong to the basic structure. I held that the first test of a conception of justice is whether its principles provide reasonable guidelines for the classical questions of social justice in this case. . . .

II

Several lines of reasoning point to the basic structure as the primary subject of justice. One is the following: suppose we begin with the initially attractive idea that society should develop over time in accordance with free agreements fairly arrived at and fully honored. Straightway we need an account of when agreements are free and the social circumstances under which they are reached are fair. In addition, while these conditions may be fair at an earlier time, the accumulated results of many separate ostensibly fair agreements, together with social and historical contingencies, are likely as time passes to alter institutions and opportunities so that the conditions for free and fair agreements no longer hold. The role of the basic structure is to secure just background conditions against which the actions of individuals and associations take place. Unless this structure is appropriately regulated and corrected, the

* From "The Basic Structure of Subject," *American Philosophical Quarterly* 14, no. 2 (April 1977). Reprinted by permission.

social process will cease to be just, however free and fair particular transactions may look when viewed by themselves.

We recognize this fact when we say, for example, that the distribution resulting from voluntary market transactions (even should all the ideal conditions for competitive efficiency obtain) is not, in general, fair unless the antecedent distribution of income and wealth as well as the structure of the system of markets is fair. The existing wealth must have been properly acquired and all must have had fair opportunities to earn income, to learn wanted skills, and so on. Again, the conditions necessary for background justice can be undermined, even though nobody acts unfairly or is aware of how the conjunction of contingencies affects the opportunities of others. There are no feasible rules that it is practicable to impose on economic agents that can prevent these undesirable consequences. These consequences are often so far in the future, or so indirect, that the attempt to forestall them by restrictive rules that apply to individuals would be an excessive if not impossible burden. Thus we start with the basic structure and try to see how this system itself should make the corrections necessary to preserve background justice.

III

A second reflection points in the same direction. Consider the situation of individuals engaged in market transactions. We have seen that certain background conditions are necessary for these transactions to be fair. But what about the nature of individuals themselves: how did they get to be what they are? A theory of justice cannot take their final aims and interests, their attitude to themselves and their life, as given. Everyone recognizes that the form of society affects its members and determines in large part the kind of persons they want to be as well as the kind of persons they are. It also limits people's ambitions and hopes in different ways, for they will with reason view themselves in part according to their place in it and take account of the means and opportunities they can realistically expect. Thus an economic regime is not only an institutional scheme for satisfying existing desires and aspirations but a way of fashioning desires and aspirations in the future.

Nor, similarly, can we view the abilities and talents of individuals as fixed natural gifts, even if there is an important genetic component. These abilities and talents cannot come to fruition apart from social conditions and as realized they always take but one of many possible forms. An ability is not, for example, a computer in the head with a definite measurable capacity unaffected by social circumstances. Among the elements affecting the realization of natural capacities are social attitudes of encouragement and support and the institutions concerned with their training and use. Thus even a potential ability at any given time is not something unaffected by existing social forms and particular contingencies over the course of life up to that moment. So not only our final ends and hopes for ourselves but our realized abilities and talents reflect, to a large degree, our personal history, opportunities, and social position. What we might have been had these things been different, we cannot know.

Finally, both of the preceding considerations are strengthened by the fact that the basic structure most likely contains significant social and economic inequalities. These I assume to be necessary, or else highly advantageous, in maintaining effective social cooperation; presumably there are various reasons for this, among which the need for incentives is but one. Even if these inequalities are not very great, they seem bound to have a considerable effect and so to favor some over others depending upon their social origins, their realized natural endowments, and the chance coincidences and opportunities that have come their way. The basic structure includes inequalities between certain starting-places, so to speak, and this feature, together with the earlier observations, prompts us to take this structure as the primary subject.

IV

In the conception of justice as fairness the institutions of the basic structure are viewed as just provided they (reasonably) satisfy the principles that free and equal moral persons, in a situation that is fair between them, would adopt for the purpose of regulating that structure. The main two principles read as follows: (1) Each person has an equal right to the most extensive scheme of equal basic liberties compatible with a similar scheme of liberties for all. (2) Social and economic inequalities are permissible provided that (a) they are to the greatest expected benefit of the least advantaged; and (b) attached to positions and offices open to all under conditions of fair equality of opportunity.

Let us consider how the special features of the basic structure affect the conditions of the initial agreement and hence the content of these principles. Now by assumption the basic structure is the all-inclusive social system that determines background justice; so any fair situation between individuals conceived as free and equal moral persons must be one that suitably evens out the contingencies within this system. Agreements reached when people know their present place in an ongoing society would be influenced by disparate social and natural contingencies. The principles adopted would then be selected by the historical course of events that took place within that structure. We would not have gotten beyond social happenstance in order to find an independent standard.

It is also clear why, when we interpret the parties as free and equal moral persons, they are to reason as if they know very little about themselves (referring here to the restrictions of the veil of ignorance). For to proceed otherwise is still to allow the disparate and deep contingent effects of the social system to influence the principles adopted; and this is true even if the parties have no particular information about themselves but only general facts about their own society (which is perhaps all that a condition of impartiality requires). When we as contemporaries are influenced by a general description of the present state of society in agreeing how we are to treat each other, and those generations that come after us, we have not yet left out of account the accidents of the basic structure. And so one arrives at the thicker rather than the thinner veil of ignorance: the parties are to be understood so far as possible solely as moral persons, that is, in abstraction from all those contingencies that the basic structure over time has shaped and influenced; and to be fair between them, the initial situation must situate them equally for as moral persons they are equal: the same essential properties qualify each.

Finally, the social contract must be regarded as hypothetical. Of course, any actual agreement is liable to the distortions just noted; but in any case, historically valid compacts, were such to exist, would have but limited force and could not serve as the basis of a general theory. Equally decisive is the fact that society is a system of cooperation that extends over time: it is cooperation between generations and not just cooperation among contemporaries. If we are to account for the duties and obligations between generations, there is no clear way to do this in a contract view without interpreting the initial agreement as hypothetical. The correct principles for the basic structure are those that the members of any generation (and hence all generations) would agree to as the ones their generation is to follow and as the principles they would want other generations to have followed and to follow subsequently, no matter how far back or forward in time.

Once we note the distinctive role of the basic structure and abstract from the various contingencies within it to find an appropriate conception of justice to regulate it, something like the notion of the original position seems inevitable. It is a natural extension of the idea of the social contract when the basic structure is taken as the primary subject of justice. . . .

NOTES

1. As the text suggests, I shall regard Locke's *Second Treatise of Government*, Rousseau's *The Social Contract*, and Kant's ethical works beginning with *The Foundations of the Metaphysics of Morals* as definitive of the contract tradition. For all of its greatness, Hobbes's *Leviathan* raises special problems. A general historical survey is provided by J. W. Gough, *The Social Contract*, 2nd ed. (Oxford, The Clarendon Press, 1957), and Otto Gierke, *Natural Law and the Theory of Society*, trans. with an introduction by Ernest Barker (Cambridge, The University Press, 1934). A presentation of the contract view as primarily an ethical theory is to be found in G. R. Grice, *The Grounds of Moral Judgment* (Cambridge, The University Press, 1967). . . .

2. Kant is clear that the original agreement is hypothetical. See *The Metaphysics of Morals*, pt. I (*Rechtslehre*), especially §§47, 52; and pt. II of the essay "Concerning

the Common Saying: This May Be True in Theory but It Does Not Apply in Practice," in *Kant's Political Writings,* ed. Hans Reiss and trans. by H. B. Nisbet (Cambridge, The University Press, 1970), pp. 73-87. See Georges Vlachos, *La Pensée politique de Kant* (Paris, Presses Universitaires de France, 1962), pp. 326-335; and J. G. Murphy, *Kant: The Philosophy of Right* (London, Macmillan, 1970), pp. 109-112, 133-136, for a further discussion.

3. For the formulation of this intuitive idea I am indebted to Allan Gibbard.

4. The process of mutual adjustment of principles and considered judgments is not peculiar to moral philosophy. See Nelson Goodman, *Fact, Fiction, and Forecast* (Cambridge, Mass., Harvard University Press, 1955), pp. 65-68, for parallel remarks concerning the justification of the principles of deductive and inductive inference.

5. Henri Poincaré remarks: "Il nous faut une faculté qui nous fasse voir le but de loin, et, cette faculté, c'est l'intuition." *La Valeur de la science* (Paris, Flammarion, 1909), p. 27.

6. The veil of ignorance is so natural a condition that something like it must have occurred to many. The closest express statement of it known to me is found in J. C. Harsanyi, "Cardinal Utility in Welfare Economics and in the Theory of Risk-Taking," *Journal of Political Economy,* vol. 61 (1953). Harsanyi uses it to develop a utilitarian theory. . . .

7. This fact is generally recognized in welfare economics, as when it is said that efficiency is to be balanced against equity. See for example Tibor Scitovsky, *Welfare and Competition* (London, George Allen and Unwin, 1952), pp. 60-69 and I. M. D. Little, *A Critique of Welfare Economics,* 2nd ed. (Oxford, The Clarendon Press, 1957), ch. VI, esp. pp. 112-116. See Sen's remarks on the limitations of the principle of efficiency, *Collective Choice and Social Welfare,* pp. 22, 24-26, 83-86.

8. This definition follows Sidgwick's suggestion in *The Methods of Ethics,* p. 285n. See also R. H. Tawney, *Equality* (London, George Allen and Unwin, 1931), ch. II, sec. ii; and B. A. O. Williams, "The Idea of Equality," in *Philosophy, Politics, and Society,* ed. Peter Laslett and W. G. Runciman (Oxford, Basil Blackwell, 1962), pp. 125f.

9. This formulation of the aristocratic ideal is derived from Santayana's account of aristocracy in ch. IV of *Reason and Society* (New York, Charles Scribner, 1905), pp. 109f. He says, for example, "an aristocratic regimen can only be justified by radiating benefit and by proving that were less given to those above, less would be attained by those beneath them." I am indebted to Robert Rodes for pointing out to me that natural aristocracy is a possible interpretation of the two principles of justice and that an ideal feudal system might also try to fulfill the difference principle.

10. See Herbert Spiegelberg, "A Defense of Human Equality," *Philosophical Review,* vol. 53 (1944), pp. 101, 113-123; and D. D. Raphael, "Justice and Liberty," *Proceedings of the Aristotelian Society,* vol. 51 (1950–1951), pp. 187f.

11. See, for example, Spiegelberg, pp. 120f.

12. An accessible discussion of this and other rules of choice under uncertainty can be found in W. J. Baumol, *Economic Theory and Operations Analysis,* 2nd ed. (Englewood Cliffs, N.J., Prentice-Hall, Inc., 1965), ch. 24. Baumol gives a geometric interpretation of these rules . . . See pp. 558-562. See also R. D. Luce and Howard Raiffa, *Games and Decisions* (New York, John Wiley and Sons, Inc., 1957), ch. XIII, for a fuller account.

13. Here I borrow from William Fellner, *Probability and Profit* (Homewood, Ill., R. D. Irwin, Inc., 1965), pp. 140-142, where these features are noted.

14. See *The Foundations of the Metaphysics of Morals,* pp. 427-430 of vol. IV of *Kants Gesammelten Schriften,* Preussische Academie der Wissenschaften (Berlin, 1913), where the second formulation of the categorical imperative is introduced.

libertarianism

John Rawls, as we have seen, presents an elegant and powerful case for his theory of justice. Adopting his principles would require extensive changes in our national priorities, even if we retained a basically capitalistic system of production. Nonetheless, he does provide a revamped theoretical foundation for the dominant liberalism of our time, which is committed to personal liberty and to reducing social and economic inequalities. Thus it should not be surprising that his strongest critics should come from thinkers outside this political mainstream. Although a challenge to Rawls has arisen from the left, from those committed more strongly to equality than to economic liberty, among his most trenchant opponents has been Robert Nozick, a libertarian.

As a libertarian, Nozick places individual liberty at center stage as the prime political value. Nozick challenges the assumption, common to liberal political thought, that justice demands extensive economic redistribution. He denies that the state may legitimately tax us—take our money by threat of coercion—to accomplish that redistribution. As a defender of laissez-faire capitalism and a critic of governmental authority, Nozick stands along with many contemporary American con-

servatives in the tradition of the seventeenth- and eighteenth-
century liberalism of John Locke and Adam Smith.

Nozick assumes, in accordance with this tradition, a perspective of individual rights—rights which may not be transgressed
by others, either as individuals or collectively as the state.
Commonly called Lockean, or negative, these rights constitute
"side constraints" on the actions of others, ensuring a person's
freedom from interference in the pursuit of his or her own life.
They are negative because they require only that others refrain
from acting in certain ways, in particular, that they refrain from
interfering with us. Beyond this, no one is obliged to do anything positive for us; we have no right, for example, to expect
others to provide us with satisfying work or with any material
goods we might need. Each individual is to be seen as autonomous and responsible, and should be left to fashion his or her
own life free from the interference of others—as long as this is
compatible with the right of others to do the same. Only the
acknowledgment of this almost absolute right to be free from
coercion, argues Nozick, fully respects the distinctiveness of
persons, each with a unique life to lead.

This framework of individual rights and corresponding
duties constitutes the basis of what power the government may
legitimately have. In Nozick's view, the only morally legitimate
state is the so-called night-watchman state, one whose functions
are restricted to protecting the negative rights of citizens, that
is, to protect them against force, theft, fraud, and so on. Yet
even this limited state is not obviously consistent with libertarian constraints, since consent is the only basis of political
obligation (beyond that imposed by others' natural rights) and
people have never expressly consented to the rule of government. Nozick's first task, then, is to justify his minimal state in
the face of the anarchist claim that *no* government is morally
legitimate. Nozick answers the anarchist by sketching how the
minimal state could arise legitimately from a state of nature
without violating the rights of any individual (by an invisible
hand process, analogous to the invisible hand of Adam Smith's
economics, in which the free choices of separate individuals,
each pursuing his or her own private interest, promote a result
—namely, the formation of a state—not intended by any one of
them.) For this reason, the night-watchman state is morally
acceptable.

Nozick claims further that this is the most extensive kind
of state that can be justified, and rejects in particular the claim
that a larger state is necessary in order to achieve justice in
economic distribution. He argues for this by presenting his own
libertarian conception of economic justice and by criticizing
alternative views. In contrast to theories he calls end-state and
patterned, Nozick proposes what he terms a historical entitle-

ment theory of justice. End-state principles hold that distributive justice depends upon certain structural features of the situation (for example, which distribution results in the greatest utility), regardless of the origins of and entitlements to the distributed goods. By contrast, historical principles hold that past circumstances "can create differential entitlements or differential deserts to things." A principle is patterned, on the other hand, if it specifies that distribution is to vary along some natural (that is, biological or social) dimension, for example, according to I.Q. (or need or height). A patterned principle may be historical if it looks to past action, as in "distribute according to moral merit."

Nozick's entitlement theory is historical and unpatterned since it holds that a distribution is just if it arises from a prior just distribution by just means. Things may be acquired originally by one's taking something that belongs to no one else, if this does not make others worse off than before. There are a number of ways of legitimately transferring justly acquired objects; gift and voluntary exchange are among them—theft and blackmail are not. There is, however, no pattern to which a just distribution should conform. In the absence of force and fraud, people may do what they wish with their goods or holdings. A parent has the right, for example, to leave an inheritance for her daughter (or anyone else's for that matter). The daughter does not necessarily deserve her inheritance and the advantage in life which it gives her, any more than she merits her native intelligence. But, in Nozick's view, she would be entitled to both; neither is a social good which society is free to distribute. One has a right to acquire and dispose of one's property as one sees fit, and an individual is entitled to his personal talents and characteristics and to whatever property he can obtain with them, so long as the negative rights of others are not violated in the process.

To disturb the free market is to tread on liberty, and the redistribution of wealth through taxation, claims Nozick, is on a par with forced labor. Justice forbids it. Nozick further argues that any patterned principle of distribution will conflict with liberty. For whatever pattern is chosen, free people will exchange labor and goods and thus upset the pattern. Enforcement of patterned conceptions of justice is thus incompatible with liberty since any nonlibertarian society would have to "forbid capitalist acts between consenting adults."

Nozick's critique of Rawls also strengthens the case for the entitlement view. He emphasizes that social goods do not come into the world unattached, like manna from heaven. To focus exclusively on distribution, as he contends Rawls does, is to ignore production, to ignore the fact that those goods must be created by someone who in doing so establishes a title to them.

Why should society be viewed as a cooperative project in the
first place, or the talents and endowments of each person be
seen as part of the collective assets of society to which all have
a title? Indeed, the terms of Rawls' contract seem unfair to the
well-endowed because their skill and talent is exploited by
others in society. It is hardly unjust, argues Nozick, to let
economic holdings vary with the abilities, interests, and endeavors of individuals. Rawls' whole procedure, he believes,
is biased against the entitlement view because the model of the
original position behind a veil of ignorance guarantees that an
end-state principle will be chosen.

ROBERT NOZICK

Harvard University

Distributive Justice

The minimal state is the most extensive state that can be justified. Any state more extensive violates people's rights. Yet many persons have put forth reasons purporting to justify a more extensive state. It is impossible within the compass of this book to examine all the reasons that have been put forth. Therefore, I shall focus upon those generally acknowledged to be most weighty and influential, to see precisely wherein they fail. In this chapter we consider the claim that a more extensive state is justified, because necessary (or the best instrument) to achieve distributive justice . . .

The term "distributive justice" is not a neutral one. Hearing the term "distribution," most people presume that some thing or mechanism uses some principle or criterion to give out a supply of things. Into this process of distributing shares some error may have crept. So it is an open question, at least, whether *redistribution* should take place; whether we should do again what has already been done once, though poorly. However, we are not in the position of children who have been given portions of pie by someone who now makes last minute adjustments to rectify careless cutting. There is no *central* distribution, no person or group entitled to control all the resources, jointly deciding how they are to be doled out. What each person gets, he gets from others who give to him

From *Anarchy, State, and Utopia,* Chapter Seven, "Distributive Justice" (New York: Basic Books, 1974). Reprinted by permission.

in exchange for something, or as a gift. In a free society, diverse persons control different resources, and new holdings arise out of the voluntary exchanges and actions of persons. There is no more a distributing or distribution of shares than there is a distributing of mates in a society in which persons choose whom they shall marry. The total result is the product of many individual decisions which the different individuals involved are entitled to make. Some uses of the term "distribution," it is true, do not imply a previous distributing appropriately judged by some criterion (for example, "probability distribution"): nevertheless, despite the title of this chapter, it would be best to use a terminology that clearly is neutral. We shall speak of people's holdings; a principle of justice in holdings describes (part of) what justice tells us (requires) about holdings. I shall state first what I take to be the correct view about justice in holdings, and then turn to the discussion of alternate views.[1]

Section I: The Entitlement Theory

The subject of justice in holdings consists of three major topics. The first is the *original acquisition of holdings,* the appropriation of unheld things. This includes the issues of how unheld things may come to be held, the process, or processes, by which unheld things may come to be held, the things that may come to be held by these processes, the extent of what comes to be held by a particular process, and so on. We shall refer to the complicated truth about this topic, which we shall not formulate here, as the principle of justice in acquisition. The second topic concerns the *transfer of holdings* from one person to another. By what processes may a person transfer holdings to another? How may a person acquire a holding from another who holds it? Under this topic come general descriptions of voluntary exchange, and gift and (on the other hand) fraud, as well as reference to particular conventional details fixed upon in a given society. The complicated truth about this subject (with placeholders for conventional details) we shall call the principle of justice in transfer. (And we shall suppose it also includes principles governing how a person may divest himself of a holding, passing it into an unheld state.)

If the world were wholly just, the following inductive definition would exhaustively cover the subject of justice in holdings.

1. A person who acquires a holding in accordance with the principle of justice in acquisition is entitled to that holding.

2. A person who acquires a holding in accordance with the principle of justice in transfer, from someone else entitled to the holding, is entitled to the holding.

3. No one is entitled to a holding except by (repeated) applications of 1 and 2.

The complete principle of distributive justice would say simply that a distribution is just if everyone is entitled to the holdings they possess under the distribution.

A distribution is just if it arises from another just distribution by legitimate means. The legitimate means of moving from one distribution to another are specified by the principle of justice in transfer. The legitimate first "moves" are specified by the principle of justice in acquisition.* Whatever arises from a just situation by just steps is itself just. The means of change specified by the principle of justice in transfer preserve justice. As correct rules of inference are truth-preserving, and any conclusion deduced via repeated application of such rules from only true premises is itself true, so the means of transition from one situation to another specified by the principle of justice in transfer are justice-preserving, and any situation actually arising from repeated transitions in accordance with the principle from a just situation is itself just. The parallel between justice-preserving transformations and truth-preserving transformations illuminates where it fails as well as where it holds. That a conclusion could have been deduced by truth-preserving means from premises that are true suffices to show its truth. That from a just situation a situation *could* have arisen via justice-preserving means does *not* suffice to show its justice. The fact that a thief's victims voluntarily *could* have presented him with gifts does not entitle the thief to his ill-gotten gains. Justice in holdings is historical; it depends upon what actually has happened. We shall return to this point later.

Not all actual situations are generated in accordance with the two principles of justice in holdings: the principle of justice in acquisition and the principle of justice in transfer. Some people steal from others, or defraud them, or enslave them, seizing their product and preventing them from living as they choose, or forcibly exclude others from competing in exchanges. None of these are permissible modes of transition from one situation to another. And some persons acquire holdings by means not sanctioned by the principle of justice in acquisition. The existence of past injustice (previous violations of the first two principles of justice in holdings) raises the third major topic under justice in holdings: the rectification of injustice in holdings. If past injustice has shaped present holdings in various ways, some identifiable and some not, what now, if anything, ought to be done to rectify these injustices? What obligations do the performers of injustice have toward those whose position is worse than it would have been had the injustice not been done? Or, than it would have been had compensation been paid promptly? How, if at all, do things change if the beneficiaries and those made worse off are not the direct parties in the act of injustice, but, for example, their descendants? Is an injustice done to someone whose holding was itself based upon an unrectified injustice? How far back must one go in wiping clean the historical slate of injustices? What may

---

* Applications of the principle of justice in acquisition may also occur as part of the move from one distribution to another. You may find an unheld thing now and appropriate it. Acquisitions also are to be understood as included when, to simplify, I speak only of transitions by transfers.

victims of injustice permissibly do in order to rectify the injustices being done to them, including the many injustices done by persons acting through their government? I do not know of a thorough or theoretically sophisticated treatment of such issues.[2] Idealizing greatly, let us suppose theoretical investigation will produce a principle of rectification. This principle uses historical information about previous situations and injustices done in them (as defined by the first two principles of justice and rights against interference), and information about the actual course of events that flowed from these injustices, until the present, and it yields a description (or descriptions) of holdings in the society. The principle of rectification presumably will make use of its best estimate of subjunctive information about what would have occurred (or a probability distribution over what might have occurred, using the expected value) if the injustice had not taken place. If the actual description of holdings turns out not to be one of the descriptions yielded by the principle, then one of the descriptions yielded must be realized.*

The general outlines of the theory of justice in holdings are that the holdings of a person are just if he is entitled to them by the principles of justice in acquisition and transfer, or by the principle of rectification of injustice (as specified by the first two principles). If each person's holdings are just, then the total set (distribution) of holdings is just. To turn these general outlines into a specific theory we would have to specify the details of each of the three principles of justice in holdings: the principle of acquisition of holdings, the principle of transfer of holdings, and the principle of rectification of violations of the first two principles. I shall not attempt that task here. (Locke's principle of justice in acquisition is discussed below.)

HISTORICAL PRINCIPLES AND END-RESULT PRINCIPLES

The general outlines of the entitlement theory illuminate the nature and defects of other conceptions of distributive justice. The entitlement theory of justice in distribution is *historical*; whether a distribution is just depends upon how it came about. In contrast, *current time-slice principles* of justice hold that the justice of a distribution is determined by how things are distributed (who has what) as judged by some *structural* principle(s) of just distribution. A utilitarian who judges between any two distributions by seeing which has the greater sum of utility and, if the sums tie, applies some fixed equality criterion to choose the more equal distribution, would hold a current time-slice principle of justice. As would someone who had a fixed schedule of trade-offs between the

---

* If the principle of rectification of violations of the first two principles yields more than one description of holdings, then some choice must be made as to which of these is to be realized. Perhaps the sort of considerations about distributive justice and equality that I argue against play a legitimate role in *this* subsidiary choice. Similarly, there may be room for such considerations in deciding which otherwise arbitrary features a statute will embody, when such features are unavoidable because other considerations do not specify a precise line; yet a line must be drawn.

sum of happiness and equality. According to a current time-slice principle, all that needs to be looked at, in judging the justice of a distribution, is who ends up with what; in comparing any two distributions one need look only at the matrix presenting the distributions. No further information need be fed into a principle of justice. It is a consequence of such principles of justice that any two structurally identical distributions are equally just. (Two distributions are structurally identical if they present the same profile, but perhaps have different persons occupying the particular slots. My having ten and your having five, and my having five and your having ten are structurally identical distributions.) Welfare economics is the theory of current time-slice principles of justice. The subject is conceived as operating on matrices representing only current information about distribution. This, as well as some of the usual conditions (for example, the choice of distribution is invariant under relabeling of columns), guarantees that welfare economics will be a current time-slice theory, with all of its inadequacies.

Most persons do not accept current time-slice principles as constituting the whole story about distributive shares. They think it relevant in assessing the justice of a situation to consider not only the distribution it embodies, but also how that distribution came about. If some persons are in prison for murder or war crimes, we do not say that to assess the justice of the distribution in the society we must look only at what this person has, and that person has, and that person has, . . . at the current time. We think it relevant to ask whether someone did something so that he *deserved* to be punished, deserved to have a lower share. Most will agree to the relevance of further information with regard to punishments and penalties. Consider also desired things. One traditional socialist view is that workers are entitled to the product and full fruits of their labor; they have earned it; a distribution is unjust if it does not give the workers what they are entitled to. Such entitlements are based upon some past history. No socialist holding this view would find it comforting to be told that because the actual distribution *A* happens to coincide structurally with the one he desires *D*, *A* therefore is no less just than *D*; it differs only in that the "parasitic" owners of capital receive under *A* what the workers are entitled to under *D*, and the workers receive under *A* what the owners are entitled to under *D*, namely very little. This socialist rightly, in my view, holds onto the notions of earning, producing, entitlement, desert, and so forth, and he rejects current time-slice principles that look only to the structure of the resulting set of holdings. (The set of holdings resulting from what? Isn't it implausible that how holdings are produced and come to exist has no effect at all on who should hold what?) His mistake lies in his view of what entitlements arise out of what sorts of productive processes.

We construe the position we discuss too narrowly by speaking of *current* time-slice principles. Nothing is changed if structural principles operate upon a time sequence of current time-slice profiles and, for example, give someone more now to counterbalance the less he has had earlier. A utilitarian or an egalitarian or any mixture of the two over time will inherit the difficulties of his more myopic comrades. He is not helped by the fact that *some* of the information others consider relevant in assessing a distribution is reflected, unrecoverably, in past matrices. Henceforth, we shall refer to such unhistorical principles of distributive justice, including the current time-slice principles, as *end-result principles* or *end-state principles.*

In contrast to end-result principles of justice, *historical principles* of justice hold that past circumstances or actions of people can create differential entitlements or differential deserts to things. An injustice can be worked by moving from one distribution to another structurally identical one, for the second, in profile the same, may violate people's entitlements or deserts; it may not fit the actual history.

PATTERNING

The entitlement principles of justice in holdings that we have sketched are historical principles of justice. To better understand their precise character, we shall distinguish them from another subclass of the historical principles. Consider, as an example, the principle of distribution according to moral merit. This principle requires that total distributive shares vary directly with moral merit; no person should have a greater share than anyone whose moral merit is greater. (If moral merit could be not merely ordered but measured on an interval or ratio scale, stronger principles could be formulated.) Or consider the principle that results by substituting "usefulness to society" for "moral merit" in the previous principle. Or instead of "distribute according to moral merit," or "distribute according to usefulness to society," we might consider "distribute according to the weighted sum of moral merit, usefulness to society, and need," with the weights of the different dimensions equal. Let us call a principle of distribution *patterned* if it specifies that a distribution is to vary along with some natural dimension, weighted sum of natural dimensions, or lexicographic ordering of natural dimensions. And let us say a distribution is patterned if it accords with some patterned principle. (I speak of natural dimensions, admittedly without a general criterion for them, because for any set of holdings some artificial dimensions can be gimmicked up to vary along with the distribution of the set.) The principle of distribution in accordance with moral merit is a patterned historical principle, which specifies a patterned distribution. "Distribute according to I.Q." is a patterned principle that looks to information not contained in distributional matrices. It is not historical, however, in that it does not look to any past actions creating differential entitlements to evaluate a distribution; it requires only distributional matrices whose columns are labeled by I.Q. scores. The distribution in a society, however, may be composed of such simple patterned distributions, without itself being simply patterned. Different sectors may operate different patterns, or some combination of patterns may operate in different proportions across a society. A distribution composed in this manner, from a small number of patterned distributions, we also shall term "patterned." And we extend the use of "pattern" to include the overall designs put forth by combinations of end-state principles.

Almost every suggested principle of distributive justice is patterned: to each according to his moral merit, or needs, or marginal product, or how hard he tries, or the weighted sum of the foregoing, and so on. The principle of entitlement we have sketched is *not* patterned.* There is no one natural dimension or weighted sum or combination of a small number of natural dimensions that yields the distributions generated in accordance with the principle of entitlement. The set of holdings that results when some persons receive their marginal products, others win at gambling, others receive a share of their mate's income, others receive gifts from foundations, others receive interest on loans, others receive gifts from admirers, others receive returns on investment, others make for themselves much of what they have, others find things, and so on, will not be patterned. Heavy strands of patterns will run through it; significant portions of the variance in holdings will be accounted for by pattern-variables. If most people most of the time choose to transfer some of their entitlements to others only in exchange for something from them, then a large part of what many people hold will vary with what they held that others wanted. More details are provided by the theory of marginal productivity. But gifts to relatives, charitable donations, bequests to children, and the like, are not best conceived, in the first instance, in this manner. Ignoring the strands of pattern, let us suppose for the moment that a distribution actually arrived at by the operation of the principle of entitlement is random with respect to any pattern. Though the resulting set of holdings will be unpatterned, it will not be incomprehensible, for it can be seen as arising from the operation of a small number of principles. These principles specify how an initial distribution may arise (the principle of acquisition of holdings) and how distributions may be transformed into others (the principle of transfer of holdings). The process whereby the set of holdings is generated will be intelligible, though the set of holdings itself that results from this process will be unpatterned.

* One might try to squeeze a patterned conception of distributive justice into the framework of the entitlement conception, by formulating a gimmicky obligatory "principle of transfer" that would lead to the pattern. For example, the principle that if one has more than the mean income one must transfer everything one holds above the mean to persons below the mean so as to bring them up to (but not over) the mean. We can formulate a criterion for a "principle of transfer" to rule out such obligatory transfers, or we can say that no correct principle of transfer, no principle of transfer in a free society will be like this. The former is probably the better course, though the latter also is true.

Alternatively, one might think to make the entitlement conception instantiate a pattern, by using matrix entries that express the relative strength of a person's entitlements as measured by some real-valued function. But even if the limitation to natural dimensions failed to exclude this function, the resulting edifice would *not* capture our system of entitlements to *particular* things.

The writings of F. A. Hayek focus less than is usually done upon what patterning distributive justice requires. Hayek argues that we cannot know enough about each person's situation to distribute to each according to his moral merit (but would justice demand we do so if we did have this knowledge?); and he goes on to say, "our objection is against all attempts to impress upon society a deliberately chosen pattern of distribution, whether it be an order of equality or of inequality." [3] However, Hayek concludes that in a free society there will be distribution in accordance with value rather than moral merit; that is, in accordance with the perceived value of a person's actions and services to others. Despite his rejection of a patterned conception of distributive justice, Hayek himself suggests a pattern he thinks justifiable: distribution in accordance with the perceived benefits given to others, leaving room for the complaint that a free society does not realize exactly this pattern. Stating this patterned strand of a free capitalist society more precisely, we get "To each according to how much he benefits others who have the resources for benefiting those who benefit them." This will seem arbitrary unless some acceptable initial set of holdings is specified, or unless it is held that the operation of the system over time washes out any significant effects from the initial set of holdings. As an example of the latter, if almost anyone would have bought a car from Henry Ford, the supposition that it was an arbitrary matter who held the money then (and so bought) would not place Henry Ford's earnings under a cloud. In any event, *his* coming to hold it is not arbitrary. Distribution according to benefits to others *is* a major patterned strand in a free capitalist society, as Hayek correctly points out, but it is only a strand and does not constitute the whole pattern of a system of entitlements (namely, inheritance, gifts for arbitrary reasons, charity, and so on) or a standard that one should insist a society fit. Will people tolerate for long a system yielding distributions that they believe are unpatterned? [4] No doubt people will not long accept a distribution they believe is *unjust*. People want their society to be and to look just. But must the look of justice reside in a resulting pattern rather than in the underlying generating principles? We are in no position to conclude that the inhabitants of a society embodying an entitlement conception of justice in holdings will find it unacceptable. Still, it must be granted that were people's reasons for transferring some of their holdings to others always irrational or arbitrary, we would find this disturbing. (Suppose people always determined what holdings they would transfer, and to whom, by using a random device.) We feel more comfortable upholding the justice of an entitlement system if most of the transfers under it are done for reasons. This does not mean necessarily that all deserve what holdings they receive. It means only that there is a purpose or point to someone's transferring a holding to one person rather than to another; that usually we can see what the transferrer thinks he's gaining, what cause he thinks he's serving, what goals he thinks he's helping to achieve, and so forth. Since in a capitalist society people often transfer holdings to others in accordance with how much they perceive these others benefiting them, the fabric constituted by the individual transactions and transfers is largely reasonable and intelligible.* (Gifts to loved ones, bequests to children, charity to the needy also are nonarbitrary components of the fabric.) In stressing the large strand of distribution in accordance with benefit to others, Hayek shows the point of many transfers, and so shows that the system of transfer of entitlements is not just spinning its gears aimlessly. The system of entitlements is defensible when constituted by the individual aims of individual transactions. No overarching aim is needed, no distributional pattern is required.

To think that the task of a theory of distributive justice is to fill in the blank in "to each according to his _____" is to be predisposed to search for a pattern; and the separate treatment of "from each according to his _____" treats production and distribution as two separate and independent issues. On an entitlement view these are *not* two separate questions. Whoever makes something, having bought or contracted for all other held resources used in the process (transferring some of his holdings for these cooperating factors), is entitled to it. The situation is *not* one of something's getting made, and there being an open question of who is to get it. Things come into the world already attached to people having entitlements over them. From the point of view of the historical entitlement conception of justice in holdings, those who start afresh to complete "to each according to his _____" treat objects as if they appeared from nowhere, out of nothing. A complete theory of justice might cover this limit case as well; perhaps here is a use for the usual conceptions of distributive justice.[5]

So entrenched are maxims of the usual form that perhaps we should present the entitlement conception as a competitor. Ignoring acquisition and rectification, we might say:

> From each according to what he chooses to do, to each according to what he makes for himself (perhaps with the contracted aid of others) and what others choose to do for him and choose to give him of what they've been given previously (under this maxim) and haven't yet expended or transferred.

This, the discerning reader will have noticed, has its defects as a slogan.

---

* We certainly benefit because great economic incentives operate to get others to spend much time and energy to figure out how to serve us by providing things we will want to pay for. It is not mere paradox mongering to wonder whether capitalism should be criticized for most rewarding and hence encouraging, not individualists like Thoreau who go about their own lives, but people who are occupied with serving others and winning them as customers. But to defend capitalism one need not think businessmen are the finest human types. (I do not mean to join here the general maligning of businessmen, either.) Those who think the finest should acquire the most can try to convince their fellows to transfer resources in accordance with *that* principle.

So as a summary and great simplification (and not as a maxim with any independent meaning) we have:

From each as they choose, to each as they are chosen.

How Liberty Upsets Patterns

It is not clear how those holding alternative conceptions of distributive justice can reject the entitlement conception of justice in holdings. For suppose a distribution favored by one of these non-entitlement conceptions is realized. Let us suppose it is your favorite one and let us call this distribution D_1; perhaps everyone has an equal share, perhaps shares vary in accordance with some dimension you treasure. Now suppose that Wilt Chamberlain is greatly in demand by basketball teams, being a great gate attraction. (Also suppose contracts run only for a year, with players being free agents.) He signs the following sort of contract with a team: In each home game, twenty-five cents from the price of each ticket of admission goes to him. (We ignore the question of whether he is "gouging" the owners, letting them look out for themselves.) The season starts, and people cheerfully attend his team's games; they buy their tickets, each time dropping a separate twenty-five cents of their admission price into a special box with Chamberlain's name on it. They are excited about seeing him play; it is worth the total admission price to them. Let us suppose that in one season one million persons attend his home games, and Wilt Chamberlain winds up with $250,000, a much larger sum than the average income and larger even than anyone else has. Is he entitled to this income? Is this new distribution D_2, unjust? If so, why? There is *no* question about whether each of the people was entitled to the control over the resources they held in D_1; because that was the distribution (your favorite) that (for the purposes of argument) we assumed was acceptable. Each of these persons *chose* to give twenty-five cents of their money to Chamberlain. They could have spent it on going to the movies, or on candy bars, or on copies of *Dissent* magazine, or of *Monthly Review*. But they all, at least one million of them, converged on giving it to Wilt Chamberlain in exchange for watching him play basketball. If D_1 was a just distribution, and people voluntarily moved from it to D_2, transferring parts of their shares they were given under D_1 (what was it for if not to do something with?), isn't D_2 also just? If the people were entitled to dispose of the resources to which they were entitled (under D_1), didn't this include their being entitled to give it to, or exchange it with, Wilt Chamberlain? Can anyone else complain on grounds of justice? Each other person already has his legitimate share under D_1. Under D_1, there is nothing that anyone has that anyone else has a claim of justice against. After someone transfers something to Wilt Chamberlain, third parties *still* have their legitimate shares; *their* shares are not changed. By what process could such a transfer among two persons give rise to a legitimate claim of distributive justice on a portion of what was transferred, by a third party who had no claim of justice on any

holding of the others *before* the transfer?* To cut off objections irrelevant here, we might imagine the exchanges occurring in a socialist society, after hours. After playing whatever basketball he does in his daily
work, or doing whatever other daily work he does, Wilt Chamberlain
decides to put in *overtime* to earn additional money. (First his work
quota is set; he works time over that.) Or imagine it is a skilled juggler
people like to see, who puts on shows after hours.

Why might someone work overtime in a society in which it is assumed
their needs are satisfied? Perhaps because they care about things other
than needs. I like to write in books that I read, and to have easy access
to books for browsing at odd hours. It would be very pleasant and con-
venient to have the resources of Widener Library in my back yard. No
society, I assume, will provide such resources close to each person who
would like them as part of his regular allotment (under D_1). Thus, persons either must do without some extra things that they want, or be
allowed to do something extra to get some of these things. On what basis
could the inequalities that would eventuate be forbidden? Notice also
that small factories would spring up in a socialist society, unless forbidden. I melt down some of my personal possessions (under D_1) and build
a machine out of the material. I offer you, and others, a philosophy
lecture once a week in exchange for your cranking the handle on my
machine, whose products I exchange for yet other things, and so on. (The
raw materials used by the machine are given to me by others who possess
them under D_1, in exchange for hearing lectures.) Each person might
participate to gain things over and above their allotment under D_1. Some
persons even might want to leave their job in socialist industry and
work full time in this private sector. I shall say something more about
these issues in the next chapter. Here I wish merely to note how private
property even in means of production would occur in a socialist society
that did not forbid people to use as they wished some of the resources
they are given under the socialist distribution D_1.[6] The socialist society
would have to forbid capitalist acts between consenting adults.

The general point illustrated by the Wilt Chamberlain example and
the example of the entrepreneur in a socialist society is that no end-state

---

* Might not a transfer have instrumental effects on a third party, changing his
feasible options? (But what if the two parties to the transfer independently had used
their holdings in this fashion?) I discuss this question below, but note here that this
question concedes the point for distributions of ultimate intrinsic noninstrumental
goods (pure utility experiences, so to speak) that are transferable. It also might be
objected that the transfer might make a third party more envious because it worsens
his position relative to someone else. I find it incomprehensible how this can be
thought to involve a claim of justice. . . .

Here and elsewhere in this chapter, a theory which incorporates elements of
pure procedural justice might find what I say acceptable, *if* kept in its proper place;
that is, if background institutions exist to ensure the satisfaction of certain conditions
on distributive shares. But if these institutions are not themselves the sum or invisible-
hand result of people's voluntary (nonaggressive) actions, the constraints they impose
require justification. At no point does our argument assume any background institutions more extensive than those of the minimal night-watchman state, a state limited
to protecting persons against murder, assault, theft, fraud, and so forth.

principle or distributional patterned principle of justice can be continuously realized without continuous interference with people's lives.
Any favored pattern would be transformed into one unfavored by the
principle, by people choosing to act in various ways; for example, by
people exchanging goods and services with other people, or giving things
to other people, things the transferrers are entitled to under the favored
distributional pattern. To maintain a pattern one must either continually
interfere to stop people from transferring resources as they wish to, or
continually (or periodically) interfere to take from some persons resources
that others for some reason chose to transfer to them. (But if some time
limit is to be set on how long people may keep resources others voluntarily transfer to them, why let them keep these resources for *any* period
of time? Why not have immediate confiscation?) It might be objected
that all persons voluntarily will choose to refrain from actions which
would upset the pattern. This presupposes unrealistically (1) that all
will most want to maintain the pattern (are those who don't, to be "re-
educated" or forced to undergo "self-criticism"?), (2) that each can gather
enough information about his own actions and the ongoing activities of
others to discover which of his actions will upset the pattern, and (3) that
diverse and far-flung persons can coordinate their actions to dovetail
into the pattern. Compare the manner in which the market is neutral
among persons' desires, as it reflects and transmits widely scattered information via prices, and coordinates persons' activities.

It puts things perhaps a bit too strongly to say that every patterned
(or end-state) principle is liable to be thwarted by the voluntary actions
of the individual parties transferring some of their shares they receive
under the principle. For perhaps some *very* weak patterns are not so
thwarted.* Any distributional pattern with any egalitarian component
is overturnable by the voluntary actions of individual persons over time;
as is every patterned condition with sufficient content so as actually to
have been proposed as presenting the central core of distributive justice.
Still, given the possibility that some weak conditions or patterns may not
be unstable in this way, it would be better to formulate an explicit description of the kind of interesting and contentful patterns under discussion, and to prove a theorem about their instability. Since the weaker
the patterning, the more likely it is that the entitlement system itself
satisfies it, a plausible conjecture is that any patterning either is unstable
or is satisfied by the entitlement system. . . .

REDISTRIBUTION AND PROPERTY RIGHTS

Apparently, patterned principles allow people to choose to spend
upon themselves, but not upon others, those resources they are entitled
to (or rather, receive) under some favored distributional pattern D_1. For
if each of several persons chooses to expend some of his D_1 resources
upon one other person, then that other person will receive more than
his D_1 share, disturbing the favored distributional pattern. Maintaining

* [Footnote omitted.]

a distributional pattern is individualism with a vengeance! Patterned distributional principles do not give people what entitlement principles do, only better distributed. For they do not give the right to choose what to do with what one has; they do not give the right to choose to pursue an end involving (intrinsically, or as a means) the enhancement of another's position. To such views, families are disturbing; for within a family occur transfers that upset the favored distributional pattern. Either families themselves become units to which distribution takes place, the column occupiers (on what rationale?), or loving behavior is forbidden. We should note in passing the ambivalent position of radicals toward the family. Its loving relationships are seen as a model to be emulated and extended across the whole society, at the same time that it is denounced as a suffocating institution to be broken and condemned as a focus of parochial concerns that interfere with achieving radical goals. Need we say that it is not appropriate to enforce across the wider society the relationships of love and care appropriate within a family, relationships which are voluntarily undertaken?* Incidentally, love is an interesting instance of another relationship that is historical, in that (like justice) it depends upon what actually occurred. An adult may come to love another because of the other's characteristics; but it is the other person, and not the characteristics, that is loved.[9] The love is not transferrable to someone else with the same characteristics, even to one who "scores" higher for these characteristics. And the love endures through changes of the characteristics that gave rise to it. One loves the particular person one actually encountered. Why love is historical, attaching to persons in this way and not to characteristics, is an interesting and puzzling question.

Proponents of patterned principles of distributive justice focus upon criteria for determining who is to receive holdings; they consider the reasons for which someone should have something, and also the total picture of holdings. Whether or not it is better to give than to receive, proponents of patterned principles ignore giving altogether. In considering the distribution of goods, income, and so forth, their theories are theories of recipient justice; they completely ignore any right a person might have to give something to someone. Even in exchanges where each party is simultaneously giver and recipient, patterned principles of justice focus only upon the recipient role and its supposed rights. Thus discussions tend to focus on whether people (should) have a right to inherit, rather than on whether people (should) have a right to bequeath or on

---

* One indication of the stringency of Rawls' difference principle, which we attend to in the second part of this chapter, is its inappropriateness as a governing principle even within a family of individuals who love one another. Should a family devote its resources to maximizing the position of its least well off and least talented child, holding back the other children or using resources for their education and development only if they will follow a policy through their lifetimes of maximizing the position of their least fortunate sibling? Surely not. How then can this even be considered as the appropriate policy for enforcement in the wider society? (I discuss below what I think would be Rawls' reply: that some principles apply at the macro level which do not apply to micro-situations.)

whether persons who have a right to hold also have a right to choose that others hold in their place. I lack a good explanation of why the usual theories of distributive justice are so recipient oriented; ignoring givers and transferrers and their rights is of a piece with ignoring producers and their entitlements. But why is it *all* ignored?

Patterned principles of distributive justice necessitate *re*distributive activities. The likelihood is small that any actual freely-arrived-at set of holdings fits a given pattern; and the likelihood is nil that it will continue to fit the pattern as people exchange and give. From the point of view of an entitlement theory, redistribution is a serious matter indeed, involving, as it does, the violation of people's rights. (An exception is those takings that fall under the principle of the rectification of injustices.) From other points of view, also, it is serious.

Taxation of earnings from labor is on a par with forced labor.* Some persons find this claim obviously true: taking the earnings of n hours labor is like taking n hours from the person; it is like forcing the person to work n hours for another's purpose. Others find the claim absurd. But even these, *if* they object to forced labor, would oppose forcing unemployed hippies to work for the benefit of the needy.† And they would also object to forcing each person to work five extra hours each week for the benefit of the needy. But a system that takes five hours' wages in taxes does not seem to them like one that forces someone to work five hours, since it offers the person forced a wider range of choice in activities than does taxation in kind with the particular labor specified. (But we can imagine a gradation of systems of forced labor, from one that specifies a particular activity, to one that gives a choice among two activities, to . . . ; and so on up.) Furthermore, people envisage a system with something like a proportional tax on everything above the amount necessary for basic needs. Some think this does not force someone to work extra hours, since there is no fixed number of extra hours he is forced to work, and since he can avoid the tax entirely by earning only enough to cover his basic needs. This is a very uncharacteristic view of forcing for those who *also* think people are forced to do something *whenever* the alternatives they face are considerably worse. However, *neither* view is correct. The fact that others intentionally intervene, in violation of a side constraint against aggression, to threaten force to limit the alternatives, in this case to paying taxes or (presumably the worse alternative) bare subsistence, makes the taxation system one of forced labor and dis-

---

*I am unsure as to whether the arguments I present below show that such taxation merely *is* forced labor; so that "is on a par with" means "is one kind of." Or alternatively, whether the arguments emphasize the great similarities between such taxation and forced labor, to show it is plausible and illuminating to view such taxation in the light of forced labor. This latter approach would remind one of how John Wisdom conceives of the claims of metaphysicians.

† Nothing hangs on the fact that here and elsewhere I speak loosely of *needs*, since I go on, each time, to reject the criterion of justice which includes it. If, however, something did depend upon the notion, one would want to examine it more carefully. For a skeptical view, see Kenneth Minogue, *The Liberal Mind* (New York: Random House, 1963), pp. 103-112.

tinguishes it from other cases of limited choices which are not forcings.[10]

The man who chooses to work longer to gain an income more than sufficient for his basic needs prefers some extra goods or services to the leisure and activities he could perform during the possible nonworking hours; whereas the man who chooses not to work the extra time prefers the leisure activities to the extra goods or services he could acquire by working more. Given this, if it would be illegitimate for a tax system to seize some of a man's leisure (forced labor) for the purpose of serving the needy, how can it be legitimate for a tax system to seize some of a man's goods for that purpose? Why should we treat the man whose happiness requires certain material goods or services differently from the man whose preferences and desires make such goods unnecessary for his happiness? Why should the man who prefers seeing a movie (and who has to earn money for a ticket) be open to the required call to aid the needy, while the person who prefers looking at a sunset (and hence need earn no extra money) is not? Indeed, isn't it surprising that redistributionists choose to ignore the man whose pleasures are so easily attainable without extra labor, while adding yet another burden to the poor unfortunate who must work for his pleasures? If anything, one would have expected the reverse. Why is the person with the nonmaterial or nonconsumption desire allowed to proceed unimpeded to his most favored feasible alternative, whereas the man whose pleasures or desires involve material things and who must work for extra money (thereby serving whomever considers his activities valuable enough to pay him) is constrained in what he can realize? Perhaps there is no difference in principle. And perhaps some think the answer concerns merely administrative convenience. (These questions and issues will not disturb those who think that forced labor to serve the needy or to realize some favored end-state pattern is acceptable.) In a fuller discussion we would have (and want) to extend our argument to include interest, entrepreneurial profits, and so on. Those who doubt that this extension can be carried through, and who draw the line here at taxation of income from labor, will have to state rather complicated patterned *historical* principles of distributive justice, since end-state principles would not distinguish *sources* of income in any way. It is enough for now to get away from end-state principles and to make clear how various patterned principles are dependent upon particular views about the sources or the illegitimacy or the lesser legitimacy of profits, interest, and so on; which particular views may well be mistaken.

What sort of right over others does a legally institutionalized end-state pattern give one? The central core of the notion of a property right in X, relative to which other parts of the notion are to be explained, is the right to determine what shall be done with X; the right to choose which of the constrained set of options concerning X shall be realized or attempted.[11] The constraints are set by other principles or laws operating in the society; in our theory, by the Lockean rights people possess (under the minimal state). My property rights in my knife allow me to leave it where I will, but not in your chest. I may choose which of the acceptable options involving the knife is to be realized. This notion of property helps us to understand why earlier theorists spoke of people as having property in themselves and their labor. They viewed each person as having a right to decide what would become of himself and what he would do, and as having a right to reap the benefits of what he did.

This right of selecting the alternative to be realized from the constrained set of alternatives may be held by an *individual* or by a *group* with some procedure for reaching a joint decision; or the right may be passed back and forth, so that one year I decide what's to become of X, and the next year you do (with the alternative of destruction, perhaps, being excluded). Or, during the same time period, some types of decisions about X may be made by me, and others by you. And so on. We lack an adequate, fruitful, analytical apparatus for classifying the *types* of constraints on the set of options among which choices are to be made, and the *types* of ways decision powers can be held, divided, and amalgamated. A *theory* of property would, among other things, contain such a classification of constraints and decision modes, and from a small number of principles would follow a host of interesting statements about the *consequences* and effects of certain combinations of constraints and modes of decision.

When end-result principles of distributive justice are built into the legal structure of a society, they (as do most patterned principles) give each citizen an enforceable claim to some portion of the total social product; that is, to some portion of the sum total of the individually and jointly made products. This total product is produced by individuals laboring, using means of production others have saved to bring into existence, by people organizing production or creating means to produce new things or things in a new way. It is on this batch of individual activities that patterned distributional principles give each individual an enforceable claim. Each person has a claim to the activities and the products of other persons, independently of whether the other persons enter into particular relationships that give rise to these claims, and independently of whether they voluntarily take these claims upon themselves, in charity or in exchange for something.

Whether it is done through taxation on wages or on wages over a certain amount, or through seizure of profits, or through there being a big *social pot* so that it's not clear what's coming from where and what's going where, patterned principles of distributive justice involve appropriating the actions of other persons. Seizing the results of someone's labor is equivalent to seizing hours from him and directing him to carry on various activities. If people force you to do certain work, or unrewarded work, for a certain period of time, they decide what you are to do and what purposes your work is to serve apart from your decisions. This process whereby they take this decision from you makes them a *part-owner* of you; it gives them a property right in you. Just as having such partial control and power of decision, by right, over an animal or inanimate object would be to have a property right in it.

End-state and most patterned principles of distributive justice institute (partial) ownership by others of people and their actions and labor.

These principles involve a shift from the classical liberals' notion of self-ownership to a notion of (partial) property rights in *other* people.

Considerations such as these confront end-state and other patterned conceptions of justice with the question of whether the actions necessary to achieve the selected pattern don't themselves violate moral side constraints. Any view holding that there are moral side constraints on actions, that not all moral considerations can be built into end states that are to be achieved (see Chapter 3, pp. 28–30), must face the possibility that some of its goals are not achievable by any morally permissible available means. An entitlement theorist will face such conflicts in a society that deviates from the principles of justice for the generation of holdings, if and only if the only actions available to realize the principles themselves violate some moral constraints. Since deviation from the first two principles of justice (in acquisition and transfer) will involve other persons' direct and aggressive intervention to violate rights, and since moral constraints will not exclude defensive or retributive action in such cases, the entitlement theorist's problem rarely will be pressing. And whatever difficulties he has in applying the principle of rectification to persons who did not themselves violate the first two principles are difficulties in balancing the conflicting considerations so as correctly to formulate the complex principle of rectification itself; he will not violate moral side constraints by applying the principle. Proponents of patterned conceptions of justice, however, often will face head-on clashes (and poignant ones if they cherish each party to the clash) between moral side constraints on how individuals may be treated and their patterned conception of justice that presents an end state or other pattern that *must* be realized.

May a person emigrate from a nation that has institutionalized some end-state or patterned distributional principle? For some principles (for example, Hayek's) emigration presents no theoretical problem. But for others it is a tricky matter. Consider a nation having a compulsory scheme of minimal social provision to aid the neediest (or one organized so as to maximize the position of the worst-off group); no one may opt out of participating in it. (None may say, "Don't compel me to contribute to others and don't provide for me via this compulsory mechanism if I am in need.") Everyone above a certain level is forced to contribute to aid the needy. But if emigration from the country were allowed, anyone could choose to move to another country that did not have compulsory social provision but otherwise was (as much as possible) identical. In such a case, the person's *only* motive for leaving would be to avoid participating in the compulsory scheme of social provision. And if he does leave, the needy in his initial country will receive no (compelled) help from him. What rationale yields the result that the person be permitted to emigrate, yet forbidden to stay and opt out of the compulsory scheme of social provision? If providing for the needy is of overriding importance, this does militate against allowing internal opting out; but it also speaks against allowing external emigration. (Would it also support, to some extent, the kidnapping of persons living in a place without compulsory social provision, who could be forced to make a contribution to the needy in your community?) Perhaps the crucial component of the position that allows emigration solely to avoid certain arrangements, while not allowing anyone internally to opt out of them, is a concern for fraternal feelings within the country. "We don't want anyone here who doesn't contribute, who doesn't care enough about the others to contribute." That concern, in this case, would have to be tied to the view that forced aiding tends to produce fraternal feelings between the aided and the aider (or perhaps merely to the view that the knowledge that someone or other voluntarily is not aiding produces unfraternal feelings).

LOCKE'S THEORY OF ACQUISITION

Before we turn to consider other theories of justice in detail, we must introduce an additional bit of complexity into the structure of the entitlement theory. This is best approached by considering Locke's attempt to specify a principle of justice in acquisition. Locke views property rights in an unowned object as originating through someone's mixing his labor with it. This gives rise to many questions. What are the boundaries of what labor is mixed with? If a private astronaut clears a place on Mars, has he mixed his labor with (so that he comes to own) the whole planet, the whole uninhabited universe, or just a particular plot? Which plot does an act bring under ownership? The minimal (possibly disconnected) area such that an act decreases entropy in that area, and not elsewhere? Can virgin land (for the purposes of ecological investigation by high-flying airplane) come under ownership by a Lockean process? Building a fence around a territory presumably would make one the owner of only the fence (and the land immediately underneath it).

Why does mixing one's labor with something make one the owner of it? Perhaps because one owns one's labor, and so one comes to own a previously unowned thing that becomes permeated with what one owns. Ownership seeps over into the rest. But why isn't mixing what I own with what I don't own a way of losing what I own rather than a way of gaining what I don't? If I own a can of tomato juice and spill it in the sea so that its molecules (made radioactive, so I can check this) mingle evenly throughout the sea, do I thereby come to own the sea, or have I foolishly dissipated my tomato juice? Perhaps the idea, instead, is that laboring on something improves it and makes it more valuable; and anyone is entitled to own a thing whose value he has created. (Reinforcing this, perhaps, is the view that laboring is unpleasant. If some people made things effortlessly, as the cartoon characters in *The Yellow Submarine* trail flowers in their wake, would they have lesser claim to their own products whose making didn't *cost* them anything?) Ignore the fact that laboring on something may make it less valuable (spraying pink enamel paint on a piece of driftwood that you have found). Why should one's entitlement extend to the whole object rather than just to the *added value* one's labor has produced? (Such reference to value might also serve to delimit the extent of ownership; for example, substitute "increases the value of" for "decreases entropy in" in the above entropy criterion.) No workable or coherent value-added property scheme has yet been devised, and any such scheme presumably would fall to objections (similar to those) that fell the theory of Henry George.

It will be implausible to view improving an object as giving full ownership to it, if the stock of unowned objects that might be improved is limited. For an object's coming under one person's ownership changes the situation of all others. Whereas previously they were at liberty (in Hohfeld's sense) to use the object, they now no longer are. This change in the situation of others (by removing their liberty to act on a previously unowned object) need not worsen their situation. If I appropriate a grain of sand from Coney Island, no one else may now do as they will with *that* grain of sand. But there are plenty of other grains of sand left for them to do the same with. Or if not grains of sand, then other things. Alternatively, the things I do with the grain of sand I appropriate might improve the position of others, counterbalancing their loss of the liberty to use that grain. The crucial point is whether appropriation of an unowned object worsens the situation of others.

Locke's proviso that there be "enough and as good left in common for others" (sect. 27) is meant to ensure that the situation of others is not worsened. (If this proviso is met is there any motivation for his further condition of nonwaste?) It is often said that this proviso once held but now no longer does. But there appears to be an argument for the conclusion that if the proviso no longer holds, then it cannot ever have held so as to yield permanent and inheritable property rights. Consider the first person Z for whom there is not enough and as good left to appropriate. The last person Y to appropriate left Z without his previous liberty to act on an object, and so worsened Z's situation. So Y's appropriation is not allowed under Locke's proviso. Therefore the next to last person X to appropriate left Y in a worse position, for X's act ended permissible appropriation. Therefore X's appropriation wasn't permissible. But then the appropriator two from last, W, ended permissible appropriation and so, since it worsened X's position, W's appropriation wasn't permissible. And so on back to the first person A to appropriate a permanent property right.

This argument, however, proceeds too quickly. Someone may be made worse off by another's appropriation in two ways: first, by losing the opportunity to improve his situation by a particular appropriation or any one; and second, by no longer being able to use freely (without appropriation) what he previously could. A *stringent* requirement that another not be made worse off by an appropriation would exclude the first way if nothing else counterbalances the diminution in opportunity, as well as the second. A *weaker* requirement would exclude the second way, though not the first. With the weaker requirement, we cannot zip back so quickly from Z to A, as in the above argument; for though person Z can no longer *appropriate*, there may remain some for him to *use* as before. In this case Y's appropriation would not violate the weaker

Lockean condition. (With less remaining that people are at liberty to use, users might face more inconvenience, crowding, and so on; in that way the situation of others might be worsened, unless appropriation stopped far short of such a point.) It is arguable that no one legitimately can complain if the weaker provision is satisfied. However, since this is less clear than in the case of the more stringent proviso, Locke may have intended this stringent proviso by "enough and as good" remaining, and perhaps he meant the nonwaste condition to delay the end point from which the argument zips back.

Is the situation of persons who are unable to appropriate (there being no more accessible and useful unowned objects) worsened by a system allowing appropriation and permanent property? Here enter the various familiar social considerations favoring private property: it increases the social product by putting means of production in the hands of those who can use them most efficiently (profitably); experimentation is encouraged, because with separate persons controlling resources, there is no one person or small group whom someone with a new idea must convince to try it out; private property enables people to decide on the pattern and types of risks they wish to bear, leading to specialized types of risk bearing; private property protects future persons by leading some to hold back resources from current consumption for future markets; it provides alternate sources of employment for unpopular persons who don't have to convince any one person or small group to hire them, and so on. These considerations enter a Lockean theory to support the claim that appropriation of private property satisfies the intent behind the "enough and as good left over" proviso, *not* as a utilitarian justification of property. They enter to rebut the claim that because the proviso is violated no natural right to private property can arise by a Lockean process. The difficulty in working such an argument to show that the proviso is satisfied is in fixing the appropriate base line for comparison. Lockean appropriation makes people no worse off than they would be *how?* [12] This question of fixing the baseline needs more detailed investigation than we are able to give it here. It would be desirable to have an estimate of the general economic importance of original appropriation in order to see how much leeway there is for differing theories of appropriation and of the location of the baseline. Perhaps this importance can be measured by the percentage of all income that is based upon untransformed raw materials and given resources (rather than upon human actions), mainly rental income representing the unimproved value of land, and the price of raw material *in situ*, and by the percentage of current wealth which represents such income in the past.*

We should note that it is not only persons favoring *private* property

---

* I have not seen a precise estimate. David Friedman, *The Machinery of Freedom* (N.Y.: Harper & Row, 1973), pp. xiv, xv, discusses this issue and suggests 5 percent of U.S. national income as an upper limit for the first two factors mentioned. However he does not attempt to estimate the percentage of current wealth which is based upon such income in the past. (The vague notion of "based upon" merely indicates a topic needing investigation.)

who need a theory of how property rights legitimately originate. Those believing in collective property, for example those believing that a group of persons living in an area jointly own the territory, or its mineral resources, also must provide a theory of how such property rights arise; they must show why the persons living there have rights to determine what is done with the land and resources there that persons living elsewhere don't have (with regard to the same land and resources).

THE PROVISO

Whether or not Locke's particular theory of appropriation can be spelled out so as to handle various difficulties, I assume that any adequate theory of justice in acquisition will contain a proviso similar to the weaker of the ones we have attributed to Locke. A process normally giving rise to a permanent bequeathable property right in a previously unowned thing will not do so if the position of others no longer at liberty to use the thing is thereby worsened. It is important to specify *this* particular mode of worsening the situation of others, for the proviso does not encompass other modes. It does not include the worsening due to more limited opportunities to appropriate (the first way above, corresponding to the more stringent condition), and it does not include how I "worsen" a seller's position if I appropriate materials to make some of what he is selling, and then enter into competition with him. Someone whose appropriation otherwise would violate the proviso still may appropriate provided he compensates the others so that their situation is not thereby worsened; unless he does compensate these others, his appropriation will violate the proviso of the principle of justice in acquisition and will be an illegitimate one.* A theory of appropriation incorporating this Lockean proviso will handle correctly the cases (objections to the theory lacking the proviso) where someone appropriates the total supply of something necessary for life.†

* Fourier held that since the process of civilization had deprived the members of society of certain liberties (to gather, pasture, engage in the chase), a socially guaranteed minimum provision for persons was justified as compensation for the loss (Alexander Gray, *The Socialist Tradition* (New York: Harper & Row, 1968), p. 188). But this puts the point too strongly. This compensation would be due those persons, if any, for whom the process of civilization was a *net loss,* for whom the benefits of civilization did not counterbalance being deprived of these particular liberties.

† For example, Rashdall's case of someone who comes upon the only water in the desert several miles ahead of others who also will come to it and appropriates it all. Hastings Rashdall, "The Philosophical Theory of Property," in *Property, its Duties and Rights* (London: MacMillan, 1915).

We should note Ayn Rand's theory of property rights ("Man's Rights" in *The Virtue of Selfishness* (New York: New American Library, 1964), p. 94), wherein these follow from the right to life, since people need physical things to live. But a right to life is not a right to whatever one needs to live; other people may have rights over these other things (see Chapter 3 of this book). At most, a right to life would be a right to have or strive for whatever one needs to live, provided that having it does not violate anyone else's rights. With regard to material things, the question is whether having it does violate any right of others. (Would appropriation of all unowned things

A theory which includes this proviso in its principle of justice in acquisition must also contain a more complex principle of justice in transfer. Some reflection of the proviso about appropriation constrains later actions. If my appropriating all of a certain substance violates the Lockean proviso, then so does my appropriating some and purchasing all the rest from others who obtained it without otherwise violating the Lockean proviso. If the proviso excludes someone's appropriating all the drinkable water in the world, it also excludes his purchasing it all. (More weakly, and messily, it may exclude his charging certain prices for some of his supply.) This proviso (almost?) never will come into effect; the more someone acquires of a scarce substance which others want, the higher the price of the rest will go, and the more difficult it will become for him to acquire it all. But still, we can imagine, at least, that something like this occurs: someone makes simultaneous secret bids to the separate owners of a substance, each of whom sells assuming he can easily purchase more from the other owners; or some natural catastrophe destroys all of the supply of something except that in one person's possession. The total supply could not be permissibly appropriated by one person at the beginning. His later acquisition of it all does not show that the original appropriation violated the proviso (even by a reverse argument similar to the one above that tried to zip back from Z to A). Rather, it is the combination of the original appropriation *plus* all the later transfers and actions that violates the Lockean proviso.

Each owner's title to his holding includes the historical shadow of the Lockean proviso on appropriation. This excludes his transferring it into an agglomeration that does violate the Lockean proviso and excludes his using it in a way, in coordination with others or independently of them, so as to violate the proviso by making the situation of others worse than their baseline situation. Once it is known that someone's ownership runs afoul of the Lockean proviso, there are stringent limits on what he may do with (what it is difficult any longer unreservedly to call) "his property." Thus a person may not appropriate the only water hole in a desert and charge what he will. Nor may he charge what he will if he possesses one, and unfortunately it happens that all the water holes in the desert dry up, except for his. This unfortunate circumstance, admittedly no fault of his, brings into operation the Lockean proviso and limits his property rights.* Similarly, an owner's property right in the only island in an area does not allow him to order a castaway from a

---

do so? Would appropriating the water hole in Rashdall's example?) Since special considerations (such as the Lockean proviso) may enter with regard to material property, one *first* needs a theory of property rights before one can apply any supposed right to life (as amended above). Therefore the right to life cannot provide the foundation for a theory of property rights.

* The situation would be different if his water hole didn't dry up, due to special precautions he took to prevent this. Compare our discussion of the case in the text with Hayek, *The Constitution of Liberty*, p. 136; and also with Ronald Hamowy, "Hayek's Concept of Freedom; A Critique," *New Individualist Review*, April 1961, pp. 28-31.

shipwreck off his island as a trespasser, for this would violate the Lockean proviso.

Notice that the theory does not say that owners do have these rights, but that the rights are overridden to avoid some catastrophe. (Overridden rights do not disappear; they leave a trace of a sort absent in the cases under discussion.)[13] There is no such external (and *ad hoc?*) overriding. Considerations internal to the theory of property itself, to its theory of acquisition and appropriation, provide the means for handling such cases. . . .

The fact that someone owns the total supply of something necessary for others to stay alive does *not* entail that his (or anyone's) appropriation of anything left some people (immediately or later) in a situation worse than the baseline one. A medical researcher who synthesizes a new substance that effectively treats a certain disease and who refuses to sell except on his terms does not worsen the situation of others by depriving them of whatever he has appropriated. The others easily can possess the same materials he appropriated; the researcher's appropriation or purchase of chemicals didn't make those chemicals scarce in a way so as to violate the Lockean proviso. Nor would someone else's purchasing the total supply of the synthesized substance from the medical researcher. The fact that the medical researcher uses easily available chemicals to synthesize the drug no more violates the Lockean proviso than does the fact that the only surgeon able to perform a particular operation eats easily obtainable food in order to stay alive and to have the energy to work. This shows that the Lockean proviso is not an "end-state principle"; it focuses on a particular way that appropriative actions affect others, and not on the structure of the situation that results.[14]

. . . The theme of someone worsening another's situation by depriving him of something he otherwise would possess may also illuminate the example of patents. An inventor's patent does not deprive others of an object which would not exist if not for the inventor. Yet patents would have this effect on others who independently invent the object. Therefore, these independent inventors, upon whom the burden of proving independent discovery may rest, should not be excluded from utilizing their own invention as they wish (including selling it to others). Furthermore, a known inventor drastically lessens the chances of actual independent invention. For persons who know of an invention usually will not try to reinvent it; and the notion of independent discovery here would be murky at best. Yet we may assume that in the absence of the original invention, sometime later someone else would have come up with it. This suggests placing a time limit on patents, as a rough rule of thumb to approximate how long it would have taken, in the absence of knowledge of the invention, for independent discovery.

I believe that the free operation of a market system will not actually run afoul of the Lockean proviso. . . . If this is correct, the proviso will not . . . provide a significant opportunity for future state action. . . .

We can bring our discussion of distributive justice into sharper focus by considering in some detail John Rawls' recent contribution to the subject. *A Theory of Justice* is a powerful, deep, subtle, wide-ranging, systematic work in political and moral philosophy which has not seen its like since the writings of John Stuart Mill, if then. It is a fountain of illuminating ideas, integrated together into a lovely whole. Political philosophers must now work within Rawls' theory or explain why not. . . . I permit myself to concentrate here on disagreements with Rawls only because I am confident that my readers will have discovered for themselves its many virtues.

Section II: Rawls' Theory

SOCIAL COOPERATION

I shall begin by considering the role of the principles of justice. Let us assume, to fix ideas, that a society is a more or less self-sufficient association of persons who in their relations to one another recognize certain rules of conduct as binding and who for the most part act in accordance with them. Suppose further that these rules specify a system of cooperation designed to advance the good of those taking part in it. Then, although a society is a cooperative venture for mutual advantage, it is typically marked by a conflict as well as by an identity of interests. There is an identity of interests since social cooperation makes possible a better life for all than any would have if each were to live solely by his own efforts. There is a conflict of interests since persons are not indifferent as to how the greater benefits produced by their collaboration are distributed, for in order to pursue their ends they each prefer a larger to a lesser share. A set of principles is required for choosing among the various social arrangements which determine this division of advantages and for underwriting an agreement on the proper distributive shares. These principles are the principles of social justice: they provide a way of assigning rights and duties in the basic institutions of society and they define the approprate distribution of the benefits and burdens of social cooperation (*A Theory of Justice,* p. 4).

. . . Why does social cooperation *create* the problem of distributive justice? Would there be no problem of justice and no need for a theory of justice, if there was no social cooperation at all, if each person got his share solely by his own efforts? If we suppose, as Rawls seems to, that this situation does *not* raise questions of distributive justice, then in virtue of what facts about social cooperation do these questions of justice emerge? What is it about social cooperation that gives rise to issues of justice? It cannot be said that there will be conflicting claims only where there is social cooperation; that individuals who produce independently and (initially) fend for themselves will not make claims of justice on each other. If there were ten Robinson Crusoes, each working alone for two years on separate islands, who discovered each other and the facts of their different allotments by radio communication via transmitters left twenty years earlier, could they not make claims on each other, supposing it were possible to transfer goods from one island to the next?[17] Wouldn't the one with least make a claim on ground of need, or on the ground that his island was naturally poorest, or on the ground that he was naturally least capable of fending for himself? Mightn't he say that justice demanded he be given some more by the others, claiming it unfair that he should receive so much less and perhaps be destitute, perhaps starving? He might go on to say that the different individual noncooperative shares stem from differential natural endowments, which are not deserved, and that the task of justice is to rectify these arbitrary facts and inequities. Rather than its being the case that no one *will* make such claims in the situation lacking social cooperation, perhaps the point is that such claims clearly would be without merit. Why would they clearly be without merit? In the social noncooperation situation, it might be said, each individual deserves what he gets unaided by his own efforts; or rather, no one else can make a claim *of justice* against this holding. It is pellucidly clear in this situation who is entitled to what, so no theory of justice is needed. On this view social cooperation introduces a muddying of the waters that makes it unclear or indeterminate who is entitled to what. Rather than saying that no theory of justice applies to this noncooperative case (wouldn't it be unjust if someone stole another's products in the noncooperative situation?), I would say that it is a clear case of application of the correct theory of justice: the entitlement theory.

How does social cooperation change this so that the same entitlement principles that apply to the noncooperative cases become inapplicable or inappropriate to cooperative ones? It might be said that one cannot disentangle the contributions of distinct individuals who cooperate; everything is everyone's joint product. On this joint product, or on any portion of it, each person plausibly will make claims of equal strength; all have an equally good claim, or at any rate no person has a distinctly better claim than any other. Somehow (this line of thought continues), it must be decided how this total product of joint social cooperation (to which individual entitlements do not apply differentially) is to be divided up: this is the problem of distributive justice.

Don't individual entitlements apply to parts of the cooperatively produced product? First, suppose that social cooperation is based upon division of labor, specialization, comparative advantage, and exchange; each person works singly to transform some input he receives, contracting with others who further transform or transport his product until it reaches its ultimate consumer. People cooperate in making things but they work separately; each person is a miniature firm.[18] The products of each person are easily identifiable, and exchanges are made in open markets with prices set competitively, given informational constraints, and so forth. In such a system of social cooperation; what is the task of a theory of justice? It might be said that whatever holdings result will depend upon the exchange ratios or prices at which exchanges are made, and therefore that the task of a theory of justice is to set criteria for "fair prices." This is hardly the place to trace the serpentine windings of theories of a just price. It is difficult to see why these issues should even arise here. People are choosing to make exchanges with other people and to transfer entitlements, with no restrictions on their freedom to trade with any other party at any mutually acceptable ratio.[19] Why does such sequential social cooperation, linked together by people's voluntary exchanges, raise any special problems about how things are to be distributed? Why isn't the appropriate (a not inappropriate) set of holdings just the one which *actually occurs* via this process of mutually-agreed-to exchanges whereby people choose to give to others what they are entitled to give or hold? . . .

Terms of Cooperation and the Difference Principle

Another entry into the issue of the connection of social cooperation with distributive shares brings us to grips with Rawls' actual discussion. Rawls imagines rational, mutually disinterested individuals meeting in a certain situation, or abstracted from their other features not provided for in this situation. In this hypothetical situation of choice, which Rawls calls "the original position," they choose the first principles of a conception of justice that is to regulate all subsequent criticism and reform of their institutions. While making this choice, no one knows his place in society, his class position or social status, or his natural assets and abilities, his strength, intelligence, and so forth.

> The principles of justice are chosen behind a veil of ignorance. This ensures that no one is advantaged or disadvantaged in the choice of principles by the outcome of natural chance or the contingency of social circumstances. Since all are similarly situated and no one is able to design principles to favor his particular condition, the principles of justice are the result of a fair agreement or bargain.[21]

What would persons in the original position agree to?

> Persons in the initial situation would choose two . . . principles: the first requires equality in the assignment of basic rights and duties, while the second holds that social and economic inequalities, for example, inequalities of wealth and authority are just only if they result in compensating benefits for everyone, and in particular for the least advantaged members of society. These principles rule out justifying institutions on the grounds that the hardships of some are offset by a greater good in the aggregate. It may be expedient but it is not just that some should have less in order that others may prosper. But there is no injustice in the greater benefits earned by a few provided that the situation of persons not so fortunate is thereby improved. The intuitive idea is that since everyone's well-being depends upon a scheme of cooperation without which no one could have a satisfactory life, the division of advantages should be such as to draw forth the willing cooperation of everyone taking part in it, including those less well situated. Yet this can be expected only if reasonable terms are proposed. The two principles mentioned seem to be a fair agreement on

the basis of which those better endowed, or more fortunate in their social position, neither of which we can be said to deserve, could expect the willing cooperation of others when some workable scheme is a necessary condition of the welfare of all.[22]

This second principle, which Rawls specifies as the difference principle, holds that the institutional structure is to be so designed that the worst-off group under it is at least as well off as the worst-off group (not necessarily the same group) would be under any alternative institutional structure. If persons in the original position follow the minimax policy in making the significant choice of principles of justice, Rawls argues, they will choose the difference principle. Our concern here is not whether persons in the position Rawls describes actually would minimax and actually would choose the particular principles Rawls specifies. Still, we should question why individuals in the original position would choose a principle that focuses upon groups, rather than individuals. Won't application of the minimax principle lead each person in the original position to favor maximizing the position of the worst-off *individual?* To be sure, this principle would reduce questions of evaluating social institutions to the issue of how the unhappiest depressive fares. Yet avoiding this by moving the focus to groups (or representative individuals) seems *ad hoc*, and is inadequately motivated for those in the individual position.[23] Nor is it clear which groups are appropriately considered; why exclude the group of depressives or alcoholics or the representative paraplegic? . . .

Rawls would have us imagine the worse-endowed persons say something like the following: "Look, better endowed: you gain by cooperating with us. If you want our cooperation you'll have to accept reasonable terms. We suggest these terms: We'll cooperate with you only if we get *as much as possible*. That is, the terms of our cooperation should give us that maximal share such that, if it was tried to give us more, we'd end up with less." How generous these proposed terms are might be seen by imagining that the better endowed make the almost symmetrical opposite proposal: "Look, worse endowed: you gain by cooperating with *us*. If you want our cooperation you'll have to accept reasonable terms. We propose these terms: We'll cooperate with you so long as *we* get as much as possible. That is, the terms of our cooperation should give us the maximal share such that, if it was tried to give us more, we'd end up with less." If these terms seem outrageous, as they are, why don't the terms proposed by those worse endowed seem the same? Why shouldn't the better endowed treat this latter proposal as beneath consideration, supposing someone to have the nerve explicitly to state it?

Rawls devotes much attention to explaining why those less well favored should not complain at receiving less. His explanation, simply put, is that because the inequality works for his advantage, someone less well favored shouldn't complain about it; he receives *more* in the unequal system than he would in an equal one. (Though he might receive still more in another unequal system that placed someone else below him.)

But Rawls discusses the question of whether those *more* favored will or should find the terms satisfactory *only* in the following passage, where *A* and *B* are any two representative men with *A* being the more favored:

> The difficulty is to show that *A* has no grounds for complaint. Perhaps he is required to have less than he might since his having more would result in some loss to *B*. Now what can be said to the more favored man? To begin with, it is clear that the well-being of each depends on a scheme of social cooperation without which no one could have a satisfactory life. Secondly, we can ask for the willing cooperation of everyone only if the terms of the scheme are reasonable. The difference principle, then, seems to be a fair basis on which those better endowed, or more fortunate in their social circumstances, could expect others to collaborate with them when some workable arrangement is a necessary condition of the good of all.[26]

What Rawls imagines being said to the more favored men does *not* show that these men have no grounds for complaint, nor does it at all diminish the weight of whatever complaints they have. That the well-being of all depends on social cooperation without which no one could have a satisfactory life could also be said to the less well endowed by someone proposing any other principle, including that of maximizing the position of the best endowed. Similarly for the fact that we can ask for the willing cooperation of everyone only if the terms of the scheme are reasonable. The question is: What terms *would be* reasonable? What Rawls imagines being said thus far merely sets up his problem; it doesn't distinguish his proposed difference principle from the almost symmetrical counterproposal that we imagined the better endowed making, or from any other proposal. Thus, when Rawls continues, "The difference principle, then, seems to be a fair basis on which those best endowed, or more fortunate in their social circumstances, could expect others to collaborate with them when some workable arrangement is a necessary condition of the good of all," the presence of the "then" in his sentence is puzzling. Since the sentences which precede it are neutral between his proposal and any other proposal, the conclusion that the difference principle presents a fair basis for cooperation *cannot* follow from what precedes it in this passage. Rawls is merely repeating that it seems reasonable; hardly a convincing reply to anyone to whom it doesn't seem reasonable.* Rawls has not shown that the more favored man *A* has no grounds for complaint at being required to have less in order that another *B* might have more than he otherwise would. And he can't show this, since *A does* have grounds for complaint. Doesn't he?

THE ORIGINAL POSITION AND
END-RESULT PRINCIPLES

How can it have been supposed that these terms offered by the less well endowed are fair? Imagine a social pie somehow appearing so that *no one* has any claim at all on any portion of it, no one has any more of

---

* [Footnote omitted.]

a claim than any other person; yet there must be unanimous agreement on how it is to be divided. Undoubtedly, apart from threats or holdouts in bargaining, an equal distribution would be suggested and found plausible as a solution. (It is, in Schelling's sense, a focal point solution.) If *somehow* the size of the pie wasn't fixed, and it was realized that pursuing an equal distribution somehow would lead to a smaller total pie than otherwise might occur, the people might well agree to an unequal distribution which raised the size of the least share. But in any actual situation, wouldn't this realization reveal something about differential claims on parts of the pie? Who is it that could make the pie larger, and would do it if given a larger share, but not if given an equal share under the scheme of equal distribution? To whom is an incentive to be provided to make this larger contribution? (There's no talk here of inextricably entangled joint product; it's known *to whom* incentives are to be offered, or at least to whom a bonus is to be paid after the fact.) Why doesn't this identifiable differential contribution lead to some differential entitlement?

If things fell from heaven like manna, and no one had any special entitlement to any portion of it, and no manna would fall unless all agreed to a particular distribution, and somehow the quantity varied depending on the distribution, then it is plausible to claim that persons placed so that they couldn't make threats, or hold out for specially large shares, would agree to the difference principle rule of distribution. But is *this* the appropriate model for thinking about how the things people produce are to be distributed? Why think the same results should obtain for situations where there *are* differential entitlements as for situations where there are not?

A procedure that founds principles of distributive justice on what rational persons who know nothing about themselves or their histories would agree to *guarantees that end-state principles of justice will be taken as fundamental.* Perhaps some historical principles of justice are derivable from end-state principles, as the utilitarian tries to derive individual rights, prohibitions on punishing the innocent, and so forth, from *his* end-state principle; perhaps such arguments can be constructed even for the entitlement principle. But no historical principle, it seems, could be agreed to in the first instance by the participants in Rawls' original position. For people meeting together behind a veil of ignorance to decide who gets what, knowing nothing about any special entitlements people may have, will treat anything to be distributed as manna from heaven.*

Suppose there were a group of students who have studied during a year, taken examinations, and received grades between 0 and 100 which

---

* Do the people in the original position ever wonder whether *they* have the *right* to decide how everything is to be divided up? Perhaps they reason that since they are deciding this question, they must assume they are entitled to do so; and so particular people can't have particular entitlements to holdings (for then they wouldn't have the right to decide together on how all holdings are to be divided); and hence everything legitimately may be treated like manna from heaven.

they have not yet learned of. They are now gathered together, having no idea of the grade any one of them has received, and they are asked to allocate grades among themselves so that the grades total to a given sum (which is determined by the sum of the grades they actually have received from the teacher). First, let us suppose they are to decide jointly upon a particular distribution of grades; they are to give a particular grade to each identifiable one of them present at the meeting. Here, given sufficient restrictions on their ability to threaten each other, they probably would agree to each person receiving the same grade, to each person's grade being equal to the total divided by the number of people to be graded. Surely they would *not* chance upon the particular set of grades they already have received. Suppose next that there is posted on a bulletin board at their meeting a paper headed ENTITLEMENTS, which lists each person's name with a grade next to it, the listing being identical to the instructor's gradings. Still, this particular distribution will not be agreed to by those having done poorly. Even if they know what "entitlement" means (which perhaps we must suppose they don't, in order to match the absence of moral factors in the calculations of persons in Rawls' original position), why should they agree to the instructor's distribution? What self-interested reason to agree to it would they have?

Next suppose that they are unanimously to agree not to a *particular* distribution of grades, but rather to general principles to govern the distribution of grades. What principle would be selected? The equality principle, which gives each person the same grade, would have a prominent chance. And if it turned out that the total was variable depending upon how they divided it, depending on which of them got what grade, and a higher grade was desirable though they were not competing among each other (for example, each of them was competing for some position with the members of separate distinct groups), then the principle of distributing grades so as to maximize the lowest grades *might* seem a plausible one. Would these people agree to the non-end-state *historical* principle of distribution: give people grades according to how their examinations were evaluated by a qualified and impartial observer? * If all the people deciding knew the particular distribution that would be yielded by this historical principle, they wouldn't agree to it. For the situation then would be equivalent to the earlier one of their deciding upon a particular distribution, in which we already have seen they would not agree to the entitlement distribution. Suppose then that the people do not know the particular distribution actually yielded by this historical principle. They cannot be led to select this historical principle because

---

* I do not mean to assume that all teachers are such, nor even that learning in universities should be graded. All I need is some example of entitlement, the details of which the reader will have some familiarity with, to use to examine decision making in the original position. Grading is a simple example, though not a perfect one, entangled as it is with whatever ultimate social purposes the ongoing practice serves. We may ignore this complication, for their selecting the historical principle on the grounds that it effectively serves those purposes would illustrate our point below that their fundamental concerns and fundamental principles are end-state ones.

it looks just, or fair, to them; for no such notions are allowed to be at work in the original position. (Otherwise people would argue there, like here, about what justice requires.) Each person engages in a calculation to decide whether it will be in his own interests to accept this historical principle of distribution. Grades, under the historical principle, depend upon nature and developed intelligence, how hard the people have worked, accident, and so on, factors about which people in the original position know almost nothing. (It would be risky for someone to think that since he is reasoning so well in thinking about the principles, he must be one of the intellectually better endowed. Who knows what dazzling argument the others are reasoning their way through, and perhaps keeping quiet about for strategic reasons.) Each person in the original position will do something like assigning probability distributons to his place along these various dimensions. It seems unlikely that each person's probability calculations would lead to the historical-entitlement principle, in preference to every other principle. Consider the principle we may call the reverse-entitlement principle. It recommends drawing up a list of the historical entitlements in order of magnitude, and giving the most anyone is entitled to, to the person entitled to the least; the second most to the person entitled to the second least, and so on.[27] Any probability calculations of self-interested persons in Rawls' original position, or any probability calculations of the students we have considered, will lead them to view the entitlement and the reverse-entitlement principles as ranked equally insofar as their own self-interest is concerned! (What calculations could lead them to view one of the principles as superior to the other?) Their calculations will not lead them to select the entitlement principle.

The nature of the decision problem facing persons deciding upon principles in an original position behind a veil of ignorance limits them to end-state principles of distribution. The self-interested person evaluates any non-end-state principle on the basis of how it works out for him; his calculations about any principle focus on how he ends up under the principle. (These calculations include consideration of the labor he is yet to do, which does not appear in the grading example except as the sunk cost of the labor already done.) Thus for any principle, an occupant of the original position will focus on the distribution D of goods that it leads to, or a probability distribution over the distributions $D_1, \ldots, D_n$ it may lead to, and upon his probabilities of occupying each position in each D_1 profile, supposing it to obtain. The point would remain the same if, rather than using personal probabilities, he uses some other decision rule of the sort discussed by decision theorists. In these calculations, the only role played by the principle is that of generating a distribution of goods (or whatever else they care about) or of generating a probability distribution over distributions of goods. Different principles are compared solely by comparing the alternative distributions they generate. Thus the principles drop out of the picture, and each self-interested person makes a choice among alternative end-state distributions. People in the original position either directly agree to an end-state distribution or they agree to a principle; if they agree to a principle, they do it solely on the basis of considerations about end-state distributions. The *fundamental* principles they agree to, the ones they can all converge in agreeing upon, *must* be end-state principles.

Rawls' construction is incapable of yielding an entitlement or historical conception of distributive justice. The end-state principles of justice yielded by his procedure might be used in an attempt to *derive*, when conjoined with factual information, historical-entitlement principles, as derivative principles falling under a nonentitlement conception of justice.[28] It is difficult to see how such attempts could derive and account for the *particular* convolutions of historical-entitlement principles. And any derivations from end-state principles of approximations of the principles of acquisition, transfer, and rectification would strike one as similar to utilitarian contortions in trying to derive (approximations of) usual precepts of justice; they do not yield the particular result desired, and they produce the wrong reasons for the sort of result they try to get. If historical-entitlement principles are fundamental, then Rawls' constructions will yield approximations of them at best; it will produce the wrong sorts of reasons for them, and its derived results sometimes will conflict with the precisely correct principles. The whole procedure of persons choosing principles in Rawls' original position presupposes that no historical-entitlement conception of justice is correct.

It might be objected to our argument that Rawls' procedure is designed to *establish* all facts about justice; there is no independent notion of entitlement, not provided by his theory, to stand on in criticizing his theory. But we do not need any *particular* developed historical-entitlement theory as a basis from which to criticize Rawls' construction. If *any* such fundamental historical-entitlement view is correct, then Rawls' theory is not. We are thus able to make this structural criticism of the type of theory Rawls presents and the type of principles it must yield, without first having formulated fully a particular historical-entitlement theory as an alternative to his. We would be ill advised to accept Rawls' theory and his construal of the problem as one of which principles would be chosen by rational self-interested individuals behind a veil of ignorance, unless we were sure that no adequate historical-entitlement theory was to be gotten.

Since Rawls' construction doesn't yield a historical or entitlement conception of justice, there will be some feature(s) of his construction in virtue of which it doesn't. Have we done anything other than focus upon the particular feature(s), and say that this makes Rawls' construction incapable in principle of yielding an entitlement or historical conception of justice? This would be a criticism without any force at all, for in this sense we would have to say that the construction is incapable in principle of yielding any conception other than the one it actually yields. It seems clear that our criticism goes deeper than this (and I hope it is clear to the reader); but it is difficult to formulate the requisite criterion of depth. Lest this appear lame, let us add that as Rawls states the root idea underlying the veil of ignorance, that feature which is the most prominent in excluding agreement to an entitlement conception, it is to prevent someone from tailoring principles to his own advantage, from designing principles to favor his particular condition. But not only does the veil of ignorance do this; it ensures that no shadow of entitlement considerations will enter the rational calculations of ignorant, nonmoral individuals constrained to decide in a situation reflecting some formal conditions of morality.* Perhaps, in a Rawls-*like* construction, some condition weaker than the veil of ignorance could serve to exclude the special tailoring of principles, or perhaps some other "structural-looking" feature of the choice situation could be formulated to mirror entitlement considerations. But as it stands there is no reflection of entitlement considerations in any form in the situation of those in the original position; these considerations do not enter even to be overridden or outweighed or otherwise put aside. Since no glimmer of entitlement principles is built into the structure of the situation of persons in the original position, there is no way these principles could be selected; and Rawls' construction is incapable in principle of yielding them. This is not to say, of course, that the entitlement principle (or "the principle of natural liberty") couldn't be *written* on the list of principles to be considered by those in the original position. Rawls doesn't do even this, perhaps because it is so transparently clear that there would be no point in including it to be considered *there*.

MACRO AND MICRO

We noted earlier the objection which doubted whether there is any independent notion of entitlement. This connects with Rawls' insistence that the principles he formulates are to be applied only to the fundamental macrostructure of the whole society, and that no micro counterexample to them will be admissible. The difference principle is, on the face of it, *unfair* (though that will be of no concern to anyone deciding in the original position); and a wide gamut of counterexamples to it can be produced that focus on small situations that are easy to take in and manage. But Rawls does *not* claim the difference principle is to apply to every situation; only to the basic structure of the society. How are we to decide if it applies to that? Since we may have only weak confidence in our intuitions and judgments about the justice of the whole structure of society, we may attempt to aid our judgment by focusing on microsituations that we do have a firm grasp of. For many of us, an important part of the process of arriving at what Rawls calls "reflective equilibrium" will consist of thought experiments in which

* Someone might think entitlement principles count as specially tailored in a morally objectionable way, and so he might reject my claim that the veil of ignorance accomplishes more than its stated purpose. Since to specially tailor principles is to tailor them *unfairly* for one's own advantage, and since the question of the fairness of the entitlement principle is precisely the issue, it is difficult to decide which begs the question: my criticism of the strength of the veil of ignorance, or the defense against this criticism which I imagine in this note.

we try out principles in hypothetical microsituations. If, in our considered judgment, they don't apply there then they are not universally applicable. And we may think that since correct principles of justice *are* universally applicable, principles that fail for microsituations cannot be correct. Since Plato, at any rate, that has been our tradition; principles may be tried out in the large and in the small. Plato thought that writ large the principles are easier to discern; others may think the reverse.

Rawls, however, proceeds as though distinct principles apply to macro and micro contexts, to the basic structure of society and to the situations we can take in and understand. Are the fundamental principles of justice *emergent* in this fashion, applying only to the largest social structure yet not to its parts? Perhaps one thinks of the possibility that a whole social structure is just, even though none of its parts is, because the injustice in each part somehow balances out or counteracts another one, and the total injustice ends up being balanced out or nullified. But can a part satisfy the most fundamental principle of justice yet still clearly be unjust, apart from its failure to perform any supposed task of counterbalancing another existing injustice? Perhaps so, if a part involves some special domain. But surely a regular, ordinary, everyday part, possessing no very unusual features, should turn out to be just when it satisfies the fundamental principles of justice; otherwise, special explanations must be offered. One cannot say merely that one is speaking of principles to apply only to the fundamental structure, so that micro counterexamples do not tell. In virtue of what features of the basic structure, features not possessed by microcases, do special moral principles apply that would be unacceptable elsewhere?

There are special disadvantages to proceeding by focusing only on the intuitive justice of described complex wholes. For complex wholes are not easily scanned; we cannot easily keep track of everything that is relevant. The justice of a whole society may depend on its satisfying a number of distinct principles. These principles, though individually compelling (witness their application to a wide range of particular microcases), may yield surprising results when combined together. That is, one may be surprised at which, and only which, institutional forms satisfy all the principles. (Compare the surprise at discovering what, and only what, satisfies a number of distinct and individually compelling conditions of adequacy; and how illuminating such discoveries are.) Or perhaps it is one simple principle which is to be writ large, and what things look like when this is done is very surprising, at first. I am not claiming that new *principles* emerge in the large, but that how the old microprinciples turn out to be satisfied in the large may surprise. If this is so, then one should not depend upon judgments about the whole as providing the only or even the major body of data against which to check one's principles. One major path to changing one's intuitive judgments about some complex whole is through seeing the larger and often surprising implications of principles solidly founded at the micro level. Similarly, discovering that one's judgments are wrong or mistaken often surely will involve overturning them by stringent applications of principles grounded on the micro level. For these reasons it is undesirable to attempt to protect principles by excluding microtests of them.

The only reason I have thought of for discounting microtests of the fundamental principles is that microsituations have particular entitlements built into them. Of course, continues the argument, the fundamental principles under consideration will run afoul of these entitlements, for the principles are to operate at a deeper level than such entitlements. Since they are to operate at the level that underlies such entitlements, no microsituation that includes entitlements can be introduced as an example by which to test these fundamental principles. Note that this reasoning grants that Rawls' procedure assumes that no fundamental entitlement view is correct, that it assumes there is some level so deep that no entitlements operate that far down.

May all entitlements be relegated to relatively superficial levels? For example, people's entitlements to the parts of their own bodies? An application of the principle of maximizing the position of those worst off might well involve forcible redistribution of bodily parts ("You've been sighted for all these years; now one—or even both—of your eyes is to be transplanted to others"), or killing some people early to use their bodies in order to provide material necessary to save the lives of those who otherwise would die young.[29] To bring up such cases is to sound slightly hysterical. But we are driven to such extreme examples in examining Rawls' prohibition on micro counterexamples. That not all entitlements in microcases are plausibly construed as superficial, and hence as illegitimate material by which to test our suggested principles, is made especially clear if we focus on those entitlements and rights that most clearly are not socially or institutionally based. On what grounds are such cases, whose detailed specifications I leave to the ghoulish reader, ruled inadmissible? On what grounds can it be claimed that the fundamental principles of justice need apply only to the fundamental institutional structure of a society? (And couldn't we build such redistributive practices concerning bodily parts or the ending of people's lives into the fundamental structure of a society?) . . .

NATURAL ASSETS AND ARBITRARINESS

Rawls comes closer to considering the entitlement system in his discussion of what he terms the system of natural liberty:

> The system of natural liberty selects an efficient distribution roughly as follows. Let us suppose that we know from economic theory that under the standard assumptions defining a competitive market economy, income and wealth will be distributed in an efficient way, and that the particular efficient distribution which results in any period of time is determined by the initial distribution of assets, that is, by the initial distribution of income and wealth, and of natural talents and abilities. With each initial distribution, a definite efficient outcome is arrived at. Thus it turns out that if we are to accept the outcome as just, and not merely as efficient, we must

accept the basis upon which over time the initial distribution of assets is determined.

In the system of natural liberty the initial distribution is regulated by the arrangements implicit in the conception of careers open to talents. These arrangements presuppose a background of equal liberty (as specified by the first principle) and a free market economy. They require a formal equality of opportunity in that all have at least the same legal rights of access to all advantaged social positions. But since there is no effort to preserve an equality or similarity, of social conditions, except insofar as this is necessary to preserve the requisite background institutions, the initial distribution of assets for any period of time is strongly influenced by natural and social contingencies. The existing distribution of income and wealth, say, is the cumulative effect of prior distributions of natural assets—that is, natural talents and abilities—as these have been developed or left unrealized, and their use favored or disfavored over time by social circumstances and such chance contingencies as accident and good fortune. Intuitively, the most obvious injustice of the system of natural liberty is that it permits distributive shares to be improperly influenced by these factors so arbitrary from a moral point of view.[33]

Here we have *Rawls'* reason for rejecting a system of natural liberty: it "permits" distributive shares to be improperly influenced by factors that are so arbitrary from a moral point of view. These factors are: "prior distribution . . . of natural talents and abilities as these have been developed over time by social circumstances and such chance contingencies as accident and good fortune." Notice that there is no mention *at all* of how persons have chosen to develop their own natural assets. Why is that simply left out? Perhaps because such choices also are viewed as being the products of factors outside the person's control, and hence as "arbitrary from a moral point of view." "The assertion that a man deserves the superior character that enables him to make the effort to cultivate his abilities is equally problematic; for his character depends in large part upon fortunate family and social circumstances for which he can claim no credit." [34] (What view is presupposed here of character and its relation to action?) "The initial endowment of natural assets and the contingencies of their growth and nurture in early life are arbitrary from a moral point of view . . . the effort a person is willing to make is influenced by his natural abilities and skills and the alternatives open to him. The better endowed are more likely, other things equal, to strive conscientiously. . . ." [35] This line of argument can succeed in blocking the introduction of a person's autonomous choices and actions (and their results) only by attributing *everything* noteworthy about the person completely to certain sorts of "external" factors. So denigrating a person's autonomy and prime responsibility for his actions is a risky line to take for a theory that otherwise wishes to buttress the dignity and self-respect of autonomous beings; especially for a theory that founds so much (including a theory of the good) upon persons' choices. One doubts that the unexalted picture of human beings Rawls' theory presupposes and rests upon can be made to fit together with the view of human dignity it is designed to lead to and embody.

Before we investigate Rawls' reasons for rejecting the system of natural liberty, we should note the situation of those in the original position. The system of natural liberty is *one* interpretation of a principle that (according to Rawls) they *do* accept: social and economic inequalities are to be arranged so that they both are reasonably expected to be to everyone's advantage, and are attached to positions and offices open to all. It is left unclear whether the persons in the original position explicitly consider and choose among *all* the various interpretations of this principle, though this would seem to be the most reasonable construal. (Rawls' chart on page 124 listing the conceptions of justice considered in the original position does *not* include the system of natural liberty.) Certainly they explicitly consider one interpretation, the difference principle. Rawls does not state why persons in the original position who considered the system of natural liberty would reject it. Their reason cannot be that it makes the resulting distribution depend upon a *morally arbitrary* distribution of natural assets. What we must suppose, as we have seen before, is that the self-interested calculation of persons in the original position does not (and cannot) lead them to adopt the entitlement principle. We, however, and Rawls, base our evaluations on different considerations.

Rawls has explicitly *designed* the original position and its choice situation so as to embody and realize his negative reflective evaluation of allowing shares in holdings to be affected by natural assets: "Once we decide to look for a conception of justice that nullifies the accidents of natural endowment and the contingencies of social circumstance. . . ." [36] (Rawls makes many scattered references to this theme of nullifying the accidents of natural endowment and the contingencies of social circumstance.) . . .

Why shouldn't holdings partially depend upon natural endowments? (They will also depend on how these are developed and on the uses to which they are put.) Rawls' reply is that these natural endowments and assets, being undeserved, are "arbitrary from a moral point of view.". . .

The Positive Argument

We shall begin with the positive argument. How might the point that differences in natural endowments are arbitrary from a moral point of view function in an argument meant to establish that differences in holdings stemming from differences in natural assets ought to be nullified? We shall consider four possible arguments. . . .

Consider next argument B:

1. Holdings ought to be distributed according to some pattern that is not arbitrary from a moral point of view.

2. That persons have different natural assets *is* arbitrary from a moral point of view.

Therefore,

3. Holdings ought not to be distributed according to natural assets.

But differences in natural assets might be *correlated* with other differences that are not arbitrary from a moral point of view and that are clearly of some possible moral relevance to distributional questions. For example, Hayek argued that under capitalism distribution generally is in accordance with perceived service to others. Since differences in natural assets will produce differences in ability to serve others, there will be some correlation of differences in distribution with differences in natural assets. The principle of the system is *not* distribution in accordance with natural assets; but differences in natural assets will lead to differences in holdings under a system whose principle is distribution according to perceived service to others. . . .

I turn now to our final positive argument which purports to derive the conclusion that distributive shares shouldn't depend upon natural assets from the statement that the distribution of natural assets is morally arbitrary. This argument focuses on the notion of equality. Since a large part of Rawls' argument serves to justify or show acceptable a particular deviation from equal shares (some may have more if this serves to improve the position of those worst off), perhaps a reconstruction of his underlying argument that places equality at its center will be illuminating. Differences between persons (the argument runs) are arbitrary from a moral point of view if there is no moral argument for the conclusion that there ought to be the differences. Not all such differences will be morally objectionable. That there is no such moral argument will seem important only in the case of those differences we believe oughtn't to obtain unless there is a moral reason establishing that they ought to obtain. There is, so to speak, a presumption against certain differences that can be overridden (can it merely be neutralized?) by moral reasons; in the absence of any such moral reasons of sufficient weight, there ought to be equality. Thus we have argument D:

1. Holdings ought to be equal, unless there is a (weighty) moral reason why they ought to be unequal.
2. People do not deserve the ways in which they differ from other persons in natural assets; there is no moral reason why people ought to differ in natural assets.
3. If there is no moral reason why people differ in certain traits, then their actually differing in these traits does not provide, and cannot give rise to, a moral reason why they should differ in other traits (for example, in holdings).

4. People's differing in natural assets is not a reason why holdings ought to be unequal.

5. People's holdings ought to be equal unless there is some other moral reason (such as, for example, raising the position of those worst off) why their holdings ought to be unequal.

Statements similar to the third premiss will occupy us shortly. Here let us focus on the first premiss, the equality premiss. Why ought people's holdings to be equal, in the absence of special moral reason to deviate from equality? (Why think there *ought* to be *any* particular pattern in holdings?) Why is equality the rest (or rectilinear motion) position of the system, deviation from which may be caused only by moral forces? Many "arguments" for equality merely *assert* that differences between persons are arbitrary and must be justified. Often writers state a presumption in favor of equality in a form such as the following: "Differences in treatment of persons need to be justified." [41] The most favored situation for this sort of assumption is one in which there is one person (or group) treating everyone, a person (or group) having *no* right or entitlement to bestow the particular treatment as they wish or even whim. But if I go to one movie theater rather than to another adjacent to it, need I justify my different treatment of the two theater owners? Isn't it enough that I felt like going to one of them? That differences in treatment need to be justified *does* fit contemporary *governments*. Here there is a centralized process treating all, with no entitlement to bestow treatment according to whim. The major portion of distribution in a free society does not, however, come through the actions of the government, nor does failure to overturn the results of the localized individual exchanges constitute "state action." When there is no *one* doing the treating, and all are entitled to bestow their holdings as they wish, it is not clear why the maxim that differences in treatment must be justified should be thought to have extensive application. Why must differences between persons be justified? Why think that we must change, or remedy, or compensate for any inequality which can be changed, remedied, or compensated for? Perhaps here is where social cooperation enters in: though there is no presumption of equality (in, say, primary goods, or things people care about) among all persons, perhaps there is one among persons cooperating together. But it is difficult to see an argument for this; surely not all persons who cooperate together explicitly agree to this presumption as one of the terms of their mutual cooperation. And its acceptance would provide an unfortunate incentive for well-off persons to refuse to cooperate with, or to allow any of their number to cooperate with, some distant people who are less well off than any among them. For entering into such social cooperation, beneficial to those less well off, would seriously worsen the position of the well-off group by creating relations of presumptive equality between themselves and the worse-off group. . . .

COLLECTIVE ASSETS

Rawls' view seems to be that everyone has some entitlement or claim on the totality of natural assets (viewed as a pool), with no one having differential claims. The distribution of natural abilities is viewed as a "collective asset." [43]

> We see then that the difference principle represents, in effect, an agreement to regard the distribution of natural talents as a common asset and to share in the benefits of this distribution whatever it turns out to be. Those who have been favored by nature, whoever they are, may gain from their good fortune only on terms that improve the situation of those who have lost out. . . . No one deserves his greater natural capacity nor merits a more favorable starting place in society. But it does not follow that one should eliminate these distinctions. There is another way to deal with them. The basic structure can be arranged so that these contingencies work for the good of the least fortunate.[44]

People will differ in how they view regarding natural talents as a common asset. Some will complain, echoing Rawls against utilitarianism,[45] that this "does not take seriously the distinction between persons"; and they will wonder whether any reconstruction of Kant that treats people's abilities and talents as resources for others can be adequate. "The two principles of justice . . . rule out even the tendency to regard men as means to one another's welfare." [46] Only if one presses *very* hard on the distinction between men and their talents, assets, abilities, and special traits. Whether any coherent conception of a person remains when the distinction is so pressed is an open question. Why we, thick with particular traits, should be cheered that (only) the thus purified men within us are not regarded as means is also unclear.

People's talents and abilities *are* an asset to a free community; others in the community benefit from their presence and are better off because they are there rather than elsewhere or nowhere. (Otherwise they wouldn't choose to deal with them.) Life, over time, is not a constant-sum game, wherein if greater ability or effort leads to some getting more, that means that others must lose. In a free society, people's talents do benefit others, and not only themselves. Is it the extraction of even more benefit to others that is supposed to justify treating people's natural assets as a collective resource? What justifies this extraction?

> No one deserves his greater natural capacity nor merits a more favorable starting place in society. But it does not follow that one should eliminate these distinctions. There is another way to deal with them. The basic structure can be arranged so that these contingencies work for the good of the least fortunate.[47]

And if there weren't "another way to deal with them?" Would it then follow that one should eliminate these distinctions? What exactly would be contemplated in the case of natural assets? If people's assets and talents *couldn't* be harnessed to serve others, would something be done to remove these exceptional assets and talents, or to forbid them from being exercised for the person's own benefit or that of someone else he chose, even though this limitation wouldn't improve the absolute position of those somehow unable to harness the talents and abilities of others for their own benefit? Is it so implausible to claim that envy underlies this conception of justice, forming part of its root notion? . . .*

We have used our entitlement conception of justice in holdings to probe Rawls' theory, sharpening our understanding of what the entitlement conception involves by bringing it to bear upon an alternative conception of distributive justice, one that is deep and elegant. Also, I believe, we have probed deep-lying inadequacies in Rawls' theory. I am mindful of Rawls' reiterated point that a theory cannot be evaluated by focusing upon a single feature or part of it; instead the whole theory must be assessed (the reader will not know how whole a theory can be until he has read all of Rawls' book), and a perfect theory is not to be expected. However we have examined an important part of Rawls' theory, and its crucial underlying assumptions. I am as well aware as anyone of how sketchy my discussion of the entitlement conception of justice in holdings has been. But I no more believe we need to have formulated a complete alternative theory in order to reject Rawls' undeniably great advance over utilitarianism, than Rawls needed a complete alternative theory before he could reject utilitarianism. What more does one need or can one have, in order to begin progressing toward a better theory, than a sketch of a plausible alternative view, which from its very different perspective highlights the inadequacies of the best existing well-worked-out theory? Here, as in so many things, we learn from Rawls.

NOTES

1. The reader who has looked ahead and seen that the second part of this chapter discusses Rawls' theory mistakenly may think that every remark or argument in the first part against alternative theories of justice is meant to apply to, or anticipate, a criticism of Rawls' theory. This is not so; there are other theories also worth criticizing.

2. See, however, the useful book by Boris Bittker, *The Case for Black Reparations* (New York: Random House, 1973).

3. F. A. Hayek, *The Constitution of Liberty* (Chicago: University of Chicago Press, 1960), p. 87.

* [Footnote omitted.]

4. This question does not imply that they will tolerate any and every patterned distribution. In discussing Hayek's views Irving Kristol has recently speculated that people will not long tolerate a system that yields distributions patterned in accordance with value rather than merit. (" 'When Virtue Loses All Her Loveliness'—Some Reflections on Capitalism and 'The Free Society,' " *The Public Interest*, Fall 1970, pp. 3-15.) Kristol, following some remarks of Hayek's, equates the merit system with justice. Since some case can be made for the external standard of distribution in accordance with benefit to others, we ask about a weaker (and therefore more plausible) hypothesis.

5. Varying situations continuously from that limit situation to our own would force us to make explicit the underlying rationale of entitlements and to consider whether entitlement considerations lexicographically precede the considerations of the usual theories of distributive justice, so that the *slightest* strand of entitlement outweighs the considerations of the usual theories of distributive justice.

6. See the selection from John Henry MacKay's novel, *The Anarchists* reprinted in Leonard Krimmerman and Lewis Perry, eds., *Patterns of Anarchy* (New York: Doubleday Anchor Books, 1966), in which an individualist anarchist presses upon a communist anarchist the following question: "Would you, in the system of society which you call free Communism prevent individuals from exchanging their labor among themselves by means of their own medium of exchange? And further: Would you prevent them from occupying land for the purpose of personal use?" The novel continues: "[the] question was not to be escaped. If he answered 'Yes!' he admitted that society had the right of control over the individual and threw overboard the autonomy of the individual which he had always zealously defended; if on the other hand, he answered 'No!' he admitted the right of private property which he had just denied so emphatically. . . . Then he answered 'In Anarchy any number of men must have the right of forming a voluntary association, and so realizing their ideas in practice. Nor can I understand how any one could justly be driven from the land and house which he uses and occupies . . . every serious man must declare himself: for Socialism, and thereby for force and against liberty, or for Anarchism, and thereby for liberty and against force.' " In contrast, we find Noam Chomsky writing, "Any consistent anarchist must oppose private ownership of the means of production," "the consistent anarchist then . . . will be a socialist . . . of a particular sort." Introduction to Daniel Guerin, *Anarchism: From Theory to Practice* (New York: Monthly Review Press, 1970), pages xiii, xv.

9. See Gregory Vlastos, "The Individual as an Object of Love in Plato" in his *Platonic Studies* (Princeton: Princeton University Press, 1973), pp. 3-34.

10. Further details which this statement should include are contained in my essay "Coercion," in *Philosophy, Science, and Method*, ed. S. Morgenbesser, P. Suppes, and M. White (New York: St. Martin, 1969).

11. On the themes in this and the next paragraph, see the writings of Armen Alchian.

12. Compare this with Robert Paul Wolff's "A Refutation of Rawls' Theorem on Justice," *Journal of Philosophy*, March 31, 1966, sect. 2. Wolff's criticism does not apply to Rawls' conception under which the baseline is fixed by the difference principle.

13. I discuss overriding and its moral traces in "Moral Complications and Moral Structures," *Natural Law Forum*, 1968, pp. 1-50.

14. Does the principle of compensation (Chapter 4) introduce patterning considerations? Though it requires compensation for the disadvantages imposed by those seeking security from risks, it is not a patterned principle. For it seeks to remove only those disadvantages which prohibitions inflict on those who might present risks to others, not all disadvantages. It specifies an obligation on those who impose the prohibition, which stems from their own particular acts, to remove a particular complaint those prohibited may make against them.

17. See Milton Friedman, *Capitalism and Freedom* (Chicago: University of Chicago Press, 1962), p. 165.

18. On the question of why the economy contains firms (of more than one person), and why each individual does not contract and recontract with others, see

Ronald H. Coase, "The Nature of the Firm," in *Readings in Price Theory*, ed. George Stigler and Kenneth Boulding (Homewood, Ill.: Irwin, 1952); and Armen A. Alchian and Harold Demsetz, "Production, Information Costs and Economic Organization," *American Economic Review*, 1972, 777-795.

19. We do not, however, assume here or elsewhere the satisfaction of those conditions specified in economists' artificial model of so-called "perfect competition." One appropriate mode of analysis is presented in Israel M. Kirzner, *Market Theory and the Price System* (Princeton, N.J.: Van Nostrand, 1963); see also his *Competition and Entrepreneurship* (Chicago: University of Chicago Press, 1973).

21. Rawls, *Theory of Justice*, p. 12.

22. Rawls, *Theory of Justice*, pp. 14-15.

23. Rawls, *Theory of Justice*, sect. 16, especially p. 98.

26. Rawls, *Theory of Justice*, p. 103.

27. But recall the reasons why using magnitudes of entitlement does not capture accurately the entitlement principle (note on p. 63, this volume).

28. Some years ago, Hayek argued (*The Constitution of Liberty*, chap. 3) that a free capitalist society, over time, raises the position of those worst off more than any alternative institutional structure; to use present terminology, he argued that it best satisfies the end-state principle of justice formulated by the difference principle.

29. This is especially serious in view of the weakness of Rawls' reasons (sect. 82) for placing the liberty principle prior to the difference principle in a lexicographic ordering.

33. Rawls, *Theory of Justice*, p. 72. Rawls goes on to discuss what he calls a liberal interpretation of his two principles of justice, which is designed to eliminate the influence of social contingencies, but which "intuitively, still appears defective . . . [for] it still permits the distribution of wealth and income to be determined by the natural distribution of abilities and talents . . . distributive shares are decided by the outcome of the natural lottery; and this outcome is arbitrary from a moral perspective. There is no more reason to permit the distribution of income and wealth to be settled by the distribution of natural assets than by historical and social fortune" (pp. 73-74).

34. Rawls, *Theory of Justice*, p. 104.

35. Rawls, *Theory of Justice*, pp. 311-312.

36. Rawls, *Theory of Justice*, p. 15.

41. "No reason need be given for . . . an equal distribution of benefits—for that is 'natural'—self-evidently right and just, and needs no justification, since it is in some sense conceived as being self-justified. . . . The assumption is that equality needs no reasons, only inequality does so, that uniformity, regularity, similarity, symmetry, . . . need not be specially accounted for, whereas differences, unsystematic behavior, changes in conduct, need explanation and, as a rule, justification. If I have a cake and there are ten persons among whom I wish to divide it, then if I give exactly one-tenth to each, this will not, at any rate automatically, call for justification; whereas if I depart from this principle of equal division I am expected to produce a special reason. It is some sense of this, however latent, that makes equality an idea which has never seemed intrinsically eccentric. . . ." Isaiah Berlin, "Equality," reprinted in Frederick A. Olafson, ed. *Justice and Social Policy* (Englewood Cliffs, N.J.: Prentice-Hall, 1961), p. 131. To pursue the analogy with mechanics further, note that it is a substantive theoretical position which specifies a particular state or situation as one which requires no explanation, whereas deviations from it are to be explained in terms of external forces. See Ernest Nagel's discussion of D'Alembert's attempts to provide an *a priori* argument for Newton's first law of motion. [*The Structure of Science* (New York: Harcourt, Brace, and World, 1961), pp. 175-177.]

43. Rawls, *Theory of Justice*, p. 179.

44. Rawls, *Theory of Justice*, p. 102.

45. Rawls, *Theory of Justice*, p. 27.

46. Rawls, *Theory of Justice*, p. 183.

47. Rawls, *Theory of Justice*, p. 102.

utilitarianism

Although every philosophy has its precursors, utilitarianism received its classic formulation by Jeremy Bentham in the early nineteenth century and was developed further by John Stuart Mill. Both were English legal and social reformers, as well as philosophers. Bentham, in particular, was concerned with applying the utilitarian principle "promote the greatest happiness of the greatest number" to legislation, and today utilitarianism remains an underlying assumption of many political programs, as well as one of the most important moral and political philosophies.

According to utilitarianism, the rightness or wrongness of actions is determined by the goodness or badness of their consequences—not just for the actor, but for all affected. Bentham was a philosophical hedonist and held that pleasure was the only good. Utilitarians from Mill onward have frequently disagreed with this, but most utilitarians today would equate goodness with happiness (or, alternatively, with satisfied desire). The principle of utility constitutes the only moral standard; considerations of justice, for example, have no moral weight independent of the goodness or badness of the consequences of an action. Thus, Bentham viewed talk of a social contract or state of nature as purely "fictitious" and of natural rights as "nonsense on stilts." For utilitarians the right (or just or best) distribution of economic goods will be that which results in the most happiness for society as a whole.

Among the most important contemporary descendants of Bentham and Mill are J. J. C. Smart and R. M. Hare. Each subscribes to a version of the utilitarian principle, although very different methods are used to justify that conclusion.

For Smart acceptance of the principle of utility depends on whether or not—and to what extent—we feel a "sentiment of generalized benevolence." By this is meant a desire or wish for the well-being and happiness of other persons. To the extent that this general attitude is present and overrides other feelings we may have, we will be inclined toward utilitarianism. Smart believes that the moral views which one accepts rest ultimately on emotional preferences and sentiment and so no normative system—including utilitarianism—can be *proved*. Instead, his concern in what follows is to explain what a utilitarian would say about economic justice and to do so in such a way that others will find the utilitarian view acceptable and attractive. He also criticizes alternative positions, showing that each is inconsistent with a desire for the well-being of others and so to that extent unacceptable. Throughout his essay Smart appeals to our intuitive moral sense, our natural feelings of benevolence, as a basis for choosing between the principle of utility and its rivals.

R. M. Hare argues to a similar conclusion by a very different route. Hare, as we have seen before, views skeptically the appeal to moral intuitions or attitudes, to which most moral philosophers have recourse in their arguments. These attitudes reflect to a large extent simply those values and beliefs which happened to be instilled in us by our society and family when we were young. Hare desires a more secure foundation on which to base our moral claims.

He begins by considering the function of ethical language, which is, he argues, to prescribe or commend a certain type of behavior and to do so universally, that is, for everyone in similar circumstances. Thus, the moral claim "You ought to aid the poor" expresses both (1) a recommendation that you behave a certain way, and (2) the idea that anyone in similar circumstances ought also to give aid. Not all prescriptions are universal, however. For example, "Eat your peas" does not logically commit the speaker to saying that everybody should eat peas! All of this can be seen by considering only the formal or metaethical aspects of moral language.

Intuitively, the idea behind Hare's metaethical analysis of moral language is this: If a person makes a moral judgment—for example, says that a theft is wrong—then he must be willing to say that similar thefts are wrong also. Thus, it won't do for a person to condemn someone's taking his property but to fail to condemn his own theft under similar circumstances. The logic of moral language commits its user to this "universal prescriptivism." To fail to do so is to use the words *right* and *wrong* incorrectly. To claim, "It's wrong for you to do that, but not for me," if we are both performing an action of the same type, is a misuse of language, a kind of inconsistency.

Hare further holds that these logical characteristics of language provide the basis for utilitarianism. In *Freedom and Reason* he writes that as we "endeavor to find lines of conduct which we can prescribe universally in a given situation . . . we find ourselves bound to give equal weight to the desires of all parties (the foundation of distributive justice); and this in turn leads to such views as that we should seek to maximize satisfactions." This is because, in deciding which conduct can be universally prescribed, we should imagine ourselves successively in the position of each affected party. Having done this, a moral agent will be inclined to prescribe that act which would do the most good for the most people—which is what utilitarianism recommends.

In his essay, "Justice and Equality," Hare again begins by looking to the formal properties of ethical reasoning. He discusses three "levels" of moral thinking (metaethical, intuitive, and critical) and distinguishes several senses of "justice." He argues that both Rawls and he treat distributive justice (who gets what goods?) and retributive justice (who gets punished or rewarded?) as analogous problems. Rawls would appeal to the procedure of the original position while Hare himself uses "universalizability" and the idea of occupying "successive positions" to achieve similar results in determining how punishment is to be distributed.

Next Hare considers the ways in which the requirements of formal justice are able to help resolve the problems of economic distribution. His formal procedure (with its utilitarian implications), together with certain plausible factual assumptions, requires, he argues, a generally egalitarian distribution of goods. Taking slavery as an example, Hare elaborates the egalitarian consequences of his view and concludes with a discussion of methodology, relativism, intuition, and related issues.

J. J. C. SMART

The Australian National University

Distributive Justice
and Utilitarianism

INTRODUCTION

In this paper I shall not be concerned with the defense of utilitarianism against other types of ethical theory. Indeed I hold that questions of ultimate ethical principle are not susceptible of proof, though something can be done to render them more acceptable by presenting them in a clear light and by clearing up certain confusions which (for some people) may get in the way of their acceptance. Ultimately the utilitarian appeals to the sentiment of generalized benevolence, and speaks to others who feel this sentiment too and for whom it is an over-riding feeling.[1] (This does not mean that he will always act from this over-riding feeling. There can be backsliding and action may result from more particular feelings, just as an egoist may go against his own interests, and may regret this.) I shall be concerned here merely to investigate certain consequences of utilitarianism, as they relate to questions of distributive justice. The type of utilitarianism with which I am concerned is act utilitarianism, which is in its normative aspects much the same as the type of utilitarianism which was put forward by Henry Sidgwick,[2] though I differ from Sidgwick over questions of moral epistemology and of the semantics of ethical language.

The Place of Justice in Utilitarian Theory

The concept of justice as a *fundamental* ethical concept is really quite foreign to utilitarianism. A utilitarian would compromise his utilitarianism if he allowed principles of justice which might conflict with the maximization of happiness (or more generally of goodness, should he be an 'ideal' utilitarian). He is concerned with the maximization of happiness [3] and not with the distribution of it. Nevertheless he may well deduce from his ethical principle that certain ways of distributing the means to happiness (e.g. money, food, housing) are more conducive to the general good than are others. He will be interested in justice in so far as it is a political or legal or quasi-legal concept. He will consider whether the legal institutions and customary sanctions which operate in particular societies are more or less conducive to the utilitarian end than are other possible institutions and customs. Even if the society consisted entirely of utilitarians (and of course no actual societies have thus consisted) it might still be important to have legal and customary sanctions relating to distribution of goods, because utilitarians might be tempted to backslide and favour non-optimific distributions, perhaps because of bias in their own favour. They might be helped to act in a more nearly utilitarian way because of the presence of these sanctions.

As a utilitarian, therefore, I do not allow the concept of justice as a fundamental moral concept, but I am nevertheless interested in justice in a subordinate way, as a *means* to the utilitarian end. Thus even though I hold that it does not matter in what way happiness is distributed among different persons, provided that the total amount of happiness is maximized, I do of course hold that it can be of vital importance that the *means* to happiness should be distributed in some ways and not in others. Suppose that I have the choice of two alternative actions as follows: I can either give $500 to each of two needy men, Smith and Campbell, or else give $1000 to Smith and nothing to Campbell. It is of course likely to produce the greatest happiness if I divide the money equally. For this reason utilitarianism can often emerge as a theory with egalitarian consequences. If it does so this is because of the empirical situation, and not because of any moral commitment to egalitarianism as such. Consider, for example, another empirical situation in which the $500 was replaced by a half-dose of a life saving drug, in which case the utilitarian would advocate giving two half doses to Smith or Campbell and none to the other. Indeed if Smith and Campbell each possessed a half dose it would be right to take one of the half doses and give it to the other. (I am assuming that a whole dose would preserve life and that a half dose would not. I am also assuming a simplified situation: in some possible situations, especially in a society of non-utilitarians, the wide social ramifications of taking a half dose from Smith and giving it to Campbell might conceivably outweigh the good results of saving Campbell's life.) However, it is probable that in most situations the equal distribution of the means to happiness will be the right utilitarian action, even though the utilitarian has no ultimate moral commitment to egalitarianism. If a utilitarian is given the choice of two actions, one of which will give 2 units of happiness to Smith and 2 to Campbell, and the other of which will give 1 unit of happiness to Smith and 9 to Campbell, he will choose the latter course.[4] It may also be that I have the choice between two alternative actions, one of which gives −1 unit of happiness to Smith and +9 units to Campbell, and the other of which gives +2 to Smith and +2 to Campbell. As a utilitarian I will choose the former course, and here I will be in conflict with John Rawls' theory, whose maximin principle would rule out making Smith worse off.

Utilitarianism and Rawls' Theory

Rawls deduces his ethical principles from the contract which would be made by a group of rational egoists in an 'original position' in which they thought behind a 'veil of ignorance,' so that they would not know who they were or even what generation they belonged to.[5] Reasoning behind this veil of ignorance, they would apply the maximin principle. John Harsanyi earlier used the notion of a contract in such a position of ignorance, but used not the maximin principle but the principle of maximizing expected utility.[6] Harsanyi's method leads to a form of rule utilitarianism. I see no great merit in this roundabout approach to ethics *via* a contrary to fact supposition, which involves the tricky notion of a social contract and which thus appears already to presuppose a moral position. The approach seems also too Hobbesian: it is anthropologically incorrect to suppose that we are all originally little egoists. I prefer to base ethics on a principle of generalized benevolence, to which some of those with whom I discuss ethics may immediately respond. Possibly it might show something interesting about our common moral notions if it could be proved that they follow from what would be contracted by rational egoists in an 'original position,' but as a utilitarian I am more concerned to advocate a normative theory which might replace our common moral notions than I am to explain these notions. Though some form of utilitarianism might be deducible (as by Harsanyi) from a contract or original position theory, I do not think that it either ought to be or need be defended in this sort of way.

Be that as it may, it is clear that utilitarian views about distribution of happiness do differ from Rawls' view. I have made a distinction between justice as a moral concept and justice as a legal or quasi-legal concept. The utilitarian has no room for the former, but he can have strong views about the latter, though *what* these views are will depend on empirical considerations. Thus whether he will prefer a political theory which advocates a completely socialist state, or whether he will prefer one which advocates a minimal state (as Robert Nozick's book does [7]), or whether again he will advocate something between the two, is something which depends on the facts of economics, sociology, and so on. As someone not expert in these fields I have no desire to dogmatize on these empirical matters. (My own private non-expert opinion is that probably neither extreme leads to maximization of happiness, though I have a liking for rather more socialism than exists in Australia or U.S.A. at present.) As a utilitarian my approach to political theory has to be tentative and empirical. Not believing in moral rights as such I can not deduce theories about the best political arrangements by making deductions (as Nozick does) from propositions which purport to be about such basic rights.

Rawls deduces two principles of justice.[8] The first of these is that 'each person is to have an equal right to the most extensive basic liberty compatible with a similar liberty for others,' and the second one is that 'social and economic inequalities are to be arranged so that they are both (a) reasonably expected to be to everyone's advantage, and (b) attached to positions and offices open to all.' Though a utilitarian could (on empirical grounds) be very much in sympathy with both of these principles, he could not accept them as universal rules. Suppose that a society which had no danger of nuclear war could be achieved only by reducing the liberty of one per cent of the world's population. Might it not be right to bring about such a state of affairs if it were in one's power? Indeed might it not be right greatly to reduce the liberty of 100% of the world's population if such a desirable outcome could be achieved? Perhaps the present generation would be pretty miserable and would hanker for their lost liberties. However we must also think about the countless future generations which might exist and be happy provided that mankind can avoid exterminating itself, and we must also think of all the pain, misery and genetic damage which would be brought about by nuclear war even if this did not lead to the total extermination of mankind.

Suppose that this loss of freedom prevented a war so devastating that the whole process of evolution on this planet would come to an end. At the cost of the loss of freedom, instead of the war and the end of evolution there might occur an evolutionary process which was not only long lived but also beneficial: in millions of years there might be creatures descended from *homo sapiens* which had vastly increased talents and capacity for happiness. At least such considerations show that Rawls' first principle is far from obvious to the utilitarian, though in certain mundane contexts he might accede to it as a useful approximation. Indeed I do not believe that restriction of liberty, in our present society, could have beneficial results in helping to prevent nuclear war, though a case could be made for certain restrictions on the liberty of all present members of society so as to enable the government to prevent nuclear blackmail by gangs of terrorists.

Perhaps in the past considerable restrictions on the personal liberties of a large proportion of citizens may have been justifiable on utilitarian grounds. In view of the glories of Athens and its contributions to civilization it is possible that the Athenian slave society was justifiable. In one part of his paper, 'Nature and Soundness of the Contract and Coherence Arguments,' [9] David Lyons has judiciously discussed the question of whether in certain circumstances a utilitarian would condone slavery. He says that it would be unlikely that a utilitarian could condone slavery as it has existed in modern times. However he considers the possibility that less objectionable forms of slavery or near slavery have existed. The less objectionable these may have been, the more likely it is that utilitarianism would have condoned them. Lyons remarks that our judgments about the relative advantages of different societies must be very tentative because we do not know enough about human history to say what were the social alternatives at any juncture.[10]

Similar reflections naturally occur in connection with Rawls' second principle. Oligarchic societies, such as that of eighteenth century Britain, may well have been in fact better governed than they would have been if posts of responsibility had been available to all. Certainly to resolve this question we should have to go deeply into empirical investigations of the historical facts. (To prevent misunderstanding, I do think that in our present society utilitarianism would imply adherence to Rawls' second principle as a general rule.)

A utilitarian is concerned with maximizing total happiness (or goodness, if he is an ideal utilitarian). Rawls largely concerns himself with certain 'primary goods', as he calls them. These include 'rights and liberties, powers and opportunities, income and wealth.'[11] A utilitarian would regard these as mere means to the ultimate good. Nevertheless if he is proposing new laws or changes to social institutions the utilitarian will have to concern himself in practice with the distribution of these 'primary goods' (as Bentham did).[12] But if as an approximation we neglect this distinction, which may be justifiable to the extent that there is a correlation between happiness and the level of these 'primary goods,' we may say that according to Rawls an action is right only if it is to the benefit of the least advantaged person. A utilitarian will hold that a redistribution of the means to happiness is right if it maximizes the general happiness, even though some persons, even the least advantaged ones, are made worse off. A position which is intermediate between the utilitarian position and Rawls' position would be one which held that one ought to maximize some sort of trade off between total happiness and distribution of happiness. Such a position would imply that sometimes we should redistribute in such a way as to make some persons, even the least advantaged ones, worse off, but this would happen less often than it would according to the classical utilitarian theory.

Utilitarianism and Sacrifice of Interests

Now though I do not believe that ultimate moral principles are capable of proof or disproof, I wonder whether this disagreement about whether we should ever sacrifice some persons' interests for the sake of the total interest may be connected with different views which philosophers have about human personality. Are we concerned simply to produce the greatest net happiness, or is it independently important that we should take account of *whose* happiness a given quantum of happiness should be? The non-utilitarian will hold that the distinction between Smith on the one hand and Campbell on the other hand is different in an ethically important way from the distinction between two different temporal segments of the same man, say Smith throughout his twenties and Smith throughout his forties. (The non-utilitarian generally feels no puzzlement about the rightness of the twenty-five year old Smith sacrificing himself for the sake of the forty-five year old Smith.) I find it hard to see what the morally relevant difference would be. It is true that we do in fact feel a special concern for future temporal segments of ourselves, perhaps because we are most of the time planning for these future temporal segments. However, sometimes we plan for the welfare of temporal segments of other people, and the man who plans martyr-dom, for example, is certainly not planning for any future temporal segment of himself (at least if he does not believe in immortality). Since the utilitarian principle is an expression of the sentiment of generalized benevolence, the utilitarian sees no relevant different between the happi-ness of one person and the happiness of another.

I have suggested that those who see the matter differently may have a strong metaphysical concept of personality. In the context of modern scientific psychology the notion of a person tends to dissolve into a welter of talk in terms of neurophysiology, cybernetics and information theory. Sidgwick may have been similarly sceptical about our ordinary notions of personality. Using an earlier philosophical idiom he remarks (as a *tu quoque* to the Egoist who asks why he should sacrifice his own present happiness for the happiness of another) that one might equally ask why one should sacrifice a present pleasure for a greater one in the future. He points out that if one accepted Hume's theory of the mind, according to which the mind is just a cluster of feelings, sensations, and images, one might ask why one part of the series of feelings which con-tribute to the mind should feel concern for another part.[13]

Returning from this speculative excursion, let us simply note that according to classical utilitarianism it can be right to diminish the happi-ness of Smith in order to bring about a more than compensating increase of the happiness of Campbell. What matters is simply the maximization of happiness, and distribution of happiness is irrelevant. Sidgwick him-self qualified this uncompromising stand in a minor way when he intro-duced a principle of equal distribution which would come into play when each of two alternative actions would produce the same amount of total happiness, each greater than that which would be produced by any other alternative action. Of course there must be an almost zero probability that two alternative actions would produce *exactly* the same total happi-ness, but as Sidgwick points out, it may be quite common *that as far as we know* the two alternatives would produce equal total happiness. Sidgwick introduces his principle of equal distribution in order to break this sort of tie,[14] and he claims that the principle is implicit in Bentham's somewhat obscure formula 'Everybody to count for one, and nobody for more than one.' Actually, if Sidgwick's principle is needed only to break ties (but why not toss a coin?) then it merely postpones the problem.

It would lead us to prefer giving 3 units of happiness to Smith plus 3 to Campbell to giving 2 to Smith plus 4 to Campbell. We could still have a tie between giving 2 units to Smith and 4 to Campbell, on the one hand, and giving 4 units to Smith and 2 to Campbell, on the other hand.

It is not clear to me that in proposing this supplementary principle of distribution Sidgwick is being quite consistent. Suppose that alternative *A* maximizes happiness and also that *B* is the alternative action which comes nearest to *A* in producing happiness, producing only slightly less. Suppose also that *A* would distribute happiness rather unequally and that *B* would distribute happiness quite equally. Nevertheless because *A* produces more happiness Sidgwick would say that *A* should be done. Since, given a suitable example, the difference between the amounts of happiness produced can be supposed as small as one pleases, it appears that Sidgwick gives equal distribution a vanishingly small value compared with that which he gives to maximization. In fact, according to usual mathematical theories such a vanishingly small value could be no other than zero, and so instead of applying his principle of distribution in order to break ties Sidgwick could surely just as well have tossed a coin. The only way for him to avoid this conclusion, I think, would have been for him to say that the value of equal distribution is non-zero but infinitesimal.[15] However, it does seem to be an odd ethical position that one should give an *infinitesimal* value to equal distribution. It seems more plausible to reject Sidgwick's supplementary principle altogether (as I am inclined to do) or else to try to work out a theory in which equality of distribution comes into the calculation of consequences in all cases, and not just in order to break ties. According to the second alternative, we should be concerned with maximizing some sort of compromise between total happiness and equal distribution of it. Such a theory might make more concessions to common sense notions of distributive justice than classical utilitarianism does.

One proposal for compromising between maximization of happiness and distribution of it is given by Nicholas Rescher in his book *Distributive Justice*.[16] (Rescher modifies utilitarianism in other ways too, but I shall not be concerned with these here.) Rescher's proposal is not for a compromise between *total* happiness and distribution but between *average* happiness and distribution, though an analogous account would hold for the case of total happiness. Rescher proposes that we should maximize an *effective average*, which is the average happiness less half the standard deviation from it. Lawrence H. Powers has argued that Rescher's definition of an effective average leads to unacceptable consequences, and has suggested replacing Rescher's definition by a new one, according to which the effective average is the average happiness less half the average deviation.[17] He gives an example which shows that Rescher's criterion could forbid a change which made everybody better off (a Pareto improvement). Powers claims that his modified criterion does not have bad consequences of this sort. Some philosophers may find this sort of compromise between utilitarianism and egalitarianism more palatable than classical utilitarianism. However, I shall now return to the consideration of distributive justice as it relates to the classical utilitarian position.

SAVINGS FOR FUTURE GENERATIONS AND FOR OTHER COUNTRIES

In thinking about distributive justice we commonly think about the problem of distributing happiness between members of a set of contemporary individuals. However this is to oversimplify the situation with which the utilitarian should be concerned. The consequences of his actions stretch indefinitely into the future, and the happiness to be maximized is that of all sentient beings, whatever their positions in space and time.[18] It is in the context of future generations that the question of whether we should maximize *average* happiness or whether we should maximize *total* happiness becomes particularly relevant. Like Sidgwick [19] I am inclined to advocate the latter type of utilitarianism. In thinking about this issue it is useful once more to compare the question of the happiness of different temporal segments of one person with the question of the happiness of a number of distinct persons. If we think that it is better to have 50 happy years of life than it is to have 20 happy years, then we should also think that it is better to have 50 happy people than to have 20 happy people, and this not just because the 50 happy people would raise the average happiness of the total population of the universe more than the 20 happy people would. (Even if the total population of the universe were 50 or 20, as the case may be, the universe with 50 happy people would be better than the universe with 20.) My argument here is of course meant to be persuasive rather than logically compelling. I suppose that a proponent of average utility could consistently reply that 50 happy years of life are intrinsically no better than 20 such years, though we may prefer a man to live the longer life because of extrinsic considerations, for example the sorrow of a widow with small children to bring up and no husband to help her.

As a utilitarian I hold that we should think of future generations no less than we should think of members of our own generation. Distance in time is no more pertinent to utilitarian considerations than is distance in space. Just as we would not conduct a bomb test on a distant island without considering the possibility that the island contained inhabitants, so also we ought to consider the effects of our actions on our remote or unknown descendants or possible descendants. I have heard it argued that the two cases are not parallel: what inhabitants are now on the island does not depend on our present actions, but who our descendants are does depend in part on our present actions. I cannot see myself why this should be a morally relevant difference. Suppose that one action would cause an island to have in the next generation a population of 1000 whereas an alternative action would cause the island to have a population of 2000 and that the question of the larger or smaller population has no significant effect on the rest of the world. Then as a utilitarian I want to prefer causing the larger population to exist, though a proponent of maximizing average utility would be indifferent between the two cases. Some philosophers might say that we have no duties towards merely possible people. If we opt for the population of 1000 then these 1000 will be actual and we will have duties towards them, but the remainder of the possible population of 2000 would not be actual and would not have rights. However such an argument should not be accepted by a utilitarian, who should not have the notion of 'duty' as a fundamental concept of his system.[20]

Anyway, let us take it that we are concerned here with utilitarianism as a theory of maximizing *total* happiness (not *average* happiness). Let us consider the question of the distribution of happiness and of the means to happiness between different generations. Just as in the case of distribution between contemporaries, utilitarianism is indifferent to various patterns of distribution of total happiness provided that the total is the same. (However the theory will not be indifferent in this sort of way to questions of the distribution of the *means* to happiness.) We must ask what sacrifices we should make now for the sake of the greater happiness of our descendants. Not so long ago it seemed that the fruits of science and technology were bringing the human species towards a golden age. (Unfortunately we have tended to forget the deleterious effect of modern technology—e.g., factory farms—on animal happiness.[21]) People are nowadays more sceptical about a future golden age: they point to problems of overpopulation, environmental pollution, the danger of nuclear war, possible accidents in genetic engineering, and so on. But let us consider what would be the right policy about savings for future generations, assuming that future generations would be happier than ours. In 'future generations' I would want to include 'future generations of non-humans' too, but I shall neglect this point in comparing utilitarianism with Rawls' theory. It indeed is a defect in the contractual theory that it neglects the sufferings of animals: the veil of ignorance prevents us from knowing who we are, i.e. which human being, but it does not, I think, prevent us from knowing that we are at least human. Now if future generations are going to be happier than our generation, it would seem to follow from Rawls' difference principle that we should make no savings for future generations. If we did we should be disadvantaging the worse off for the benefit of the better off. Rawls escapes this consequence by what seems to be an *ad hoc* modification of his original theory: he modifies the egoistic inclinations of people in his 'original position' by allowing them some altruistic feelings, namely feelings for the welfare of their children and grandchildren.

Utilitarianism might seem to imply an opposite conclusion. Instead of implying zero savings (as Rawls' theory could if it did not have the above mentioned modification) utilitarianism would seem to require what many people would regard as an unacceptably high amount of savings. In a discussion of F. P. Ramsey's pioneering paper 'A Mathematical Theory of Saving,'[22] John C. Harsanyi has pointed out[23] that on certain plausible assumptions about the relation between increments of wealth to increments of happiness (assumptions about utility functions), Ramsey's argument might well imply that the present generation should save more than half of their national incomes. However, Harsanyi has argued that utility functions applicable to the present generation do not properly relate savings to future felicity. New technological discoveries may well make present capital investments of little use in the future. For this reason, as well as others which I shall not go into here, Harsanyi has argued that optimal savings would be less than might at first have been supposed on the basis of Ramsey's argument.

Nevertheless it may well be that utilitarian considerations imply that savings for future generations should be much greater than many people think. The less we think that a golden age is coming the stronger these reasons will be. Very much expense and effort need to be made, for example, to show that radio-active waste materials do not harm our remote descendants, or failing that, we must forgo the use of nuclear reactors for generating power. Similarly with respect to the rich countries in relation to the third world, the wasteful technologies, certain fishing areas, and so on, for the benefit of the poorer ones. The fact that such savings or renunciations that are enjoined by utilitarian considerations may well come to far more than would be politically acceptable is no criticism of utilitarianism: it is a reflection of the fact that people are usually more swayed by self-interest than they ought to be. Of course utilitarianism is a theory for individual decision making, and prevailing political attitudes constitute part of the empirical facts about the world with which, like it or not, a utilitarian decision maker will have to contend. Some actions which would be right if they were generally imitated would be merely Quixotic if there were no prospect of such imitation. For example when there was a proposal to raise the salaries of Australian professors, some friends of mine wrote letters to the newspapers saying that it would be better to use this amount of taxpayers' money to increase the number of junior faculty members. When this idea did not catch on, there was obviously no point in their refusing (as individuals) the proposed salary increases. (I neglect the fact here that there would have been great administrative difficulties in putting such individual decisions into effect.) Though utilitarianism is *in theory* not egalitarian, because it does not protect the interests of the worst off people in the way that Rawls' theory does, it is possible that there might be situations in which Rawls' constraint of not making the worst off even more badly off would force Rawls into a decision which would lead to a greater difference between rich and poor than would utilitarian theory. This is because removal of the constraint might, at the cost of making a very few of the worst off members of society still worse off, bring about a more general levelling off on the whole. (Here we must of course make allowance for the fact that if we are concerned with the redistribution of the *means* to happiness, taking what people have may produce more unhappiness than not giving it to them in the first place.) To take a rather fanciful example, suggested to me by some remarks of Harsanyi's,[24] suppose that society spent astronomical sums on very badly off mentally defective people, thus making them able to perform some simple tasks which would otherwise be beyond them, and that this vast expenditure for the mentally defective prevented ordinary health care for the ordinary poor but not handicapped people. On the above supposition utilitarianism would suggest a redistribution of resources *from* the mentally defective *to* better health care for the generality of the poor. This would seem to be forbidden by Rawls' difference principle. Whether in any actual situations Rawls' theory or utilitarian theory would lead to the greater egalitarianism in practice depends on many empirical considerations, and I would not like to pronounce on this matter.

UTILITARIANISM AND NOZICK'S THEORY

General adherence to Robert Nozick's theory (in his *Anarchy, State, and Utopia*) [25] would be compatible with the existence of very great inequality indeed. This is because the whole theory is based quite explicitly on the notion of *rights*: in the very first sentence of the preface of his book we read 'Individuals have rights. . . .' The utilitarian would demur here. A utilitarian legislator might tax the rich in order to give aid to the poor, but a Nozickian legislator would not do so. A utilitarian legislator might impose a heavy tax on inherited wealth, whereas Nozick would allow the relatively fortunate to become even more fortunate, provided that they did not infringe the *rights* of the less fortunate. The utilitarian legislator would hope to increase the total happiness by equalizing things a bit. How far he should go in this direction would depend on empirical considerations. He would not want to equalize things too much if this led to too much weakening of the incentive to work, for example. Of course according to Nozick's system there would be no reason why members of society should not set up a utilitarian utopia, and voluntarily equalize their wealth, and also give wealth to poorer communities outside. However it is questionable whether such isolated utopias could survive in a modern environment, but if they did survive, the conformity of the behaviour of their members to utilitarian theory, rather than the conformity to Nozick's theory, would be what would commend their societies to me.

SUMMARY

In this article I have explained that the notion of justice is not a fundamental notion in utilitarianism, but that utilitarians will characteristically have certain views about such things as the distribution of wealth, savings for the benefit of future generations and for the third world countries and other practical matters. Utilitarianism differs from John Rawls' theory in that it is ready to contemplate some sacrifice to certain individuals (or classes of individuals) for the sake of the greater good of all, and in particular may allow certain limitations of personal freedom which would be ruled out by Rawls' theory. *In practice*, however, the general tendency of utilitarianism may well be towards an egalitarian form of society.

NOTES

1. In hoping that utilitarianism can be rendered acceptable to some people by presenting it in a clear light, I do not deny the possibility of the reverse happening. Thus I confess to a bit of a pull the other way when I consider Nozick's example of an 'experience machine'. See Robert Nozick, *Anarchy, State and Utopia* (Oxford: Blackwell, 1975), pp. 42-45, though I am at least partially reassured by Peter Singer's remarks towards the end of his review of Nozick, *New York Review of Books*, March 6, 1975. Nozick's example of an experience machine is more worrying than the more familiar one of a pleasure inducing machine, because it seems to apply to ideal as well as to hedonistic utilitarianism.

2. Henry Sidgwick, *Methods of Ethics*, Seventh Edition (Chicago: University of Chicago Press, 1962), especially Book IV.

3. In this paper I shall assume a hedonistic utilitarianism, though most of what I have to say will be applicable to ideal utilitarianism too.

4. There are of course difficult problems about the assignment of cardinal utilities to states of mind, but for the purposes of this paper I am assuming that we can intelligibly talk, as utilitarians do, about units of happiness.

5. John Rawls, *A Theory of Justice* (Cambridge, Mass.: Harvard University Press, 1971).

6. John C. Harsanyi, 'Cardinal Utility in Welfare Economics and the Theory of Risk-Taking', *Journal of Political Economy*, 61 (1953), 434-435, and 'Cardinal Welfare, Individualistic Ethics, and Interpersonal Comparisons of Utility', *ibid.*, 63 (1955), 309-321. Harsanyi has discussed Rawls' use of the maximin principle and has defended the principle of maximizing expected utility instead, in a paper 'Can the Maximin Principle Serve as a Basis for Morality? A Critique of John Rawls's Theory', *The American Political Science Review*, 69 (1975), 594-606. These articles have been reprinted in John C. Harsanyi, *Essays on Ethics, Social Behavior, and Scientific Explanation* (Dordrecht, Holland: D. Reidel, 1976).

7. Robert Nozick, *Anarchy, State and Utopia*. (See fn. 1 above).

8. Rawls, *A Theory of Justice*, p. 60.

9. In Norman Daniels (ed.), *Reading Rawls* (Oxford: Blackwell, 1975), pp. 141-167. See pp. 148-149.

10. Lyons, *op. cit.*, p. 149, near top.

11. Rawls, *op. cit.*, p. 62.

12. On this point see Brian Barry, *The Liberal Theory of Justice* (London: Oxford University Press, 1973), p. 55.

13. See Sidgwick, *Methods of Ethics*, Seventh Edition, pp. 418-419.

14. *Ibid.*, pp. 416-417.

15. Of course during the nineteenth century the notion of an infinitesimal fell into disrepute among mathematicians, for very good reasons, but it has recently been made mathematically respectable by Abraham Robinson. See Abraham Robinson, *Non-Standard Analysis* (Amsterdam: North-Holland, 1970). A simple account of Robinson's idea can be found in an article by Martin Davis and Reuben Hersh, 'Non-Standard Analysis', *Scientific American*, June 1972, pp. 78-86.

16. Nicholas Rescher, *Distributive Justice* (Indianapolis: The Bobbs-Merrill Company, 1966). See pp. 31-41.

17. Lawrence H. Powers, 'A More Effective Average: A Note on Distributive Justice', *Philosophical Studies*, 21 (1970), 74-78.

18. There is a question as to whether Jeremy Bentham himself thought in this universalistic way or whether the interests with which he was concerned were re-

stricted in various ways. See David Lyons 'Was Bentham a Utilitarian?', in *Reason and Reality, Royal Institute of Philosophy Lectures,* Vol. 5, 1970–1971. (London: Macmillan, 1972), pp. 196-221.

19. For Sidgwick's remarks on the question of average happiness *versus* total happiness see *Methods of Ethics,* Seventh Edition, pp. 414-416.

20. An interesting discussion of the problem of future generations is to be found in Jan Narveson, 'Utilitarianism and New Generations', *Mind,* 76 (1967), 62-72. Narveson is a utilitarian, though his view differs somewhat from my own form of utilitarianism, and his conclusions about future generations are opposed to mine. On p. 63 Narveson says 'Whenever one has a duty, it *must* be possible to say on whose account the duty arises—i.e. *whose* happiness is in question'. I want to deny this statement: I think that I ought to maximize happiness, and I can work out the best ways of achieving this end without knowing *who* are the people who will be happy or miserable. This is why I expect that Narveson's notion of 'duty' differs from my notion of 'ought' and that his notion is perhaps even related to the correlative and non-utilitarian notion of a right. But I am not clear about this and I could easily have misunderstood Narveson's notion of 'duty'.

21. On this matter see Peter Singer's important book, *Animal Liberation* (New York: Random House, 1975).

22. *Economic Journal,* 38 (1928), 543-559.

23. 'Can the Maximin Principle Serve as a Basis for Morality? A Critique of John Rawls' Theory', *loc. cit.*

24. *Ibid.*

25. See footnote 1.

R. M. HARE

Corpus Christi College, Oxford

Justice and Equality

THE SENSES OF 'JUST'

There are several reasons why a philosopher of my persuasion should wish to write about justice. The first is the general one that ethical theory ought to be applied to practical issues, both for the sake of improving the theory and for any light it may shed on the practical issues, of which many of the most important involve questions of justice. This is shown by the frequency with which appeals are made to justice and fairness and related ideals when people are arguing about political or economic questions (about wages for example, or about schools policy or about relations between races or sexes). If we do not know what 'just' and 'fair' mean (and it looks as if we do not) and therefore do not know what would settle questions involving these concepts, then we are unlikely to be able to sort out these very difficult moral problems. I have also a particular interest in the topic: I hold a view about moral reasoning which has at least strong affinities with utilitarianism; [1] and there is commonly thought to be some kind of antagonism between justice and utility or, as it is sometimes called, expediency. I have therefore a special need to sort these questions out.

We must start by distinguishing between different kinds of justice, or

between different senses or uses of the word 'just' (the distinction between
these different ways of putting the matter need not now concern us).
In distinguishing between different kinds of justice we shall have to make
crucial use of a distinction between different levels of moral thinking
which I have explained at length in other places.[2] It is perhaps simplest to
distinguish three levels of thought, one ethical or meta-ethical and two
moral or normative-ethical. At the meta-ethical level we try to establish the
meanings of the moral words, and thus the formal properties of the moral
concepts, including their logical properties. Without knowing these a theory of normative moral reasoning cannot begin. Then there are two levels
of (normative) moral thinking which have often been in various ways distinguished. I have myself in the past called them 'level 2' and 'level 1';
but for ease of remembering I now think it best to give them names, and
propose to call level 2 the *critical* level and level 1 the *intuitive* level. At
the intuitive level we make use of *prima facie* moral principles of a fairly
simple general sort, and do not question them but merely apply them
to cases which we encounter. This level of thinking cannot be (as intui-
tionists commonly suppose) self-sustaining; there is a need for a critical
level of thinking by which we select the *prima facie* principles for use at
the intuitive level, settle conflicts between them, and give to the whole
system of them a justification which intuition by itself can never provide.
It will be one of the objects of this paper to distinguish those kinds of
justice whose place is at the intuitive level and which are embodied in
prima facie principles from those kinds which have a role in critical and
indeed in meta-ethical thinking.

The principal result of meta-ethical enquiry in this field is to isolate
a sense or kind of justice which has come to be known as 'formal justice'.
Formal justice is a property of all moral principles (which is why Profes-
sor Rawls heads his chapter on this subject not 'Formal constraints of the
concept of *just*' but 'Formal constraints of the concept of *right*',[3] and
why his disciple David Richards is able to make a good attempt to found
the whole of morality, and not merely a theory of justice, on a similar
hypothetical-contract basis).[4] Formal justice is simply another name for
the formal requirement of universality in moral principles on which, as
I have explained in detail elsewhere,[5] golden-rule arguments are based.
From the formal, logical properties of the moral words, and in particular
from the logical prohibition of individual references in moral principles,
it is possible to derive formal canons of moral argument, such as the rule
that we are not allowed to discriminate morally between individuals unless there is some qualitative difference between them which is the ground
for the discrimination; and the rule that the equal interests of different
individuals have equal moral weight. Formal justice consists simply in the
observance of these canons in our moral arguments; it is widely thought
that this observance by itself is not enough to secure justice in some more
substantial sense. As we shall see, one is not offending against the first rule
if one says that extra privileges should be given to people just because
they have white skins; and one is not offending against either rule if one
says that one should take a cent from everybody and give it to the man

with the biggest nose, provided that he benefits as much in total as they lose. The question is, How do we get from formal to substantial justice?

This question arises because there are various kinds of material or substantial justice whose content cannot be established directly by appeal to the uses of moral words or the formal properties of moral concepts (we shall see later how much can be done indirectly by appeal to these formal properties *in conjunction with* other premises or postulates or presuppositions). There is a number of different kinds of substantial justice, and we can hardly do better than begin with Aristotle's classification of them,[6] since it is largely responsible for the different senses which the word 'just' still has in common use. This is a case where it is impossible to appeal to common use, at any rate of the word 'just' (the word 'fair' is better) in order to settle philosophical disputes, because the common use is itself the product of past philosophical theories. The expressions 'distributive' and 'retributive' justice go back to Aristotle,[7] and the word 'just' itself occupies the place (or places) that it does in our language largely because of its place in earlier philosophical discussions.

Aristotle first separated off a generic sense of the Greek word commonly translated 'just', a sense which had been used a lot by Plato: the sense in which justice is the whole of virtue in so far as it concerns our relations with other people.[8] The last qualification reminds us that this is not the most generic sense possible. Theognis had already used it to include the whole of virtue, full stop.[9] These very generic senses of the word, as applied to men and acts, have survived into modern English to confuse philosophers. One of the sources of confusion is that, in the less generic sense of 'just' to be discussed in most of this paper, the judgment that an act would be unjust is sometimes fairly easily overridden by other moral considerations ('unjust', we may say, 'but right as an act of mercy'; or 'unjust, but right because necessary in order to avert an appalling calamity'). It is much more difficult for judgments that an act is required by justice in the generic sense, in which 'unjust' is almost equivalent to 'not right', to be overridden in this way.

Adherents of the *'fiat justitia ruat caelum'*[10] school seldom make clear whether, when they say 'Let justice be done though the heavens fall', they are using a more or less generic sense of 'justice'; and they thus take advantage of its non-overridability in the more generic sense in order to claim unchallengeable sanctity for judgments made using one of the less generic senses. It must be right to do the just thing (whatever that may be) in the sense (if there still is one in English) in which 'just' *means* 'right'. In this sense, if it were right to cause the heavens to fall, and therefore just in the most generic sense, it would of course be right. But we might have to take into account, in deciding whether it would be right, the fact that the heavens would fall (that causing the heavens to fall would be one of the things we were doing if we did the action in question). On the other hand, if it were merely the just act in one of the less generic senses, we might hold that, though just, it was not right, because it would not be right to cause the heavens to fall merely in order to secure justice in this more limited sense; perhaps some concession to mercy, or even to common sense, would be in order.

This is an application of the 'split-level' structure of moral thinking sketched above. One of the theses I wish to maintain is that principles of justice in these less generic senses are all *prima facie* principles and therefore overridable. I shall later be giving a utilitarian account of justice which finds a place, at the intuitive level, for these *prima facie* principles of justice. At this level they have great importance and utility, but it is in accordance with utilitarianism, as indeed with common sense, to claim that they can on unusual occasions be overriden. Having said this, however, it is most important to stress that this does *not* involve conceding the overridability of either the generic kind of justice, which has its place at the critical level, or of formal justice, which operates at the meta-ethical level. These are preserved intact, and therefore defenders of the sanctity of justice ought to be content, since these are the core of justice as of morality. We may call to mind here Aristotle's [11] remarks about the 'better justice' or 'equity' which is required in order to rectify the crudities, giving rise to unacceptable results in particular cases, of a justice whose principles are, as they have to be, couched in general (i.e. simple) terms. The lawgiver who, according to Aristotle, 'would have' given a special prescription if he had been present at this particular case, and to whose prescription we must try to conform if we can, corresponds to the critical moral thinker, who operates under the constraints of formal justice and whose principles are not limited to simple general rules but can be specific enough to cover the peculiarities of unusual cases.

RETRIBUTIVE AND DISTRIBUTIVE JUSTICE

After speaking briefly of generic justice, Aristotle goes on [12] to distinguish two main kinds of justice in the narrower or more particular sense in which it means 'fairness'. He calls these retributive and distributive justice. They have their place, respectively, in the fixing of penalties and rewards for bad and good actions, and in the distribution of goods and the opposite between the possible recipients. One of the most important questions is whether these two sorts of justice are reducible to a single sort. Rawls, for example, thinks that they are, and so do I. By using the expression 'justice as fairness', he implies that all justice can be reduced to kinds of distributive justice, which itself is founded on procedural justice (i.e. on the adoption of fair procedures) in distribution.[13]

We may (without attempting complete accuracy in exposition) explain how Rawls might effect this reduction as follows. The parties in his 'original position' are prevented by his 'veil of ignorance' from knowing what their own positions are in the world in which they are to live; so they are unable when adopting principles of justice to tailor them to suit their own individual interests. Impartiality (a very important constituent, at least, of justice) is thus secured. Therefore the principles which govern *both* the distribution of wealth and power and other good things

and the assignment of rewards and penalities (and indeed all other matters which have to be regulated by principles of justice) will be impartial
as between individuals, and in this sense just. In this way Rawls in effect
reduces the justice of acts of retribution to justice in distributing between
the affected parties the good and bad effects of a system of retributions,
and reduces this distributive justice in turn to the adoption of a just
procedure for selecting the system of retributions to be used.

This can be illustrated by considering the case of a criminal facing a
judge (a case which has been thought to give trouble to me too, though
I dealt with it adequately, on the lines which I am about to repeat here,
in my book *Freedom and Reason*).[14] A Rawlsian judge, when sentencing
the criminal, could defend himself against the charge of injustice or unfairness by saying that he was faithfully observing the principles of justice
which would be adopted in the original position, whose conditions are
procedurally fair. What these principles would be requires, no doubt, a
great deal of discussion, in the course of which I might find myself in
disagreement with Rawls. But my own view on how the judge should
justify his action is, in its formal properties, very like his. On my view
likewise, the judge can say that, when he asks himself what universal
principles he is prepared to adopt for situations exactly like the one
he is in, and considers examples of such logically possible situations in
which *he* occupies, successively, the positions of judge, and of criminal,
and of all those who are affected by the administration and enforcement
of the law under which he is sentencing the criminal, including, of course,
potential victims of possible future crimes—he can say that when he asks
himself this, he has no hesitation in accepting the principle which bids
him impose such and such a sentence in accordance with the law.

I am assuming that the judge is justifying himself at the critical level.
If he were content with justifying himself at the intuitive level, his task
would be easier, because, we hope, he, like most of us, has intuitions
about the proper administration of justice in the courts, embodying
prima facie principles of a sort whose inculcation in judges and in the
rest of us has a high social utility. I say this while recognizing that *some*
judges have intuitions about these matters which have a high social *dis-*
utility. The question of what intuitions judges ought to have about
retributive justice is a matter for *critical* moral thinking.

On both Rawls' view and mine retributive justice has thus been reduced to distributive; on Rawls' view the principles of justice adopted
are those which *distribute* fairly between those affected the good and the
evil consequences of having or not having certain enforced criminal laws;
on my own view likewise it is the impartiality secured by the requirement
to universalize one's prescriptions which makes the judge say what he
says, and here too it is an impartiality in distributing good and evil
consequences between the affected parties. For the judge to let off the
rapist would not be *fair* to all those who would be raped if the law were
not enforced. I conclude that retributive justice can be reduced to distributive, and that therefore we shall have done what is required of us
if we can give an adequate account of the latter.

What is common to Rawls' method and my own is the recognition that to get solutions to particular questions about what is just or unjust, we have to have a way of selecting principles of justice to answer such questions, and that to ask them in default of such principles is senseless. And we both recognize that the method for selecting the principles has to be founded on what he calls 'the formal constraints of the concept of right'. This measure of agreement can extend to the method of selecting principles of distributive justice as well as retributive. Neither Rawls nor I need be put off our stride by an objector who says that we have not addressed ourselves to the question of what acts are just, but have divagated on to the quite different question of how to select principles of justice. The point is that the first question cannot be answered without answering the second. Most of the apparently intractable conflicts about justice and rights that plague the world have been generated by taking certain answers to the first question as obvious and requiring no argument. We shall resolve these conflicts only by asking what arguments are available for the principles by which questions about the justice of individual acts are to be answered. In short, we need to ascend from intuitive to critical thinking; as I have argued in my review of his book, Rawls is to be reproached with not *completing* the ascent.[15]

Nozick, however, seems hardly to have begun it.[16] Neither Rawls nor I have anything to fear from him, so long as we stick to the formal part of our systems which we in effect share. When it comes to the application of this formal method to produce substantial principles of justice, I might find myself in disagreement with Rawls, because he relies much too much on his own intuitions which are open to question. Nozick's intuitions differ from Rawls', and sometimes differ from, sometimes agree with mine. This sort of question is simply not to be settled by appeal to intuitions, and it is time that the whole controversy ascended to a more serious, critical level. At this level, the answer which both Rawls and I should give to Nozick is that whatever sort of principles of justice we are after, whether structural principles, as Rawls thinks, or historical principles, as Nozick maintains, they have to be supported by critical thinking, of which Nozick seems hardly to see the necessity. This point is quite independent of the structural-historical disagreement.

For example, if Nozick thinks that it is just for people to retain whatever property they have acquired by voluntary exchange which benefited all parties, starting from a position of equality but perhaps ending up with a position of gross inequality, and if Rawls, by contrast, thinks that such inequality should be rectified in order to make the position of the least advantaged in society as good as possible, how are we to decide between them? Not by intuition, because there seems to be a deadlock between their intuitions. Rawls has a procedure, which *need* not appeal to intuition, for justifying distributions; this would give him the game, if he were to base the procedure on firm logical grounds, and if he followed it correctly. Actually he does not so base it, and mixes up so many intuitions in the argument that the conclusions he reaches are not such as the procedure really justifies. But Nozick has no procedure at all: only a variety of considerations of different sorts, all in the end based on intuition. Sometimes he seems to be telling us what arrangements in society would be arrived at if bargaining took place in accordance with games-theory between mutually disinterested parties; sometimes what arrangements would maximize the welfare of members of society; and sometimes what arrangements would strike them as fair. He does not often warn us when he is switching from one of these grounds to another; and he does little to convince us by argument that the arrangements so selected would be in accordance with justice. He hopes that we will think what he thinks; but Rawls at least thinks otherwise.

Formal Justice and Substantial Equality

How then do we get from formal to substantial justice? We have had an example of how this is done in the sphere of retributive justice; but how is this method to be extended to cover distributive justice as a whole, and its relation, if any, to equality in distribution? The difficulty of using formal justice in order to establish principles of substantial justice can indeed be illustrated very well by asking whether, and in what sense, justice demands equality in distribution. The complaint is often made that a certain distribution is unfair or unjust because unequal; so it looks, at least, as if the substantial principle that goods ought to be distributed equally in default of reasons to the contrary forms part of some people's conception of justice. Yet, it is argued, this substantial principle cannot be established simply on the basis of the formal notions we have mentioned. The following kind of schematic example is often adduced: consider two possible distributions of a given finite stock of goods, in one of which the goods are distributed equally, and in the other of which a few of the recipients have nearly all the goods, and the rest have what little remains. It is claimed with some plausibility that the second distribution is unfair, and the first fair. But it might also be claimed that impartiality and formal justice alone will not establish that we ought to distribute the goods equally.

There are two reasons which might be given for this second claim, the first of them a bad one, the other more cogent. The bad reason rests on an underestimate of the powers of golden-rule arguments. It is objected, for example, that people with white skins, if they claimed privileges in distribution purely on the ground of skin-colour, would not be offending against the formal principle of impartiality or universalizability, because no individual reference need enter into the principle to which they are appealing. Thus the principle that blacks ought to be subservient to whites is impartial as between *individuals*; any individual whatever who has the bad luck to find himself with a black skin or the good luck to find himself with a white skin is impartially placed by the principle in the appropriate social rank. This move receives a brief answer in my *Freedom and Reason*,[17] and a much fuller one in a forthcoming paper.[18] If the whites are faced with the decision, not merely of whether to frame this principle, but of whether to prescribe its adoption universally in all cases, including hypothetical ones in which their own skins turn black, they will at once reject it.

The other, more cogent-sounding argument is often used as an argument against utilitarians by those who think that justice has a lot to do with equality. It could also, at first sight, be used as an argument against the adequacy of formal justice or impartiality as a basis for distributive justice. That the argument could be leveled against both these methods is no accident; as I have tried to show elsewhere,[19] utilitarianism of a certain sort is the embodiment of—the method of moral reasoning which fulfils in practice—the requirement of universalizability or formal justice. Having shown that neither of these methods can produce a direct justification for equal distribution, I shall then show that both can produce indirect justifications, which depend, not on a priori reasoning alone, but on likely assumptions about what the world and the people in it are like.

The argument is this. Formal impartiality only requires us to treat everybody's interest as of equal weight. Imagine, then, a situation in which utilities are equally distributed. (There is a complication here which we can for the moment avoid by choosing a suitable example. Shortly I shall be mentioning the so-called principle of diminishing marginal utility, and shall indeed be making important use of it. But for now let us take a case in which it does not operate, so that we can, for ease of illustration, treat money as a linear measure of utility.) Suppose that we can vary the equal distribution that we started with by taking a dollar each away from everybody in the town, and that the loss of purchasing power is so small that they hardly notice it, and therefore the utility enjoyed by each is not much diminished. However, when we give the resulting large sum to one man, he is able to buy himself a holiday in Acapulco, which gives him so much pleasure that his access of utility is equal to the sum of the small losses suffered by all the others. Many would say that this redistribution was unfair. But we were, in the required sense, being impartial between the equal interests of all the parties; we were treating an equal access or loss of utility to any party as of equal value or disvalue. For, on our suppositions, the taking away of a dollar from one of the unfortunate parties deprived him of just as much utility as the addition of that dollar gave to the fortunate one. But if we are completely impartial, we have to regard *who has* that dollar or that access of utility as irrelevant. So there will be nothing to choose, from an impartial point of view, between our original equal distribution and our later highly unequal one, in which everybody else is deprived of a cent in order to give one person a holiday in Acapulco. And that is why people say that formal impartiality alone is not enough to secure social justice, nor even to secure impartiality itself in some more substantial sense.

What is needed, in the opinion of these people, is some principle which says that it is unjust to give a person more when he already has more than the others—some sort of egalitarian principle. Egalitarian principles are only one possible kind of principles of distributive justice; and it is so far an open question whether they are to be preferred to alternative inegalitarian principles. It is fairly clear as a matter of history that different principles of justice have been accepted in different societies. As Aristotle says, 'everybody agrees that the just distribution is one in accordance with desert of some kind; but they do not call desert the same thing, but the democrats say it is being a free citizen, the oligarchs being rich, others good lineage, and the aristocrats virtue'.[20] It is not difficult to think of some societies in which it would be thought unjust for one man to have privileges not possessed by all men, and of others in which it would be thought unjust for a slave to have privileges which a free man would take for granted, or for a commoner to have the sort of house which a nobleman could aspire to. Even Aristotle's democrats did not think that slaves, but only citizens, had equal rights; and Plato complains of democracy that it 'bestows equality of a sort on equals and unequals alike'.[21] We have to ask, therefore, whether there are any reasons for preferring one of these attitudes to another.

At this point some philosophers will be ready to step in with their intuitions, and tell us that some distributions or ways of achieving distributions are *obviously* more just than others, or that *everyone will agree on reflection* that they are. These philosophers appeal to our intuitions or prejudices in support of the most widely divergent methods or patterns of distribution. But this is a way of arguing which should be abjured by anybody who wishes to have rational grounds for his moral judgments. Intuitions prove nothing; general consensus proves nothing; both have been used to support conclusions which *our* intuitions and our consensus may well find outrageous. We want arguments, and in this field seldom get them.

However, it is too early to despair of finding some. The utilitarian, and the formalist like me, still have some moves to make. I am supposing that we have already made the major move suggested above, and have ruled out discrimination on grounds of skin colour and the like, in so far as such discrimination could not be accepted by all for cases where they were the ones discriminated against. I am supposing that our society has absorbed this move, and contains no racists, sexists or in general discriminators, but does still contain economic men who do not think it wrong, in pursuit of Nozickian economic liberty, to get what they can, even if the resulting distribution is grotesquely unequal. Has the egalitarian any moves to make against them, and are they moves which can be supported by appeal to formal justice, in conjunction with the empirical facts?

TWO ARGUMENTS FOR EQUAL DISTRIBUTION

He has two. The first is based on that good old prop of egalitarian policies, the diminishing marginal utility, within the ranges that matter, of money and of nearly all goods. Almost always, if money or goods are taken away from someone who has a lot of them already, and given to someone who has little, total utility is increased, other things being equal. As we shall see, they hardly ever are equal; but the principle is all right. Its ground is that the poor man will get more utility out of what he is given than the rich man from whom it is taken would have got. A millionaire minds less about the gain or loss of a dollar than I do, and I than a pauper.

It must be noted that this is not an *a priori* principle. It is an empirical fact (if it is) that people are so disposed. The most important thing I have to say in this paper is that when we are, as we now are, trying to establish *prima facie* principles of distributive justice, it is enough if they can be justified in the world as it actually is, among people as they actually are. It is a wholly illegitimate argument against formalists or utilitarians that states of society or of the people in it could be *conceived of* in which gross inequalities could be justified by formal or utilitarian arguments. We are seeking principles for practical use in the world as it is. The same applies when we ask what qualifications are required to the principles.

Diminishing marginal utility is the firmest support for policies of progressive taxation of the rich and other egalitarian measures. However, as I said above, other things are seldom equal, and there are severe empirical, practical restraints on the equality that can sensibly be imposed by governments. To mention just a few of these hackneyed other things: the removal of incentives to effort may diminish the total stock of goods to be divided up; abrupt confiscation or even very steep progressive taxation may antagonize the victims so much that a whole class turns from a useful element in society to a hostile and dangerous one; or, even if that does not happen, it may merely become demoralized and either lose all enterprise and readiness to take business risks, or else just emigrate if it can. Perhaps one main cause of what is called the English sickness is the alienation of the middle class. It is an empirical question, just when egalitarian measures get to the stage of having these effects; and serious political argument on this subject should concentrate on such empirical questions, instead of indulging in the rhetoric of equal (or for that matter of unequal) rights. Rights are the offspring of *prima facie*, intuitive principles, and I have nothing against them; but the question is, What *prima facie* principles ought we to adopt? What intuitions ought we to have? On these questions the rhetoric of rights sheds no light whatever, any more than do appeals to intuition (i.e. to prejudice, i.e. to the *prima facie* principles, good or bad, which our upbringings happen to have implanted in us). The worth of intuitions is to be known by their fruits; as in the case of the principles to be followed by judges in administering the law, the best principles are those with the highest acceptance-utility, i.e. those whose general acceptance maximizes the furtherance of the interests, in sum, of all the affected parties, treating all those interests as of equal weight, i.e. impartially, i.e. with formal justice.

We have seen that, given the empirical assumption of diminishing marginal utility, such a method provides a justification for moderately egalitarian policies. The justification is strengthened by a second move that the egalitarian can make. This is to point out that inequality itself has a tendency to produce envy, which is a disagreeable state of mind and leads people to do disagreeable things. It makes no difference to the argument whether the envy is a good or a bad quality, nor whether it is justified or unjustified—any more than it makes a difference whether the alienation of the middle class which I mentioned above is to be condemned or excused. These states of mind are facts, and moral judgments have to be made in the light of the facts as they are. We have to take account of the actual state of the world and of the people in it. We can very easily think of societies which are highly unequal, but in which the more fortunate members have contrived to find some real or metaphorical opium or some Platonic noble lie [22] to keep the people quiet, so that the people feel no envy of privileges which we should consider outrageous. Imagine, for example, a society consisting of happy slave-owners and of happy slaves, all of whom know their places and do not have ideas above their station. Since there is *ex hypothesi* no envy, this source of disutility does not exist, and the whole argument from envy collapses.

It is salutary to remember this. It may make us stop looking for purely formal, *a priori* reasons for demanding equality, and look instead at the actual conditions which obtain in particular societies. To make the investigation more concrete, albeit oversimplified, let us ask what would have to be the case before we ought to be ready to push this happy slave-owning society into a revolution—peaceful or violent—which would turn the slaves into free and moderately equal wage-earners. I shall be able only to sketch my answer to this question, without doing nearly enough to justify it.

ARGUMENTS FOR AND AGAINST EGALITARIAN REVOLUTIONS

First of all, as with all moral questions, we should have to ask what would be the actual consequences of what we were doing—which is the same as to ask what we should be *doing*, so that accusations of 'consequentialism' [23] need not be taken very seriously. Suppose, to simplify matters outrageously, that we can actually predict the consequences of the revolution and what will happen during its course. We can then consider two societies (one actual and one possible) and a possible process of transition from one to the other. And we have to ask whether the transition from one to the other will, all in all, promote the interests of all those affected more than to stay as they are, or rather, to develop as they would develop if the revolution did not occur. The question can be divided into questions about the process of transition and questions about the relative merits of the actual society (including its probable subsequent 'natural' development) and the possible society which would be produced by the revolution.

We have supposed that the slaves in the existing society feel no envy, and that therefore the disutility of envy cannot be used as an argument for change. If there *were* envy, as in actual cases is probable, this argument *could* be employed; but let us see what can be done without it. We have the fact that there is gross inequality in the actual society and much greater equality in the possible one. The principle of diminishing marginal utility will therefore support the change, provided that its effects are not outweighed by a reduction in total utility resulting from the change and the way it comes about. But we have to be sure that this condition is fulfilled. Suppose, for example, that the actual society is a happy bucolic one and is likely to remain so, but that the transition to the possible society initiates the growth of an industrial economy in which everybody has to engage in a rat-race and is far less happy. We might in that case pronounce the actual society better. In general it is not self-evident that the access of what is called wealth makes people happier, although they nearly always think that it will.

Let us suppose, however, that we are satisfied that the people in the possible society will be better off all round than in the actual. There is also the point that there will be more generations to enjoy the new regime than suffer in the transition from the old. At least, this is what revolutionaries often say; and we have set them at liberty to say it by assuming, contrary to what is likely to be the case, that the future state of society is predictable. In actual fact, revolutions usually produce states of society very different from, and in most cases worse than, what their authors expected—which does not always stop them being better than what went before, once things have settled down. However, let us waive these difficulties and suppose that the future state of society can be predicted, and that it is markedly better than the existing state, because a greater equality of distribution has, owing to diminishing marginal utility, resulted in greater total utility.

Let us also suppose that the more enterprising economic structure which results leads to increased production without causing a rat-race. There will then be more wealth to go round and the revolution will have additional justification. Other benefits of the same general kind may also be adduced; and what is perhaps the greatest benefit of all, namely liberty itself. That people like having this is an empirical fact; it may not be a fact universally, but it is at least *likely* that by freeing slaves we shall *pro tanto* promote their interests. Philosophers who ask for *a priori* arguments for liberty or equality often talk as if empirical facts like this were totally irrelevant to the question. Genuine egalitarians and liberals ought to abjure the aid of these philosophers, because they have taken away the main ground for such views, namely the fact that people are as they are.

The arguments so far adduced support the call for a revolution. They will have to be balanced against the disutilities which will probably be caused by the process of transition. If heads roll, that is contrary to the interests of their owners; and no doubt the economy will be disrupted at least temporarily, and the new rulers, whoever they are, may infringe liberty just as much as the old, and possibly in an even more arbitrary manner. Few revolutions are pleasant while they are going on. But if the revolution can be more or less smooth or even peaceful, it may well be that (given the arguments already adduced about the desirability of the future society thereby achieved) revolution can have a utilitarian justification, and therefore a justification on grounds of formal impartiality between people's interests. But it is likely to be better for all if the same changes can be achieved less abruptly by an evolutionary process, and those who try to persuade us that this is not so are often merely giving way to impatience and showing a curious indifference to the interests of those for whom they purport to be concerned.

The argument in favour of change from a slave-owning society to a wage-earning one has been extremely superficial, and has served only to illustrate the lines on which a utilitarian or a formalist might argue. If we considered instead the transition from a capitalist society to a socialist one, the same forms of argument would have to be employed, but might not yield the same result. Even if the introduction of a fully socialist economy would promote greater equality, or more equal liberties (and I can see no reason for supposing this, but rather the reverse; for socialism tends to produce very great inequalities of *power*), it needs to be argued what the consequences would be, and then an assessment has to be made of the relative benefits and harms accruing from leaving matters alone and from having various sorts of bloody or bloodless change. Here again the rhetoric of rights will provide nothing but inflamatory material for agitators on both sides. It is designed to lead to, not to resolve, conflicts.

REMARKS ABOUT METHODS

But we must now leave this argument and attend to a methodological point which has become pressing. We have not, in the last few pages, been arguing about what state of society would be just, but about what state of society would best promote the interests of its members. All the arguments have been utilitarian. Where then does justice come in? It is likely to come into the propaganda of revolutionaries, as I have already hinted. But so far as I can see it has no direct bearing on the question of what would be the better society. It has, however, an important indirect bearing which I shall now try to explain. Our *prima facie* moral principles and intuitions are, as I have already said, the products of our upbringings; and it is a very important question *what* principles and intuitions it is best to bring up people to have. I have been arguing on the assumption that this question is to be decided by looking at the consequences for society, and the effects on the interests of people in society, of inculcating different principles. We are looking for the set of principles with the highest acceptance-utility.

Will these include principles of justice? The answer is obviously 'Yes', if we think that society and the people in it are better off with *some* principles of justice than without any. A 'land without justice' (to use the title of Milovan Djilas' book) [24] is almost bound to be an unhappy one. But what are the principles to be? Are we, for example, to inculcate the principle that it is just for people to perform the duties of their station and not envy those of higher social rank? Or the principle that all inequalities of any sort are unjust and ought to be removed? For my part, I would think that neither of these principles has a very high acceptance-utility. It may be that the principle with the highest acceptance-utility is one which makes just reward vary (but not immoderately) with desert, and assesses desert according to service to the interests of one's fellow-men. It would have to be supplemented by a principle securing equality of opportunity. But it is a partly empirical question what principles would have the highest acceptance-utility, and in any case beyond the scope of this paper. If some such principle is adopted and inculcated, people will *call* breaches of it unjust. Will they *be* unjust? Only in the sense that they will be contrary to a *prima facie* principle of distributive justice which we ought to adopt (not because it is itself a just principle, but because it is the best principle). The only sense that can be given to the question of whether it is a just principle (apart from the purely circular or tautological question of whether the principle obeys itself), is by asking whether the procedure by which we have selected the principle satisfies the logical requirements of critical moral thinking, i.e. is *formally* just. We might add that the adoption of such a formally just procedure and of the principles it selects is just in the *generic* sense mentioned at the beginning of this paper: it is the right thing to do; we morally ought to do it. The reason is that critical thinking, because it follows the requirements of formal justice based on the logical properties of the moral concepts, especially 'ought' and 'right', can therefore not fail, if pursued correctly in the light of the empirical facts, to lead to principles of justice which are in accord with morality. But because the requirements are all formal, they do not by themselves determine the content of the principles of justice. We have to do the thinking.

What principles of justice are best to try to inculcate will depend on the circumstances of particular societies, and especially on psychological facts about their members. One of these facts is their readiness to accept the principles themselves. There might be a principle of justice which it would be highly desirable to inculcate, but which we have no chance of successfully inculcating. The best principles for a society to *have* are, as I said, those with the highest acceptance-utility. But the best principles to *try to inculcate* will not necessarily be these, if these are impossible to inculcate. Imagine that in our happy slave-society both slaves and slave-owners are obstinately conservative and know their places, and that the attempt to get the slaves to have revolutionary or egalitarian thoughts will result only in a very few of them becoming discontented, and probably going to the gallows as a result, and the vast majority merely becoming unsettled and therefore more unhappy. Then we ought not to try to inculcate such an egalitarian principle. On the other hand, if, as is much more likely, the principle stood a good chance of catching on, and the revolution was likely to be as advantageous as we have supposed, then we ought. The difference lies in the dispositions of the inhabitants. I am not saying that the probability of being accepted is the same thing as acceptance-utility; only that the rationality of trying to inculcate a principle (like the rationality of trying to do anything else) varies with the likelihood of success. In this sense the advisability of trying to inculcate principles of justice (though not their merit) is relative to the states of mind of those who, it is hoped, will hold them.

It is important to be clear about the extent to which what I am advocating is a kind of relativism. It is certainly not relativistic in any strong sense. Relativism is the doctrine that the truth of some moral statement depends on whether people accept it. A typical example would be the thesis that if in a certain society people think that they ought to get their male children circumcised, then they ought to get them circumcised, full stop. Needless to say, I am not supporting any such doctrine, which is usually the result of confusion, and against which there are well-known arguments. It is, however, nearly always the case that among the facts relevant to a moral decision are facts about people's thoughts or dispositions. For example, if I am wondering whether I ought to take my wife for a holiday in Acapulco, it is relevant to ask whether she would like it. What I have been saying is to be assimilated to this last example. If we take as given certain dispositions in the members of society (namely dispositions not to accept a certain principle of justice however hard we work at propagating it) then we have to decide whether, in the light of these facts, we ought to propagate it. What principles of justice we ought to propagate will vary with the probable effects of propagating them. The answer to this 'ought'-question is not relative to what we, who are asking it, think about the matter; it is to be arrived at by moral thought on the basis of the facts of the situation. But among these facts are facts about the dispositions of people in the society in question.

The moral I wish to draw from the whole argument is that ethical reasoning *can* provide us with a way of conducting political arguments about justice and rights rationally and with hope of agreement; that such rational arguments have to rest on an understanding of the concepts being used, *and* of the facts of our actual situation. The key question is 'What principles of justice, what attitudes towards the distribution of goods, what ascriptions of rights, are such that their acceptance is in the general interest?' I advocate the asking of this question as a substitute for one which is much more commonly asked, namely 'What rights do I have?' For people who ask this latter question will, being human, nearly always answer that they have just those rights, whatever they are, which will promote a distribution of goods which is in the interest of their own social group. The rhetoric of rights, which is engendered by this question, is a recipe for class war, and civil war. In pursuit of these rights, people will, because they have convinced themselves that justice demands it, inflict almost any harms on the rest of society and on themselves. To live at peace, we need principles such as critical thinking can provide, based on formal justice and on the facts of the actual world in which we have to live. It is possible for all to practise this critical thinking in cooperation, if only they would learn how; for all share the same moral concepts with the same logic, if they could but understand them and follow it.

NOTES

1. See my 'Ethical Theory and Utilitarianism' (*ETU*) in *Contemporary British Philosophy 4*, ed. H. D. Lewis (London, 1976).

2. See, e.g., my 'Principles', *Ar. Soc.* 72 (1972/3), 'Rules of War and Moral Reasoning', *Ph. and Pub. Aff.* 1 (1972) and *ETU*.

3. Rawls, J., *A Theory of Justice* (Cambridge, Mass., 1971), p. 130.

4. Richards, D. A. J., *A Theory of Reasons for Action* (Oxford, 1971).

5. See my *Freedom and Reason*, pt. II (Oxford, 1963) and *ETU*.

6. *Nicomachean Ethics*, bk. V.

7. ib. 1130 b 31, 1131 b 25.

8. ib. 1130 a 8.

9. Theognis 147; also attr. to Phocylides by Aristotle, ib. 1129 b 27.

10. The earliest version of this tag is attr. by the *Oxford Dictionary of Quotations* to the Emperor Ferdinand I (1503–64).

11. ib. 1137 b 8.

12. ib. 1130 a 14 ff.

13. *A Theory of Justice*, p. 136.

14. Pp. 115-7, 124.

15. *Ph. Q.* 23 (1973), repr. in *Reading Rawls*, ed. N. Daniels (Oxford, 1975).

16. Nozick, R. D., *Anarchy, State and Utopia* (New York, 1974).

17. Pp. 106f.

18. 'Relevance', in a volume in honour of R. Brandt, W. Frankena and C. Stevenson, eds. A. Goldman and J. Kim (Reidel, forthcoming).

19. See note 2 above.

20. ib. 1131 a 25.

21. *Republic* 558 c.

22. ib. 414 b.

23. See, e.g., Anscombe, G. E. M., 'Modern Moral Philosophy', *Philosophy* 33 (1958) and Williams, B. A. O., in Smart, J. J. C. and Williams, B. A. O., *Utilitarianism: For and Against* (Cambridge, Eng., 1973), p. 82.

24. Djilas, M., *Land without Justice* (London, 1958).

part
2

criticisms and alternatives

merit and contribution

Some philosophers would argue that the three approaches presented in Part I are seriously flawed, since none of them recommends that economic goods be distributed according to how much is deserved. For all three theories desert is at best a derivative—not a primary—element. Rawls, for example, argues that once we know that the economic structure (tax policy, welfare programs, employment opportunity) is just, then people can be said to deserve whatever they get *within that structure*. Thus desert is a secondary notion, determined by the justice of the social institutions. Nozick, on the other hand, intentionally employs the notion of "entitlement" rather than "desert". On his free market view individuals may come to have just titles to material goods, but he does not wish to say that they merit what they so receive. Similarly, desert does not play a central role for utilitarians, whose sole concern is to maximize society's happiness. Still it may seem that it is a weakness in each theory that desert is omitted. What, after all, could possibly be more just than to give people exactly what they deserve?

But how can desert be measured? What precisely does it mean? Three conceptions of desert come to mind immediately.

135

First, one might hold that a person's *ability* should determine how much he or she is allowed to have. Second, the amount of *effort* or work that is put forth might be thought the best principle of distribution. Third, the amount one deserves could be determined by the *contribution* a person has made. The idea here is that a person should be rewarded according to how much of the total economic product he or she managed to produce.

However plausible each of these criteria might seem under some circumstances, each is open to serious objections. Abilities to do certain types of work or to perform a job well are often endowments with which one is born or are due to the environment in which one is raised. But if this is so, how can ability be a fair ground for distributing economic goods? In any event, ability alone would not suffice because a talented but lazy worker would not be thought very deserving.

The criterion of effort would remedy this last defect, but anyone using this measure of desert is immediately confronted with the difficult problem of comparison and measurement. The number of hours spent is clearly inadequate, since different jobs require different amounts of effort in a given period of time. Even if we could compare effort where physical labor is involved, how would an hour of construction work be compared with teaching medicine or with singing? One might also question the fairness of using effort as a guide to desert. It is frequently true that people with greater abilities tend to be more motivated and so work harder. Thus, effort itself turns out to be, to some extent, a function of natural abilities, which are not themselves deserved.

Similar problems arise for contribution. Here again measurement poses a difficulty. It might seem that allowing the market to determine economic benefits would be to distribute according to the criterion of contribution because market price indicates the worth to others of what is being offered for sale, and worth to others is fairly close to a measure of contribution. Still, a person might make a contribution of great significance, but one whose market worth is unrecognized at the time. More generally, certain contributions which are of the greatest benefit to society as a whole may not be the kinds of things which the market itself can reward. Imagine a person who does great service to his or her community during an emergency or whose life is devoted to serving the poor. Yet measuring one's contribution to society in this broader sense would be difficult. A second problem is suggested by the fact that what one is able to contribute and whether or not one is able to make a really important contribution would seem to depend upon all sorts of fortuitous circumstances, which are morally irrelevant. At the very least, equality of opportunity would have to be required if contribution were to be a fair distributive criterion, but even this might not suffice. Those with a favorable family upbringing and a natural industriousness would be better suited to contribute, and lady luck would place only certain individuals in the right place at the right time to make a key contribution.

Acknowledging the limitations of the market and the arbitrariness of circumstance, one might argue that distribution should be based simply on a person's overall *moral* worth. Once effort and contribution are rejected as indicators of what a person deserves, however, it is unclear how moral worth is to be ascertained. Perhaps the criterion of moral worth would be appropriate for a small religious community where there is consensus on the relevant moral standard, but its general applicability is doubtful. Further, one might well wonder why the intrinsic moral worth of a person should be rewarded economically. Virtue, some have thought, is its own reward.

Despite these difficulties, desert still seems relevant to justice. Must not justice at least take some account of what people merit? Must it not at least inquire into what individuals have done in the past? The contributors in this section believe it should. So our original problem remains, and desert, in one or other of the senses mentioned above, is discussed in each of the following essays.

In a wide-ranging review of the major, rival theories of justice, Michael Lessnoff argues, in part, that economic inequalities are justified where they are deserved because of harder work. Likewise, James Rachels analyzes carefully the relation between justice and desert, and argues for desert (as measured by work completed) as a basis for distribution. Focusing on the specific moral problem of reverse discrimination, he contends that because of the importance of work for determining desert, it is often true that less qualified members of minorities may deserve a job or admission to a school over a better qualified white male.

Finally, Norman Daniels discusses what he calls "meritocracies," that is, societies in which one's abilities give one a ground for claiming to deserve a certain job. He points out that such claims derive ultimately from efficiency, and that many theories of justice are meritocratic in his sense. His argument leads to considerations of the basis of claims by some that reverse discrimination is unjust, and to a discussion of the distinction between how much jobs should provide in economic rewards, on one hand, and whether one is entitled to a certain job on the other. Against Nozick, he contends that our natural characteristics and assets should not be used as a basis for distributing major economic rewards, even if those characteristics are used as a basis for distributing jobs.

M. H. LESSNOFF

University of Glasgow

Capitalism, Socialism and Justice

In this paper I shall try to illuminate the contrasting theories of Rawls and Nozick by placing them in the context of the wider contrast between capitalism and socialism.* The latter are the names of economic systems, not of theories of distributive justice. Nonetheless, their supporters characteristically defend them, and their opponents attack them, on the basis of views as to what constitutes a just distribution. We may thus talk of capitalist and socialist conceptions of justice. Marx's views on distribution may be taken to exemplify the socialist conception, while to find a version of the capitalist conception we need look no further than Nozick himself. Nozick in fact defends a notably libertarian version of capitalism. Rawls' theory, on the other hand, does not fall neatly into either camp. I shall therefore be concerned with three conceptions of justice: socialist (exemplified by Marx), capitalist (exemplified by Nozick's libertarian version) and Rawlsian. None of these, I believe, is completely satisfactory in itself, and I shall end by trying to adumbrate a theory of justice, based on hints furnished by the three conceptions, that combines due regard for individual freedom with the avoidance of unjust exploitation. This, it seems to me, is the challenge any such theory must confront, though I have no great confidence that I have done so successfully.

* I should like to thank the Editors for helpful suggestions regarding this paper.

THREE CONCEPTIONS OF JUSTICE:
CAPITALIST, SOCIALIST AND RAWLSIAN

I turn first to a comparison of my three conceptions of justice. For this purpose it is useful, if perhaps a little dangerous, to express each conception as a brief slogan. Nozick himself has summed up his libertarian version of the capitalist conception roughly as follows: "From each according to what he chooses to do, to each according to what he makes for himself (perhaps with the contracted aid of others) and what others choose to do for him or give him of what (under this maxim) they rightfully own." Since this slogan is scarcely brief, Nozick condensed it to:

"From each as they choose, to each as they are chosen." [1]

This libertarian capitalist conception can now be contrasted with the socialist, as expressed in Marx's famous formulation.[2] While recognizing the need for a transitional stage in which consumption goods would be distributed in proportion to labour contribution, Marx held that the "higher phase of communist society" would be governed by this principle (first enunciated, it seems, by Louis Blanc): [3]

"From each according to his ability, to each according to his needs."

Unfortunately, this slogan has some drawbacks as a conception of justice. I shall not worry unduly as to the imprecision of the terms "needs" (does it refer to what is needed for mere survival, or for some minimum level of comfort, or for "self-realisation"? Who decides what is needed by each individual? etc.). I shall assume these problems to be soluble. What is more troublesome is the apparent incompleteness of the principle, "To each according to his needs." For it appears perfectly possible (though this depends to some éxtent on how "needs" are interpreted) that the goods required to satisfy needs may exceed or fall short of the quantity of goods that are or could be produced. Marx certainly did not envisage the "higher phase of communism" as being a state of severe economic scarcity, quite the contrary—which lands us with the opposite problem, what to do about the distribution of any surplus over and above needs. Marx's slogan, taken alone, seems perfectly compatible with distribution of such a surplus in accordance with market forces—so that it could plausibly be claimed that the Marxist demand is satisfied by welfare capitalism. But it is not credible that Marx himself would have accepted this. To ensure that our second slogan expresses a Marxian socialist conception of justice, we must understand it to imply, either that the whole social product is somehow to be distributed according to need, or else (perhaps) that after needs have been satisfied the surplus is to be distributed among individuals equally.

Thirdly, the Rawlsian conception. Two parts of Rawls' famous principles of justice are relevant here, the priority of basic liberty, and the condition that inequalities of income and wealth must be arranged so as to maximize the smallest share (the Difference Principle).[4] Putting these two together, we can express the Rawlsian conception of economic justice as:

> "From each as they choose, to each in accordance with the Difference Principle."

A brief comparison of these three conceptions will bring us to the heart of the quarrel between Rawls and Nozick on economic justice. In a way that is perhaps intuitively obvious, Rawls' position falls somewhere between the capitalist and socialist conceptions. Nevertheless, it may be worth spelling the point out. The crucial variable, seized on, rightly, by Nozick[5] in his polemic against Rawls, is the attitude to the useful abilities with which individuals are endowed. For Nozick, the individuals who have these abilities are entitled to them, to what they can make with them or obtain by selling them in a free market. But they have no (pre-contractual) obligation to make any use of them whatever; such use as they do make of them, and the terms on which they do so, must depend on their own free decision. Individuals are the owners of their abilities.

The polar opposite to this view is not, as Nozick implies, Rawls' view, but rather the socialist conception of justice. At this point, though, it is necessary to ward off a possible objection: that what I have called the socialist conception of justice is not a conception of justice at all. According to Robert Tucker,[6] the socialist formula used by Blanc and Marx is "not a formula for distributive justice but expresses . . . an ethic of brotherhood." Marx, Tucker argues, was not much concerned with the concept of just distribution and even considered it to be "ideological nonsense." His hostility, for Tucker, arose from a fundamental contradiction between the idea of justice, which connotes a rightful balance between the conflicting claims of different parties (such as bourgeois and proletarian), and Marx's vision of communism as a society in which conflict has been abolished and "social justice" therefore become an irrelevance.

Much of Tucker's thesis may be accepted without damage to the present argument. What, from that point of view, matters, is not whether Marx or Blanc would have considered the socialist slogan to be a conception of justice, but whether it *is* such. That Marx thought of communism as a conflictless society does not alter the fact that the slogan he endorsed lays down a distribution of economic rights and obligations which he held to be more desirable than any other. It is, in this sense (the only sense required by the present argument), a conception of distributive justice. And it is a conception diametrically opposed to the capitalist conception, in which an individual's abilities are held to be his own, to use or not as he chooses. In the socialist conception, the individual is held to be under an obligation to contribute to society "according to his ability." Nor does he receive from society in accordance with his contribution. An individual, in other words, does not own his abilities, nor is he entitled to the fruits of them. They belong to society collectively.

What is the bearing of such a conception on individual freedom? According to Marx, in the "higher phase of communist society," with the disappearance of "the enslaving subordination of the individual to the division of labour," labour will become "not only a means of life but life's prime want." [7] Labour, in other words, will be voluntarily forthcoming from everyone in accordance with his abilities, without need for either market incentives or state coercion. One need not take this utopia seriously. Anyone practically concerned with the real world must recognise that to propose the socialist principle of distributive justice is to propose that it be *enforced*, if necessary. Men are not likely freely to place their abilities wholly at society's disposal.

Compared with the capitalist and socialist conceptions, Rawls' conception of economic justice occupies a slightly curious half-way house. Men's abilities are treated as their own to the extent that each individual is entitled to choose for himself what (and indeed whether) to contribute to production. On the other hand, the individual does not fully own his abilities in the sense that he is not fully entitled to their economic fruits. If he were, not only would he be entitled to anything he could make, he would also be entitled to whatever he could get by selling his services on a free market to others with similar entitlements. But he is not—his "holdings" are subject to upper and lower limits set by the Difference Principle. The less well-endowed, in other words, are entitled to some of the economic fruits of the abilities of the better-endowed.

Rawls' intermediate position between the capitalist and socialist conceptions has some questionable consequences. "Less well-endowed", he makes clear,[8] includes those less endowed (and even, presumably, those not endowed at all) with willingness to work. Thus, in the Rawlsian just society, receipt of economic benefit is not dependent on making any contribution to the social product, even if one is able to. For practical purposes, there is no distinction between being unable to work and being simply unwilling. There is good reason to think that, in a Rawlsian society, there would be a large group of non-workers by choice, for the application of the Difference Principle would assure that the incomes of all non-workers would be maintained, by state transfers, not just at subsistence level, but at the "maximum minimum" entailed by that Principle. Non-workers, in other words, would (neglecting complications due to inheritance etc.) constitute the poorest group in a Rawlsian society, and thus the group whose income would have to be made as high as possible. Rawls might reply that the group of deliberate idlers would be small because of the "Aristotelian Principle", that is, because "human beings enjoy the exercise of their . . . abilities and this enjoyment increases the more the ability is realized." [9] Maybe so, but can one assume that the abilities people will enjoy exercising will be socially useful— i.e. that they will enjoy *work*? Perhaps Rawls does believe this, for he writes that "experiencing the realization of self which comes from a . . .

devoted exercise of social duties" is "one of the main forms of human good." [10] This, he holds, is why all social and economic positions must be open to all. But to suppose that most jobs can be so satisfying in themselves as to make well-paid idleness a bad bargain, is reminiscent of the Marxist utopia discussed above.

This consequence of Rawls' theory may seem unpalatable, but is there any way to show that it is a mistaken conception of justice? One argument that certainly fails to show this is put forward by Nozick in Chapter 7 of *Anarchy, State and Utopia*.[11] The Difference Principle, Nozick argues, cannot be defended (as Rawls thinks) as a fair compromise between those well-endowed with useful skills (and character-traits) and those poorly-endowed with them; for the Difference Principle represents the *best possible* terms the latter could conceivably have for economic cooperation between the two groups. Any attempt to give them better terms still would be self-defeating, and would mean their getting less rather than more. But this is clearly false. One can conceive of a society in which the poorly-endowed receive the entire social product, except for what is necessary to provide subsistence wages for the well-endowed— wages which they receive only on condition that they work to the best of their abilities. No doubt such a system would have to be enforced by means of slavery, but that is beside the point, which is, that such a distribution is conceivable and that under it, while total social product would very likely be less than under the Difference Principle, the income of the poorly-endowed would probably be greater.

So this particular attack of Nozick's fails. However, I believe that the Difference Principle can be refuted on the basis of Rawls' own premises, or rather by pointing to a discrepancy between two versions of these premises. For, by Rawls' account,[12] the concept of justice is a matter of "the proper distribution of the benefits *and burdens* of social cooperation" (emphasis added). But in the Rawlsian original position, the burdens have completely disappeared. The Rawlsian contractors are asked to agree on the distribution of benefits only, in Rawls' terminology, of (primary) social *goods*.[13] But Rawlsian contractors, as rational men possessed of general social knowledge, would be aware that economic goods (income and wealth) have to be produced, that their production entails costs (primarily work), and that this burden must somehow or other be shared out among members of society. They would surely insist that this be taken properly into account in the principle governing economic distribution.

How could this be done? One superficially attractive idea would be to "maximinimize," not income and wealth simply, but a more complex index of "economic welfare," which would include some measure of the onerousness or unpleasantness of work—in which, that is, the "cost" incurred by an individual in his work would count negatively and be set against the "benefits" of income and wealth he enjoyed. The idle would then presumably get a much less good deal in terms of income and wealth alone, and there would accordingly be much less incentive to be idle.

But how to measure the onerousness of different people's work? Hours worked is clearly an inadequate measure (unless, once again indulging in Marxian fantasy, the division of labour were abolished), and I can think of none that would be adequate.[14] If the onerousness of work could somehow be measured, it might occur to Rawlsian contractors, reasoning in their familiar way, to share the burden out equally, or rather on a "minimax" basis. But this would fall foul of Rawls' priority of liberty, since it would involve compulsory labour. It looks as if the only solution is to let each person work out his own trade-off between the burdens of work and the benefits it brings, making benefits depend on work, except for a social security system to look after those *unable* to work.[15] But to say this is to abandon the Difference Principle.

END-STATE, HISTORICAL AND PATTERNED PRINCIPLES

The conclusion reached above casts doubt on another argument of Nozick against Rawls, which has to do with Nozick's celebrated distinction between "end-state" principles of justice, and "historical" principles (of which Nozick's "entitlement" principles are a species).[16] An end-state principle is one that concerns itself only with the *structure* of the distribution of goods among individuals; it is indifferent as to which individual occupies which place in the distribution and (unlike an historical principle) to the *process* by which he acquires his place. By this very token, Nozick finds end-state principles objectionable. Nozick also argues that, not only is Rawls' Difference Principle an end-state principle, but the Rawlsian "veil of ignorance" ensures that the principles of justice selected by his contractors must be of the end-state rather than the historical type. Rawls' Difference Principle is certainly an end-state principle, but I have argued that his contractors, veiled in ignorance as they are, would in fact find themselves driven to principles of a historical, if not an historical-entitlement kind. Thus, no good objection to Rawls' contractarian method stems from the distinction between end-state and historical principles.

Nozick objects not only to end-state principles of justice (because of their indifference to the means by which an individual acquires his "holdings") but also to what he calls "patterned" principles, that is, principles which specify that an individual's place in the distribution of goods vary according to some attribute or attributes of his, such as his merits, needs, or deserts.[17] Nozick's main objection to patterned principles is that they are incompatible with individual freedom—essentially the same point as has been made earlier by Friedrich Hayek in his polemic against "social justice," and which he has recently elaborated again.[18] Personally I must agree with Hayek and with Nozick that this constitutes a valid objection to patterned principles of distribution, and it provides another reason to reject the socialist conception of justice. That conception, we now see, is doubly incompatible with freedom: firstly, in that the (semi-) principle, "From each according to his ability" would have to be enforced; secondly, because "To each according to his needs" is a patterned principle of distribution.

But Nozick is wrong, it seems to me, to use the objectionableness of patterned principles as a further stick with which to beat Rawls' Difference Principle. The Difference Principle is, as we have seen, an end-state principle; according to Nozick it is also a patterned principle.[19] Furthermore, Nozick believes that not only patterned principles but also end-state principles are incompatible with freedom.[20] But he is twice mistaken: the Difference Principle is not a patterned principle, and though an end-state principle it is not incompatible with freedom. As an end-state principle it lays down a structure of distribution, but not who is to come where in the structure (not, in Nozick's terms, a pattern of distribution). Thus, while it does place some restriction on freedom, it also leaves a good deal: people are free to find their own place in the given structure. The Difference Principle is thus compatible with the Rawlsian priority of basic liberty—it is the exercise of this liberty that (partly) decides an individual's place in the distribution of income and wealth.

Indeed, there is good reason to think that Nozick is thoroughly confused as to the relation between end-state and patterned principles. Although he assigns the Difference Principle to both categories, it would appear that in fact the two categories are mutually exclusive: by definition, an end-state principle is concerned only with the structure of the distribution of a good, not with who is where in the structure; whereas a patterned principle, which lays down that a person's position in the distribution match some attribute of his, must be concerned with who is where (for example, that the more "deserving" are better off). There is perhaps one exception to this, which may have misled Nozick, namely perfect equality, which may be said to be both a structure of distribution and a pattern of distribution in Nozick's sense. But so far as I can see this is the only exception.

If end-state principles of distribution are not in general incompatible with freedom one apparently powerful objection to them dissolves. It is perhaps worth stressing how extreme a libertarian Nozick is in his total rejection of all end-state principles—much more extreme than Hayek, for example. Hayek is quite willing to countenance a state-maintained system of social security [21]—what Rawls would call a social minimum (though a considerably less generous one than Rawls envisages). Such a minimum is of course an end-state, and it is therefore only to be expected that Nozick rejects it. He does so, not out of regard for freedom as such (which, as Hayek has seen, is in any case quite compatible with a social minimum), but out of a belief in property rights so absolute that they take precedence over human life itself, and rule out practically any state interference with the free operation of the market (except perhaps to prevent monopolization of intrinsically limited resources).[22] It seems clear that anyone who values human life above private property rights must reject Nozick's libertarian capitalist conception of justice, just as anyone who values freedom must reject Marx's socialist conception.

CAPITALISM, SOCIALISM AND JUSTICE

But rejection of what I have called the socialist conception of justice does not in itself entail rejection of socialism as such; nor does rejection of Nozick's libertarian capitalist conception entail rejection of capitalism itself. Socialism, defined as public ownership of the means of production, does not entail the Marxian (or any) principle of distribution. Indeed, there is a sense in which socialism so defined entails abandoning any prescription about distributive justice at all. For public ownership, if taken seriously, means that the people collectively own the productive resources available to the society in question, which in turn means that they (or perhaps their freely elected representatives) are authorized to decide what these resources should be used to produce, *and* how the product should be distributed among individuals. If they really have this power, they must be free to decide to leave these questions to market forces, or to apply any other principle that they prefer—they cannot be constrained by any mandatory "principle of justice" laid down in advance. Thus, rejection of the so-called "socialist" conception of justice does not entail rejection of socialism.

Nor does our rejection of Nozick's extreme position entail rejection of capitalism (that is, private ownership of the means of production), which is quite compatible with a social minimum. Rawls, for his part, while he supports the free *market*, professes neutrality as between capitalism and socialism [23] (private and public *ownership*), whereas Hayek is one of capitalism's most robust defenders.[24] Is there any objection to Hayek's free market capitalism plus social minimum? The standard socialist objection to any profit-oriented capitalist system is that by definition it involves *exploitation*. That is, the social product is the product of labour, and any diversion of income from labour in the form of profits, interest payments, dividends, rents, etc. represents an exploitation of the workers by the recipients of these forms of income, and is thus unjust. The phenomenon is found at its most extreme in the person of the rentier, the completely passive recipient of unearned income, but no doubt socialists would also consider the active entrepreneur, and the salaried manager, to be exploiters, on the grounds that they owe at least part of their income to control of the means of production, which enables them to benefit at the workers' expense.

It should be noticed that this objection to exploitation is not just an objection to inequality. Capitalists no doubt are richer than workers, and are perhaps bound to be (on average) in a capitalist economy. But if the system could somehow continue unchanged except that the incomes of workers came to be, by and large, no less than those of recipients of unearned income, the latter would presumably still be considered to be exploiters of the former, in the sense of living off their labour. (By this criterion, incidentally, payment of the Rawlsian maximin to deliberate idlers would also amount to exploitation, and so would providing with income "according to their needs" those who failed to work "according to their ability.") However, there would seem to be several possible ways in which capitalist exploitation could in theory be abolished without introducing socialism, and even without abolishing capitalism. Suppose, for example, the various categories of income remained as they now are under capitalism, but instead of the present division into social classes everyone derived about the same proportion of his income from work and from property (everyone both worked and owned shares, not necessarily in the same firms). In such a situation there would presumably be considerable inequality, but it looks as if no one would be exploited, by the socialist criterion. Or if this model seems far-fetched, there is also the possibility (mentioned by Nozick)[25] of a market system composed of firms each owned and controlled by their workers (note that this is *not* socialism as defined above), which again would presumably lead to inequalities of income, but where the workers could not be exploited by any minority through its control of the means of production.

But perhaps we should not too hastily conclude that these systems *would* be free of exploitation. The trouble is that, as we saw, they would incorporate the inequalities inevitably produced by a market economy. Perhaps these inequalities do amount to exploitation. After all, as Hayek has himself acknowledged, the inequalities that arise under a free market are to a large extent not deserved, but are the result of good and bad fortune; and if these inequalities mean that some people have less than they otherwise would, though they deserve no less, because others no more deserving have more, is this not exploitation? Hayek's reply to this complaint is that free market capitalism, because of its economic efficiency, maximizes "the chances of all to have their wants satisfied." [26] But this, even if true, is not enough. Economic efficiency may maximize want satisfaction on the whole, or on average, but this abstract average is of no interest to a concrete person who is relatively disadvantaged. He is presumably interested in his own position. He should, therefore, be much more impressed by the Rawlsian argument that he should accept the relative advantages of others insofar as, in absolute terms, they benefit him.

It is perhaps possible now to sketch some tentative conclusions. The aim is to discover principles of distribution which rule out unfair exploitation without curtailing individual freedom unduly. The foregoing discussion suggests that in order to avoid unfair exploitation we must prevent undeserved inequalities that do not benefit the relatively disadvantaged. This is a departure from Rawls' Difference Principle, which is ruled out by the need to avoid exploitation—we have seen that the Difference Principle, as Rawls interprets it, represents exploitation of workers by the idle. What I am suggesting is that economic inequality may be considered just in *either* of two cases: (1) it is to the advantage of the less well-off; *or* (2) it is deserved (where advantage is due to harder work, for example).

But does this conception of justice leave enough room for freedom? Or does it fall into the trap of laying down a patterned distribution of goods? In a now classic passage of *Anarchy, State and Utopia*,[27] Nozick introduced the tale of Wilt Chamberlain, the basketball player raised to enormous riches by the free choice of millions of fans to pay extra to watch him play. Such inequality, he argued, is inseparable from freedom. Is it ruled out by my conception of justice? Not necessarily. In fact, this example requires careful analysis. It may be that, if Chamberlain's fans were not willing to make him richer than themselves, they would not be able to see him play; but, for the sake of seeing him play, they are so willing. In that case, the transaction that makes Chamberlain wealthy *is* to the advantage of his fans, who are less wealthy than he. Any attempt to prevent him from becoming more wealthy would harm them, and in fact reduce their *real* income. Such transactions, therefore, are not ruled out by my suggested principles of justice, nor indeed by Rawls' Difference Principle which, as I have already argued, is not a patterned principle. Nor does my own suggestion indicate a patterned distribution, for although it makes desert a sufficient condition for inequality, it does not make it a necessary one.

But the Wilt Chamberlain example requires further analysis, for the situation may be quite different from that described above. It may be that the basketball player's fans *could* see him play without making him richer than they are, and also without coercing him in any way. It may be, that is, that the player would still be willing to play, even if paid an income no greater than anyone else; but that the market situation is such that he is able to demand, and get, a greater income. In that case, the transaction by which his fans make him richer than they is *not* to their advantage—for they could still see him play, while paying less for the pleasure. Confiscation of the player's "excess income" would not harm his fans in this case. Furthermore, confiscation and redistribution would be just, for the situation described is one in which the player would otherwise be exploiting a favourable market position to achieve an undeserved advantage over others.

In practice, unfortunately, there are great difficulties in distinguishing these two possible situations, and most real cases are probably mixed rather than pure. Regrettably, I am not able here to go beyond the sketching of principles to their practical application. Nonetheless, it does appear that justice requires that greater advantages be either deserved, or to the benefit of the less advantaged. In a free economy, this implies state intervention to provide a social minimum both for those who work and for those unable to work, which should be as high as possible, consistently with the desert principle. Ideally, in view of that principle, transfers to those who would otherwise fall below the minimum should be financed only out of the *undeserved* extra earnings of those favoured by the luck of the market. If this is impracticable, distributive justice is impracticable.

NOTES

1. Nozick, *Anarchy, State and Utopia* (Oxford, 1974), p. 160. I have slightly simplified Nozick's longer formulation.
2. Cf. Marx and Engels, *Selected Works* (London, 1968), pp. 323-5.
3. Cf. R. Tucker, *The Marxian Revolutionary Idea* (London, 1970), pp. 37-8.
4. Rawls, *A Theory of Justice* (Harvard, 1971), pp. 60, 76 ff.
5. *Op. cit.*, pp. 213-31.
6. *Op. cit.*, p. 38.
7. Marx and Engels, *op. cit.*, p. 324.
8. *Op. cit.*, pp. 310-12.
9. *Op. cit.*, p. 426.
10. *Op. cit.*, p. 84.
11. *Op. cit.*, pp. 189-97.
12. *Op. cit.*, p. 5.
13. *Op. cit.*, pp. 62, 92-5, 150.
14. The inadequacy of hours worked as a measure seems to rule out a solution tentatively endorsed by Rawls (in his "Reply to Alexander and Musgrave," *Quarterly Journal of Economies*, 88, 1974), viz. to apply the Difference Principle to goods and leisure taken together—since leisure is simply the obverse of hours worked.
15. Being "unable to work" may result not only from physical or mental disability, but also from unavailability of work due to economic circumstances. Thus the social security envisaged includes unemployment insurance as well as disability pensions etc.
16. See Nozick, *op. cit.*, pp. 150-5, 198-204.
17. *Op. cit.*, pp. 155-64.
18. F. Hayek, *Law, Legislation and Liberty, Vol. 2: The Mirage of Social Justice* (London, 1976), ch. 9; and *The Constitution of Liberty* (London, 1960), ch. 6.
19. *Op. cit.*, p. 209.
20. *Op. cit.*, p. 163.
21. *The Mirage of Social Justice, op. cit.*, p. 87.
22. *Op. cit.*, pp. 178-82. On p. 179, Nozick denies that there is any right to life incorporating "a right to whatever one needs to live," since "other people may have rights over those things." There is only "a right to have or strive for whatever one needs to live, provided that having it does not violate anyone else's rights"—including, presumably, anyone else's rights to property to which, on Nozick's account, they are entitled.
23. *Op. cit.*, pp. 270-4.
24. See Hayek, *The Constitution of Liberty* (London, 1960), pp. 135-7, 140-2.
25. *Op. cit.*, pp. 250-5.
26. *The Mirage of Social Justice, op. cit.*, pp. 70-1, 132.
27. *Op. cit.*, pp. 160-3.

JAMES RACHELS

University of Alabama-Birmingham

What People Deserve

I shall discuss the concept of desert, and argue that what people deserve always depends on their own past actions. In order to illustrate the practical consequences of my analysis, I will consider its application to the problem of reverse discrimination.

THE RELATION BETWEEN JUSTICE AND DESERT

It is an important point of logic that if a value-judgment is true, there must be good reasons in support of it. Suppose you are told that you ought to do a certain action, or that so-and-so is a good man. You may ask *why* you ought to do it, or *why* he is a good man, and if no reasons can be given, you may reject those judgments as arbitrary. Claims of justice have this in common with other value-judgments; an action or social policy is just, or unjust, only if there is some reason why it is so. The attempt to decide questions of justice is, therefore, largely a matter of assessing the reasons that can be offered in support of the competing judgments.

Judgments of justice may be distinguished from other sorts of value-judgments by the kinds of reasons that are relevant to supporting them. The fact that an action would make someone unhappy may be a reason why that action *ought not* be done, but it is not a reason why the action would be *unjust*. On the other hand, the fact that an action would violate someone's rights is a reason why the act would be unjust. Questions of justice are narrower than questions of what should be done, in this sense: Any reason why an act would be unjust is also a reason why it should not be done; but not every reason why an act should not be done is a reason for thinking it unjust.

The fact that people are, or are not, treated as they deserve to be treated is one kind of reason why an action or social policy may be just or unjust. I say "one kind of reason" because there are also other sorts of reasons relevant to supporting claims of justice. Besides requiring that people be treated as they deserve, justice may also require that people's rights be respected, which is different, and, as Nozick emphasizes, historical backgrounds may also be relevant to determining justice. A complete theory of justice would provide, among other things, an exhaustive account of the different kinds of reasons relevant to supporting such judgments. I will not attempt to construct a complete theory; instead, I will only sketch that part of the theory having to do with desert. As a preliminary, I want to cite two instances from recent philosophical writing on justice in which the neglect of desert, as one consideration among others, has caused difficulty.

(a) The problem of reverse discrimination is one aspect of the more general problem of distributive justice, having to do with justice in the distribution of jobs and educational opportunities. Black people, women, and members of other groups have often been denied access to jobs and educational opportunities. It is easy enough to say that this is wrong, but it is not so easy to say exactly what should now be done about it. Some believe it is enough that we simply stop discriminating against them. Others think we ought to go further and give such persons preferential treatment, at least temporarily, in order to help rectify the past injustices. And in many cases this is already being done. The problem is whether this sort of preferential treatment is itself unjust to the whites, males, or others who are disadvantaged by it.

The term "distributive justice" is commonly used by philosophers, but as Nozick points out, it can be misleading.[1] It suggests that there is a central supply of things which some authority has to dole out; but for most goods, there is no such supply and no such authority. Goods are produced by diverse individuals and groups who then have rights with respect to them, and the "distribution" of holdings at any particular time will depend, at least in part, on the voluntary exchanges and agreements those people have made. Jobs, for example, do not come from some great stockpile, to be handed out by a master "distributor" who may or may not follow principles of "justice." Jobs are created by the independent decisions of countless business people, who are entitled, within some limits of course, to operate their own businesses according to their own judgments. In a free society those people get to choose with whom they will make what sorts of agreements, and this means, among other things, that they get to choose who is hired from among the various job applicants.

These observations suggest an argument in defense of reverse discrimination: If private business people have a right to hire whomever they please, don't they have a right to hire blacks and women in preference to others? In her paper on "Preferential Hiring" Judith Jarvis Thomson [2] advances an argument based on exactly this idea. The argument begins with this principle:

> No perfect stranger has a right to be given a benefit which is yours to dispose of; no perfect stranger even has a right to be given an equal chance at getting a benefit which is yours to dispose of.[3]

Since many jobs are benefits which private employers have a right to dispose of, those employers violate no one's rights in hiring whomever they wish. If they choose to hire blacks, or women, rather than other applicants, they have a perfect right to do so. Therefore, she concludes, "there is no problem about preferential hiring," at least in the case of private businesses.

Thomson's principle is plausible. If something is *yours*, then no one else has a right to it—at least, no perfect stranger who walks in off the street wanting it. Suppose you have a book which you don't need and decide to give away as a gift. Smith and Jones both want it, and you decide to give it to Smith. Is Jones entitled to complain? Apparently not, since *he* had no claim on it in the first place. If it was your book, you were entitled to give it to whomever you chose; you violated no right of Jones in giving it to Smith. Why shouldn't the same be true of jobs? If you start a business, on your own, why shouldn't you be free to hire whomever you please to work with you? You violate no one's rights in hiring whomever you please, since no one had a right to be hired by you in the first place.

This is an important and powerful argument because it calls attention to a fact that is often overlooked, that people do not naturally have claims of right to jobs and other benefits which are privately produced. However, the argument also depends on another assumption which is false, namely, the assumption that people are treated unjustly *only if* their rights are violated. In fact, a person may be treated unjustly even though no right of his is violated, because he is not treated as he deserves to be treated. Suppose one applicant for a job has worked very hard to qualify himself for it; he has gone to night-school, at great personal sacrifice, to learn the business, and so on. Another applicant could have done all that, but chose not to; instead, he has frittered away his time and done nothing to prepare himself. In addition, the first applicant has worked hard at every previous job he has held, making a good record for himself, whereas the second is a notorious loafer—and it's his own fault; he has no good excuse. Now it may be true that neither applicant has a *right* to the job, in the sense that the employer has the right to give the job to whomever he pleases. However, the first man is clearly more deserving, and if the employer is concerned to treat job applicants fairly he will not hire the second man over the first.

(b) Now let me return briefly to Nozick.[4] In Part II of *Anarchy, State and Utopia* he defends capitalism, not merely as efficient or workable,

but as the only moral economic system, because it is the only such system which respects individual rights. Under capitalism people's holdings are determined by the voluntary exchanges (of services and work as well as goods) they make with others. Their right to liberty requires that they be allowed to make such exchanges, provided that they violate no one else's rights in doing so. Having acquired their holdings by such exchanges, they have a right to them; so it violates their rights for the government (or anyone else) to seize their property and give it to others. It is impermissible, therefore, for governments to tax some citizens in order to provide benefits for others.

The obvious objection is that such an arrangement could produce a disastrously unfair distribution of goods. Some lucky entrepreneurs could become enormously rich, while other equally deserving people are poor, and orphans starve. In reply Nozick contends that even if unmodified capitalism did lead to such a distribution, that would not necessarily be unjust. The justice of a distribution, he says, can be determined only by considering the historical process which led to it. We cannot tell whether a distribution is just simply by checking whether it conforms to some nonhistorical pattern, for example the pattern of everyone having equal shares, or everyone having what he or she needs. To show this Nozick gives a now-famous argument starring the basketball player Wilt Chamberlain. First, he says, suppose the goods in a society are distributed according to some pattern which you think just. Call this distribution D_1. Since you regard D_1 as a just distribution, you will agree that under it each person has a right to the holdings in his or her possession. Now suppose a million of these people each decide to give Wilt Chamberlain twenty-five cents to watch him play basketball. Chamberlain becomes rich, and the original pattern is upset. But if the original distribution was just, mustn't we admit that the new distribution (D_2) is also just?

> Each of these persons *chose* to give twenty-five cents of their money to Chamberlain. They could have spent it on going to the movies, or on candy bars, or on copies of *Dissent* magazine, or of *Monthly Review*. But they all, at least one million of them, converged on giving it to Wilt Chamberlain in exchange for watching him play basketball. If D_1 was a just distribution, and people voluntarily moved from it to D_2, transferring parts of their shares they were given under D_1 (what was it for if not to do something with?), isn't D_2 also just? . . . Can anyone else complain on grounds of justice? . . . After someone transfers something to Wilt Chamberlain, third parties *still* have their legitimate shares; *their* shares are not changed.[5]

The main argument here seems to depend on the principle that *If D_1 is a just distribution, and D_2 arises from D_1 by a process in which no one's rights are violated, then D_2 is also just.* Now Nozick is surely right that the historical process which produces a situation is one of the things that must be taken into account in deciding whether it is just. But that need not be the only relevant consideration. The historical process *and* other considerations, such as desert, must be weighed together to determine what is just. Therefore, it would not follow that a distribution is just *simply* because it is the result of a certain process, even a process in which no one's rights are violated. So this argument cannot answer adequately the complaint against unmodified capitalism.

To make the point less abstract, consider the justice of inherited wealth. A common complaint about inherited wealth is that some people gain fortunes which they have done nothing to deserve, while others, of equal merit, have nothing. This seems unjust on the face of it. Nozick points out that if the testators legitimately own their property—if it is *theirs*—then they have a right to give it to others as a gift. (The holdings of third parties will not be changed, etc.) Bequests are gifts; therefore property owners have a right to pass on their property to their heirs. This is fair enough, but at most it shows only that there is more than one consideration to be taken into account here. That some people have more than others, without deserving it, counts against the justice of the distribution. That they came by their holdings in a certain way may count in favor of the justice of the same distribution. It should come as no surprise that in deciding questions of justice competing claims must often be weighed against one another, for that is the way it usually is in ethics.

DESERT AND PAST ACTIONS

Deserts may be positive or negative, that is, a person may deserve to be treated well or badly; and they may be general or specific, that is, a person may deserve to be treated in a generally good or bad way, or he may deserve some specific kind of good or bad treatment. An example may make the latter distinction clear. Suppose a woman has always been kind and generous with others. As a general way of dealing with her, she deserves that others be kind and generous in return. Here we need not specify any *particular* act of kindness to say what she deserves, although of course treating her kindly will involve some particular act or other. What she deserves is that people treat her decently in *whatever* situation might arise. By way of contrast, think of someone who has worked hard to earn promotion in his job. He may deserve, *specifically*, to be promoted.

I wish to argue that the basis of all desert is a person's own past actions. In the case of negative desert, this is generally conceded. In order for a person to deserve punishment, for example, he must have *done something* to deserve it. Moreover, he must have done it "voluntarily," in Aristotle's sense, without any excuse such as ignorance, mistake, or coercion. In allowing these excuses and others like them, the law attempts to restrict punishment to cases in which it is deserved.

But not every negative desert involves punishment, strictly speaking. They may involve more informal responses to other people's misconduct. Suppose Adams and Brown work at the same factory. One morning Adams' car breaks down and he calls Brown to ask for a ride to work. Brown refuses, not for any good reason, but simply because he won't be bothered. Later, Brown finds himself in the same fix: his car won't start, and he can't get to work; so he calls Adams to ask for a lift. Now if Adams is a kind and forgiving person, he may grant Brown's request. And perhaps we all ought to be kind and forgiving. However, if Adams does choose to help Brown, he will be treating Brown better than Brown deserves. Brown deserves to be left in the lurch. Here I am not arguing that we ought to treat people as they deserve—although I do think there are reasons for so treating people, which I will mention presently— here I am only describing what the concept of desert involves. What Brown *deserves*, as opposed to what kindness or any other value might decree, is to be treated as well, *or as badly*, as he himself chooses to treat others.

If I am right, then the familiar lament "What did I do to deserve this?," asked by a victim of misfortune, is more than a mournful cliché. If there is no satisfactory answer, then in fact one does *not* deserve the misfortune. And since there is always a presumption against treating people badly, if a person does not deserve bad treatment it is likely to be wrong to treat him in that way. On the other side, in the case of positive deserts, we may notice a corresponding connection between the concept of desert and the idea of *earning* one's way, which also supports my thesis.

To elaborate an example I used earlier, think of an employer who has to decide which of two employees to give a promotion. One has worked very hard for the company for several years. He has always been willing to do more than his share of work; he has put in a lot of over-time when no one else would; and so on. The other has always done the least he could get by with, never taking on any extra work or otherwise exerting himself beyond the necessary minimum. Clearly, if the choice is between these two candidates, it is the first who deserves the promotion. It is important to notice that this conclusion does not depend on any estimate of how the two candidates are likely to perform in the future. Even if the second candidate were to reform, so that he would work just as hard (and well) in the new position as the first candidate, the first is still more deserving. What one deserves depends on what one has done, not on what one will do.

Of course there may be any number of reasons for not giving the promotion to the most deserving candidate: perhaps it is a family busi-ness, and the second candidate is the boss's son, and he will be advanced simply because of who he is. But that does not make him the most de-serving candidate; it only means that the promotion is to be awarded on grounds other than desert. Again, the boss might decide to give the position to the second candidate because he is extraordinarily smart and talented, and the boss thinks for that reason he will do a better job (he has promised to work harder in the future). This is again to award the job on grounds other than desert, for no one deserves anything *simply* in virtue of superior intelligence and natural abilities. As Rawls empha-sizes, a person no more deserves to be intelligent or talented than he deserves to be the boss's son—or, than he deserves to be born white in a society prejudiced against nonwhites. These things are all matters of chance, at least as far as the lucky individual himself is concerned.

Three questions naturally arise concerning this view. First, aren't there bases of desert *other than* a person's past actions, and if not, why not? Second, if a person may not deserve things in virtue of being naturally talented or intelligent or fortunate in some other way, how can he deserve things by working for them? After all, isn't it merely a matter of luck that one person grows up to be industrious—perhaps as the result of a rigorous upbringing by his parents—while another person is not encouraged, and ends up lazy for reasons beyond his control? And finally, even if I am right about the basis of desert, what reason is there actually to treat people according to their deserts? Why should desert matter? I will take up these questions in order. The answers, as we shall see, are interrelated.

(a) In his important article "Justice and Personal Desert" Joel Feinberg says that "If a person is deserving of some sort of treatment, he must, necessarily, be so in virtue of *some possessed characteristic* or prior activity." [6] Among the characteristics that may be the basis of desert he includes abilities, skills, physical attributes, and so on. In a tennis game, for example, the most skillful player deserves to win, and in a beauty contest the prettiest or most handsome deserves to win.

Does the most skillful player deserve to win an athletic competition? It seems a natural enough thing to say. But suppose the less skilled player has worked very hard, for weeks, to prepare himself for the match. He has practiced nine hours a day, left off drinking, and kept to a strict regimen. Meanwhile, his opponent, who is a "natural athlete," has partied, stayed drunk, and done nothing in the way of training. *But he is still the most skilled*, and as a result can probably beat the other guy anyway. Does he *deserve* to win the game, simply because he is better endowed by nature? Does he *deserve* the acclaim and benefits which go with winning? Of course, skills are themselves usually the product of past efforts. People must work to sharpen and develop their natural abilities; therefore, when we think of the most skillful as the most deserving, it may be because we think of them as having worked hardest. (Ted Williams practiced hitting more than anyone else on the Red Sox.) But sometimes that assumption is not true.

Do the prettiest and most handsome deserve to win beauty contests? Again, it seems a natural enough thing to say. There is no doubt that the *correct* decision for the judges of such a competition to make is to award the prize to the best-looking. But this may have little to do with the contestants' deserts. Suppose a judge were to base his decision on desert; we might imagine him reasoning like this: "Miss Montana isn't the prettiest, but after all, she's done her best with what nature provided. She's studied the use of make-up, had her teeth and nose fixed, and spent hours practicing walking down runways in high-heeled shoes. That smile didn't just happen; she had to learn it by spending hours before a mirror. Miss Alabama, on the other hand, is prettier, but she just entered the contest on a lark—walked in, put on a bathing suit, and here she is. Her make-up isn't even very good." If all this seems ridiculous, it is because the point of such contests is *not* to separate the more deserving from the less (and maybe because beauty contests are themselves a little ridiculous, too). The criterion is beauty, not desert, and the two have little to do with one another. The same goes for athletic games: the purpose is to see who is the best player, or at least who is able to defeat all the others, and not to discover who is the most deserving competitor.

There is a reason why past actions are the only bases of desert. A fair amount of our dealings with other people involves holding them responsible, formally or informally, for one thing or another. It is unfair to hold people responsible for things over which they have no control. People have no control over their native endowments—over how smart, or athletic, or beautiful they naturally are—and so we may not hold them responsible for those things. They are, however, in control of (at least some of) their own actions, and so they may rightly be held responsible for the situations they create, or allow to exist, by their voluntary behavior. But those are the *only* things for which they may rightly be held responsible. The concept of desert serves to signify the ways of treating people that are appropriate responses to them, *given that* they are responsible for those actions or states of affairs. That is the role played by desert in our moral vocabulary. And, as ordinary-language philosophers used to like to say, if there weren't such a term, we'd have to invent one. Thus the explanation of why past actions are the only bases of desert connects with the fact that *if* people were never responsible for their own conduct—if hard determinism were true—no one would ever deserve anything, good or bad.

(b) According to the view I am defending, we may deserve things by working for them, but not simply by being naturally intelligent or talented or lucky in some other way. Now it may be thought that this view is inconsistent, because whether someone is willing to work is just another matter of luck, in much the same way that intelligence and talent are matters of luck. Rawls takes this position when he says:

> Perhaps some will think that the person with greater natural endowments deserves those assets and the superior character that made their development possible. Because he is more worthy in this sense, he deserves the greater advantages that he could achieve with them. This view, however, is surely incorrect. It seems to be one of the fixed points of our considered judgments that no one deserves his place in the distribution of native endowments, any more than one deserves one's initial starting place in society. The assertion that a man deserves the superior character that enables him to make the effort to cultivate his abilities is equally problematic; for his character depends in large part upon fortunate family and social circumstances for which he can claim no credit. The notion of desert seems not to apply to these cases.[7]

So if a person does not deserve anything on account of his intelligence or natural abilities, how can he deserve anything on account of his industriousness? Isn't willingness to work just another matter of luck?

The first thing to notice here is that people do not deserve things on account of their *willingness* to work, but only on account of their actually having worked. The candidate for promotion does not deserve it because he has been willing to work hard in his old job, or because he is willing to work hard in the new job. Rather he deserves the promotion because he actually *has* worked hard. Therefore it is no objection to the view I am defending to say that willingness to work is a character trait that one does not merit. For, on this view, the basis of desert is not a character trait of any kind, not even industriousness. The basis of desert is a person's past actions.

Now it may be that some people have been so psychologically devastated by a combination of poor native endowment and unfortunate family and social circumstances that they no longer have the capacity for making anything of their lives. If one of these people has a job, for example, and doesn't work very hard at it, it's no use blaming him because, as we would say, he just hasn't got it in him to do any better. On the other hand, there are those in whom the capacity for effort has not been extinguished. Among these, some choose to work hard, and others, who *could* so choose, do not. It is true of everyone in this latter class that he is *able*, as Rawls puts it, "to strive conscientiously." The explanation of why some strive, while others don't, has to do with their own choices. When I say that those who work hard are more deserving of success, promotions, etc., than those who don't, I have in mind comparisons made among people in this latter class, in whom the capacity for effort has not been extinguished.[8]

There is an important formal difference between industriousness, considered as a lucky asset, and other lucky assets such as intelligence. For only by exercising this asset—i.e., by working—can one utilize his other assets, and achieve anything with them. Intelligence alone produces nothing; intelligence plus work can produce something. And the same relation holds between industriousness and every other natural talent or asset. Thus "willingness to work," if it is a lucky asset, is a sort of super-asset which enables one's other assets to be utilized. Working is simply the way one uses whatever else one has. This point may help to explain why the concept of desert is tied to work in a way in which it is not tied to intelligence or talents. And at the same time it may also provide a rationale for the following distinction: if a person displays intelligence and talent in his work, and earns a certain benefit by it, then he deserves the benefit *not* because of the intelligence or talent shown, but only on account of the work done.

(c) Finally, we must ask why people ought to be treated according to their deserts. Why should desert matter? In one way, it is an odd question. The reason why the conscientious employee ought to be promoted is precisely that he has earned the promotion by working for it. That is a full and sufficient justification for promoting him, which does not require supplementation of any sort. If we want to know why he

should be treated in that way, that is the answer. It is not easy to see what else, by way of justification, is required.

Nevertheless, something more may be said. Treating people as they deserve is one way of treating them as autonomous beings, responsible for their own conduct. A person who is punished for his misdeeds is *held responsible* for them in a concrete way. He is not treated as a mindless automaton, whose defective performances must be "corrected," or whose good performance promoted, but as a responsible agent whose actions merit approval or resentment.[9] The recognition of deserts is bound up with this way of regarding people. Moreover, treating people as they deserve *increases* their control over their own lives and fortunes, for it allows people to determine, through their own actions, how others will respond to them. It can be argued on grounds of kindness that people should not always be treated as they deserve, when they deserve ill. But this should not be taken to imply that deserts count for nothing. They can count for something, and still be overridden in some cases. To deny categorically that desert matters would not only excuse the malefactors; it would leave all of us impotent to earn the good treatment and other benefits which others have to bestow, and thus would deprive us of the ability to control our own destinies as social beings.

REVERSE DISCRIMINATION

Is it right to give preferential treatment to blacks, women, or members of other groups who have been discriminated against in the past? I will approach this issue by considering the deserts of the individuals involved. "Reverse Discrimination" is not a particularly good label for the practices in question because the word "discrimination" has come to have such unsavory connotations. Given the way that word is now used, to ask whether reverse *discrimination* is justified already prejudices the question in favor of a negative answer. But in other ways the term is apt: the most distinctive thing about reverse discrimination is that it *reverses* past patterns, so that those who have been discriminated against are now given preferential treatment. At any rate, the label is now part of our common vocabulary, so I will stay with it.

The following example incorporates the essential elements of reverse discrimination. The admissions committee of a certain law school assesses the qualifications of applicants by assigning numerical values to their college grades, letters of recommendation, and test scores, according to some acceptable formula. (The better the grades, etc., the higher the numerical values assigned.) From past experience the committee judges that a combined score of 600 is necessary for a student to have a reasonable chance of succeeding in the school's program. Thus in order to be minimally qualified for admission an applicant must score at least 600. However, because there are more qualified applicants than places available, many who score over 600 are nevertheless rejected.

Against this background two students, one black and one white, apply for admission. The black student's credentials are rated at 700, and the white student's credentials are rated at 720. So although both exceed the minimum requirement by a comfortable margin, the white student's qualifications are somewhat better. But the white applicant is rejected and the black applicant is accepted. The officials of the school explain that this decision is part of a policy designed to bring more blacks into the legal profession. The scores of the white applicants are generally higher than those of the blacks; so, some blacks with lower scores must be admitted in order to have a fair number of black students in the entering class.

I should point out that this example is patterned after an actual case. In 1971 a student named Marco DeFunis applied for admission to the University of Washington Law School, and was rejected. He then learned that one-fourth of those accepted were minority-group students with academic records inferior to his own. The law school conceded that DeFunis had been passed over to make room for the minority students, and DeFunis brought suit charging that his rights had been violated. A lower court ruled in his favor; the Supreme Court of the state of Washington reversed this decision. The United States Supreme Court heard the case, but then declined to rule on the substance since the specific issue involved—DeFunis' admission to the University of Washington Law School—had become a moot point. DeFunis had been enrolled in the School when he filed suit, and by the time the case reached the highest court he had already graduated! So the example is not merely a philosopher's invention.

Now a number of arguments can be given in support of the law school's policy, and other policies like it. Black people have been, and still are, the victims of racist discrimination. One result is that they are poorly represented in the professions. In order to remedy this it is not enough that we simply stop discriminating against them. For, so long as there are not enough "role models" available—i.e., black people visibly successful in the professions, whom young blacks can recognize as models to emulate—young blacks cannot be expected to aspire to the professions and prepare for careers in the way that young whites do. It is a vicious cycle: while there are relatively few black lawyers, relatively few young blacks will take seriously the possibility of becoming lawyers, and so they will not be prepared for law school. But if relatively few young blacks are well-prepared for law school, and admissions committees hold them to the same high standards as the white applicants, there will be relatively few black lawyers. Law school admissions committees may try to help set things right, and break this cycle, by temporarily giving preferential treatment to black applicants.

Moreover, although many people now recognize that racist discrimination is wrong, prejudice against blacks is still widespread. One aspect of the problem is that a disproportionate number of blacks are still poor and hold only menial jobs, while the most prestigious jobs are occupied mostly by whites. So long as this is so, it will be easy for the white majority to continue with their old stereotyped ideas about black people.

But if there were more black people holding prestigious jobs, it would be much more difficult to sustain the old prejudices. So in the long run law school admissions policies favoring black applicants will help reduce racism throughout the society.

I believe these arguments, and others like them, show that policies of reverse discrimination can be socially useful, although this is certainly a debatable point. For one thing, the resentment of those who disapprove of such policies will diminish their net utility. For another, less qualified persons will not perform as well in the positions they attain. However, I will not discuss these issues any further. I will concentrate instead on the more fundamental question of whether policies of reverse discrimination are unjust. After all, the rejected white student may concede the utility of such policies and nevertheless still complain that he has been treated unjustly. He may point out that he has been turned down simply because of his race. If he had been black, and had had exactly the same qualifications, he would have been accepted. This, he may argue, is equally as unjust as discriminating against black people on account of their race. Moreover, he can argue that, even if black people have been mistreated, he was not responsible for it, and so it is unfair to penalize him for it now. These are impressive arguments and, if they cannot be answered, the rightness of reverse discrimination will remain in doubt regardless of its utility.

I will argue that whether the white applicant has been treated unjustly depends on *why* he has better credentials than the black, that is, it depends on what accounts for the 20-point difference in their qualifications.

Suppose, for example, that his higher qualifications are due entirely to the fact that he has worked harder. Suppose the two applicants are equally intelligent, and have had the same opportunities. But the black student has spent a lot of time enjoying himself, going to the movies, and so forth, while the white student has passed by such pleasures to devote himself to his studies. If *this* is what accounts for the difference in their qualifications, then it seems that the white applicant really has been treated unjustly. For he has earned his superior qualifications; he deserves to be admitted ahead of the black student because he has worked harder for it.

But now suppose a different explanation is given as to why the white student has ended up with a 20-point advantage in qualifications. Suppose the applicants are equally intelligent *and* they have worked equally hard. However, the black student has had to contend with obstacles which his white competitor has not had to face. For example, his early education was at the hands of ill-trained teachers in crowded, inadequate schools, so that by the time he reached college he was far behind the other students and despite his best efforts he never quite caught up. If *this* is what accounts for the difference in qualifications, things look very different. For now the white student has not earned his superior qualifications. He has done nothing to deserve them. His record is, of course, the result of things he's done, just as the black student's record is the result of things the black student has done. But the fact that he has a *better* record than the black student is not due to anything he has done. That difference is due only to his good luck in having been born into a more advantaged social position. Surely he cannot deserve to be admitted into law school ahead of the black simply because of *that*.

Now in fact black people in the United States have been, and are, systematically discriminated against, and it is reasonable to believe that this mistreatment does make a difference to black people's ability to compete with whites for such goods as law school admission. Therefore, at least some actual cases probably do correspond to the description of my example. Some white students have better qualifications for law school only because they have not had to contend with the obstacles faced by their black competitors. If so, their better qualifications do not automatically entitle them to prior admission.

Thus it is not the fact that the applicant is black that matters. What is important is that, as a result of past discriminatory practices, he has been unfairly handicapped in trying to achieve the sort of academic standing required for admission. If he has a claim to "preferential" treatment now, it is for *that* reason.

It follows that, even though a system of reverse discrimination might involve injustice for some whites, in many cases no injustice will be done. In fact, the reverse is true: If no such system is employed—if, for example, law school admissions are granted purely on the basis of "qualifications"—*that* may involve injustice for the disadvantaged who have been unfairly handicapped in the competition for qualifications.

It also follows that the most common arguments against reverse discrimination are not valid. The white student in our example cannot complain that he is being rejected simply because he is white. The effect of the policy is only to *neutralize an advantage* that he has had because he is white, and that is very different.[10] Nor will it do any good for the white to complain that, while blacks may have suffered unjust hardships, *he* is not responsible for it and so should not be penalized for it. The white applicant is not being penalized, or being made to pay reparations, for the wrongs that have been done to blacks. He is simply not being allowed to *profit* from the fact that those wrongs were done, by now besting the black in a competition that is "fair" only if we ignore the obstacles which one competitor, but not the other, has had to face.

Notes

1. Robert Nozick, *Anarchy, State and Utopia* (New York: Basic Books, 1974), pp. 149-150.

2. Judith Jarvis Thomson, "Preferential Hiring," *Philosophy and Public Affairs*, vol. 2, no. 4 (Summer 1973), pp. 364-384.

3. *Ibid.*, p. 369.

4. The following is from my review of *Anarchy, State and Utopia* in *Philosophia,* vol. 7 (1977).

5. Nozick, p. 161.

6. Joel Feinberg, *Doing and Deserving* (Princeton: Princeton University Press, 1970), p. 58 (italics added).

7. John Rawls, *A Theory of Justice* (Cambridge, Mass.: Harvard University Press, 1971), pp. 103-104.

8. What I am resisting—and what I think Rawls' view leads us towards—is a kind of determinism that would make all moral evaluation of persons meaningless. On this tendency in Rawls, see Nozick, pp. 213-214.

9. This point is elaborated by Herbert Morris in his illuminating paper "Persons and Punishment," *The Monist,* vol. 52 (1968), pp. 475-501.

10. Cf. George Sher, "Justifying Reverse Discrimination in Employment," *Philosophy and Public Affairs,* vol. 4, no. 2 (Winter 1975), pp. 159-170. Sher also argues that "reverse discrimination is justified insofar as it neutralizes competitive disadvantages caused by past privations" (p. 165). I have learned a lot from Sher's paper.

NORMAN DANIELS

Tufts University

Meritocracy *

Sometimes a person has abilities and interests which enable him or her to perform a given job, position, or office—hereafter, I will just say "job" —better than other available persons. In what sense do such abilities and interests constitute a basis for claiming the more capable person merits the job? Does the fact that someone possesses special abilities and interests which are needed for the superior performance of jobs of considerable social importance and prestige constitute a basis for claiming the person deserves or merits greater rewards for the job? I want to explore some of the issues associated with these questions, but I will do so by analyzing the notion of a meritocracy, a social order built around a particular notion of merit. My hope is that examination of such a hypothetical social order will allow me to assess the broader implications of this particular notion of merit for a theory of distributive justice. Though my model for the meritocracies I consider derives from Michael Young's satire about a world-wide technocratic society in which all assignments of jobs and rewards are organized on a merit basis,[1] I am

* This paper grew out of remarks I made as commentator on Alan Soble's "Meritocracy and Rawls' Second Principle" presented at the Western Division APA Meetings, New Orleans, April 1976. I have benefited from discussion with Hugo Bedau and from comments by John Troyer as well as from critical discussion following presentations of versions of this paper at Brown, Calgary, Tufts, and the Pacific Division APA Meetings. A different version of this paper appears in *Philosophy and Public Affairs* Vol. 7. No. 2, Spring 1978.

not concerned with the details of his construction, except for his construal of merit as *ability plus effort*.

A Meritocratic Job Placement Principle

I take a meritocracy to be a society whose basic institutions are governed by a partial theory of distributive justice consisting of principles of the following three types:

1. A principle of job placement that awards jobs to individuals on the basis of merit;
2. A principle specifying the conditions of opportunity under which the job placement principle is applied;
3. A principle specifying reward schedules (salary, benefits, etc.) for jobs.

It is obvious that such principles constitute only a partial theory of distributive justice: they say nothing, for example, about liberty or its distribution, nor about many other questions. But I will concentrate on just this much here since most meritocrats do. I will argue that there is a preferred principle for job placement and one for opportunity and that most meritocrats would agree to them. But, meritocrats will still vary widely on reward principles. My schema allows us to separate problems common to what meritocrats generally share from problems that arise from reward schedules.

Most meritocrats share certain empirical assumptions which give rise to a principle of job placement. First, they assume that different jobs require different sets of human abilities and different personality traits, including motivation, if they are to be performed with maximum competency. Certain skills, whether mental or motor, are more critical for some jobs than others. Second, they assume that people differ in the abilities and personality traits they possess. Some people possess more developed motor skills, some more developed mental skills, than others. Usually, this second assumption is not couched solely in terms of actual skills possessed. Rather, it is assumed people differ in their natively determined capacity to develop a given level of a certain skill. Often the ambiguous word "ability" does double duty here, hedging bets between claims about inequalities of skills and claims about inequalities of capacity. In any case, most meritocrats believe that it is obvious that people differ in levels of skill and that it is at least probable that they differ in the capacity to acquire levels of skills.[2]

Meritocrats infer from these two assumptions that some arrays of assignments of individuals to jobs will be more productive than others. That is, if we take care to match people with the jobs they are best able to perform, then we will have produced a relatively productive array of job assignments. Actually, we are unlikely to find just one particular array of job assignments that is more productive than any other. Rather, it seems likely that there are a number of equally productive arrays of job assignments for any group of jobs and individuals.

A warning is needed about the notion of productivity. It must be accepted as an intuitively applicable notion for a wide range of jobs, positions, or offices for which no standard measurement of productivity exists. For such jobs, economists often take market-determined wage levels to indicate average productivity levels. But, such a device is not satisfactory for many reasons. So I will assume we can meaningfully talk about the productivity of doctors, teachers, lawyers, hairdressers, and so on, even though no single quantitative measure seems acceptable. Meritocrats and non-meritocrats alike operate with intuitively acceptable, if imprecise, notions of competent or productive job performance.

The principle I believe would be preferred for job placement makes use of the idea of equally productive patterns of job assignments. This says that job assignments should be made by selecting the most productive array of job assignments; if that is not possible (because some jobs are already held), then select the next most productive array of job assignments, and so on.[3] Such a Productivity Principle seems desirable because, in the absence of arguments showing that justice or other considerations of right demand some other array than a maximally productive one, there is good reason to seek productivity in social arrangements. I want to leave it an open question how a meritocrat would respond to a claim that justice demanded—as compensation for past services or past injuries —that someone not selected by the Productivity Principle nevertheless be given a particular job. Some such claims would seem to be weighty enough to justify overriding the presumption in favor of productivity considerations. But more on this point shortly.

If the Productivity Principle is adopted, then the notion of individual merit enters the picture in the following, restricted way. An individual may claim to merit one job more than another job, or to merit one job more than another person does, if and only if his occupying that job is an assignment that is part of the assignments selected by the Productivity Principle. The claim of merit or relative merit is dependent for its basis on the rationale for the Principle. The merit does not derive from having the abilities themselves, but only from the fact that abilities can play a certain social role. We focus on the relevant abilities because of their utility, not because there is something intrinsically meritorious about having them. It should be quite clear by now that the particular notion of merit I am concerned with here should not be confused with the more general concept of desert; also it should not be confused with certain ordinary uses of "merit" which are similar to the broader notion of desert. I am concerned with merit as it plays a role in the types of meritocracies I am analyzing.

IMPLICATIONS OF THE PRODUCTIVITY PRINCIPLE

To see why the Productivity Principle is the preferred principle, consider the following case.[4] Jack and Jill both wants jobs A and B and each much prefers A to B. Jill can do either A or B better than Jack. But the situation S in which Jill performs B and Jack A is more productive than Jack doing B and Jill A (S'). The Productivity Principle selects S, not S', because it is attuned to macro, not micro, productivity considerations. It says "select people for jobs so that *overall* job performance is maximized."

It might be felt that the "real" meritocrat would balk at such a macro principle. The "real" meritocrat, it might be argued, is one who thinks a person should get a job if he or she is the best available person for *that* job. We might formulate such a view as the micro-productivity principle that, for any job J, we should select the applicant who can most productively perform J from among those desiring J more than any other job. The micro principle would select S', not S.

I think that, given the rationale for treating job-related abilities as the basis for merit claims in the first place, namely that it is socially desirable to enhance productivity where possible, the macro principle seems preferable. There is something anomalous about basing a merit claim, given our restricted notion of merit, on claims about micro-productivity considerations while at the same time ignoring macro-productivity considerations. We seem to need an explanation why macro considerations should not overrule the micro ones. Alternatively, we might try to divorce the merit claim from all productivity considerations, but this approach makes it completely mysterious why job-related abilities are made the basis of merit in the first place.[5]

I suppose one reason some may think the micro-merit principle is preferable to the Productivity Principle is that it seems *unfair* to Jill that she gets the job she prefers less even though she can do the job Jack gets better than he can. But what is the sense of unfairness here based on? After all, under this arrangement, Jack has the job he prefers more and overall productivity is enhanced. And, if Jill had her way, Jack would not have his, and macroproductivity would suffer as well. It is important to note as well that B is a job Jill wants, though not as much as she wants A. The Productivity Principle does not force people into jobs they do not want at all.

I believe the sense of unfairness here derives from particular, inessential features of our economic system. In many hiring or job-placement situations in our society, we make no effort to calculate macroproductivity from job assignments. We assume that macroproductivity is always directly proportional to microproductivity. So, in most hiring that is done on a merit basis (and of course much is not), we tend to use the microprinciple. From the micro point of view of such an habitual practice, it does look like the macro Productivity Principle makes Jill pay a price we ordinarily might not make her pay.

But if this explanation does *account for* the sense of unfairness some feel, it does not justify it in a relevant way. Our task is not just to describe the intuitions we have, influenced as they are by existing economic arrangements. Rather, where we have some reason to think the intuitions are just a by-product of existing institutions, and where our task is to find principles to establish institutions we think more just than existing ones, then we may be forced to modify or abandon some of our habitual intuitions. If the Productivity Principle appears on theoretical grounds to be a more plausible principle governing the institution of job placement, then our favoritism for micro considerations may seem unjustifiable. Moreover, if an individual's sense of fairness were molded by institutions which took macroproductivity into account, not just micro productivity, then our data on unfairness might disappear. If Jill (and others) knew the macro Productivity Principle and not the micro-principle were determining job placement, no legitimate expectations of hers (or ours) would be unsatisfied by the selection of her for B rather than A.

What I have been trying to show is the appropriateness of using the macro Productivity Principle rather than the alternative micro principle, given the rationale for worrying about job-related abilities in the first place, namely their overall connection to productivity. For purposes of my exposition, however, I do not need to rule out some version of the micro principle wherever it is construed as a rough, practical guide to the application of the macro principle. That is, given societies (like ours) in which there is no provision for a more scientific method of calculating maximally productive job arrays, in which most hiring or placement for positions is on a job-by-job basis, then the micro principle may be the best rule of thumb. Such a compromise in practice is not, however, a compromise with the rationale behind the Productivity Principle. It is important to note, however, that the Productivity Principle seems to presuppose a more sophisticated theory of productivity measurement and may also commit us to more elaborate, centralized hiring than the micro principle. Since my task here is to analyze where a particular notion of merit leads us, I need not evaluate these last considerations to determine the ultimate desirability of the macro Productivity Principle or the micro principle.

In any case, keeping in mind the compromise just proposed, I will assume that meritocrats can agree on the macro Productivity Principle. But it must be clear what this assumption implies: an individual merits a job if his or her placement on that job is part of the most productive array of job assignments. Such a derivation of a merit claim to a job does not presuppose that any kind of desert claim is present other than one derived from productivity considerations. Our obligation to honor a merit claim so derived is only as strong as the *prima facie* obligation to satisfy productivity considerations.

Some may feel that this truncated notion of merit that emerges must be an incorrect one because it omits any appeal to a stronger notion of desert. They are inclined to assert that if Jill has the greater ability, then Jill *deserves* the job. But the force of my argument is to leave us wondering whether there is a plausible basis for such a desert claim at all, given that our selection of certain abilities as relevant for job placement was based on their connection to productivity.[6]

It is worth a brief digression to mention two implications of my analysis for the problem of preferential hiring. Some people object to preferential hiring on the grounds (not necessarily the most convincing ones) that not choosing the most competent candidate, as judged by test scores or other professional criteria, is a violation of that person's presumptive rights. But, if merit claims to jobs are derived from the Productivity Principle, then macro-productivity claims may, as a matter of empirical fact, override the micro-based claims of the most competent applicant. For example, a better mix of race and sex in such professional positions as the law, teaching, or medicine might well pay dividends in terms of services rendered to those who would not otherwise get them, inspiration to long-suppressed motivation, the overcoming of race and sex stereotypes which are counterproductive in other ways, and so on. But the proponent of affirmative action should beware that the appeal to the Productivity Principle does not backfire: suppose productivity is reduced because of sexist or racist opposition to what otherwise would be a meritocratic placement. Then the Productivity Principle might play a conservative role, capitulating to existing biases.

This result leads me to a more important result of my analysis of merit. Whether my claim to merit a particular job more than another does is dependent on an appeal to the Productivity Principle or to a micro principle, it nevertheless is justified only by efficiency considerations. If consideration of right or justice demands we override efficiency considerations—to satisfy a concern for equality, to compensate for past injuries, or to reward for past service—then we are not faced with a case of pitting claims of right against other claims of right. Rather, we pit productivity against considerations of justice. And many will feel less concerned about such a compromise of productivity than they would if a claim to merit a job were really a claim of right, a claim of justice.[7]

MERIT AND REWARD

I would like to return now to discuss the remaining types of principles meritocrats share. Although there may be some exceptions, I believe that most meritocrats would view fair, rather than just formal, equality of opportunity as the appropriate precondition for application of the Productivity Principle. Formal equality of opportunity obtains when there are no legal or quasi-legal barriers to people's having equal access (based on merit) to positions and offices or to the means (education and training) needed to qualify one for access to such jobs. Fair equality of opportunity requires not only that negative legal or quasi-legal constraints on equality of opportunity be eliminated, but also that positive steps be taken to provide equality of access—and the means to achieve such equality of access—to those with inferior initial competitive positions resulting from family background or other biological or social accidents.

If we make the empirical assumption that conditions of fair opportunity maximize the availability of human abilities which would otherwise be wasted under conditions of merely formal opportunity, then considerations of productivity alone carry us some way toward the preference for fair opportunity. Of course, efficiency considerations alone may *not* always point to fair rather than formal opportunity. If there were a tremendous superfluity of abilities available just as a result of formal opportunity, then more might have to be invested through fair opportunity measures to produce increases in the maximally productive class of job assignments than is justified by the size of those increases. Similarly, if early, arbitrary selection of some individuals for special training for certain jobs were maximally efficient, other non-utilitarian arguments might be needed before fair opportunity would be preferred. Rawls, for example, does not rest his argument for fair opportunity on grounds of efficiency alone. Rather, he argues that people will feel they do not have fair access to the centrally important social good of self-realization if formal, rather than fair, opportunity is instituted.[8] In any case, I will assume that meritocrats generally treat fair, not formal, opportunity as the precondition for applying the Productivity Principle. Little in my argument hangs on this assumption.

Thus far I have said nothing about the rewards and burdens that accompany different jobs. The Productivity Principle, as I have presented it, is defined without reference to any particular schedule of rewards and burdens. So far, although an individual may claim to merit a job when his having it satisfies the principle, there is no sense given to his meriting any particular set of rewards or burdens. I have deliberately dissociated the meritocratic basis for job assignment from the process of determining the schedule of benefits and burdens associated with different jobs or positions.[9]

I think it is possible for meritocrats to differ on the reward schedules they join to the system structured by the Productivity Principle and fair equality of opportunity. Consider the following eight meritocracies which differ only in their reward schedules:

1. Status quo meritocracy: the reward schedule for jobs mirrors those inequalities in rewards and burdens which characterize the U.S. status quo.

2. Unbridled meritocracy: the reward schedule allows whatever rewards those who end up with positions of power and prestige can acquire for themselves. (Status quo and unbridled meritocracies may be identical.)

3. Desert meritocracy: the reward schedule allows rewards proportional to the contribution of the jobs (but not constrained by efficiency considerations as in (5)); alternatively, the desert basis might have nothing to do with productivity—it might be moral worthiness, for example.

4. Nationalist meritocracy: inequalities in rewards act to advance the national interest.

5. Utilitarian meritocracy: the reward schedule allows inequalities which act to maximize average or total utility.

6. Maximin meritocracy: the reward schedule allows inequalities which act to maximize the index of primary social goods of those who are worst off.

7. Strict egalitarian meritocracy: no inequalities in reward are allowed.

8. Socialist meritocracy: the reward schedule allows no inequalities in the satisfaction of (basic?) needs.

My list allows for meritocracies which no one may actually have supported. And, for the sake of brevity, it may not mention your favorite meritocracy. But the main point should be clear, namely, I do not consider it an essential feature of a meritocracy that efficiency is the sole principle governing selection of reward schedules, but I do believe that an appeal to productivity in job assignment is always involved in meritocracy through the Productivity Principle.

I believe a number of qualifying remarks are in order. First, unless certain empirical conditions obtain, meritocracy may prove to be a theory which does not determine which job assignments are to be made. If application of the Productivity Principle is effectively to determine job placement, then the number of equally productive patterns of job assignments is going to have to be fairly small. I am inclined to believe, however, that this number will be quite large under real conditions of fair equality of opportunity. With adequate education and training, most people might competently perform almost any job, or at least a very large range of jobs. Second, the Productivity Principle presupposes that we have very good ways of predicting which abilities and personality traits will lead to successful, i.e., productive, performance of a given job. But many of our current efforts in those directions are woefully inadequate.[10]

A final, most important qualification. My analysis might seem to imply that we know how to apply the Productivity Principle independently of fixing a reward schedule. But such independence is unlikely. Different reward schedules would presumably affect the motivations of individuals contemplating entering certain jobs. Just this point is at the heart of Rawls' view that material incentives will be necessary if we are to procure the greatest talent possible for certain burdensome jobs. So it seems we cannot determine the class of maximally productive job assignments, which we need for application of the Productivity Principle, until we know something of the reward structure. But this fact does not alter my main point: we can distinguish the Productivity Principle from reward principles, and what all meritocrats share is appeal to the Productivity Principle and fair equality of opportunity, however else they may differ in their use of reward schedules.[11]

If we keep our attention on the shared features of meritocracy, we can see why many varied theorists have found something attractive in it. Indeed, insisting that job placement be meritocratic under conditions of fair equality of opportunity leads to serious criticism of existing institutions. But these shared principles always operate against a background determined by the reward schedule. And in our society, the reward schedule is rarely itself the target of challenge by meritocrats. But, meritocracy

becomes controversial when we begin to see the consequences of meritocratic job placement operating in a context of certain reward schedules.

IS MERITOCRACY UNFAIR?

My concern here, which may disappoint some, is not to debate the
merits of different reward schedules in order to arrive at a comprehen-
sive theory of distributive justice. Rather, I want to concentrate on a
particular problem raised for certain reward schedules just because they
operate in conjunction with the Productivity Principle. The meritocracies I listed earlier offer three types of reward schedules. Type One
meritocracies (status quo, unbridled, desert [according to contribution],
nationalist, and utilitarian) allow for significant inequalities in rewards
with no constraints to protect those with the worst jobs. Type Two
meritocracies either allow no significant inequalities (egalitarian) or allow inequalities not based on the social functions of the jobs but rather
on the needs or other deserts of the job holder (socialist and some desert
meritocracies). Type Three meritocracies allow for inequalities but attempt to constrain them in ways that act to benefit those whose abilities
tend to lead to low reward jobs (maximin). Meritocracies of the first type
are open to a criticism that Type Two, and possibly Type Three, meritocracies avoid.

If a reward schedule allows significant inequalities of reward to be
associated with different jobs, as in Type One meritocracies, then the
fortuitous possession of certain natural abilities and traits may also make
one the beneficiary of significant social rewards as well. Rawls calls the
constellation of genetic and environmental contingencies that determine
one's natural abilities and character traits a "natural lottery." Type One,
unlike Type Two, meritocracies, reward a desirable payoff in the natural
lottery with a second payoff. Many find such a double payoff intuitively
unfair. Just as it seems unfair to many that social accidents of birth—
being born rich—lead to multiple payoffs, so too it seems unfair that
natural accidents of birth and upbringing can lead to such important
social consequences.

The basis for the intuition about unfairness is that the operation of
the natural lottery is morally arbitrary. The basis for selecting an assignment of natural assets, such as natural abilities, talents, and personality
traits, to one person rather than another has nothing to do with any
conceivable basis for desert. Rather, it is rooted in biological and psychological contingencies. The core idea seems to be that the person *did*
nothing to deserve or earn his natural assets. But is this idea accurate?
Are our job-related abilities and talents never assets we did anything to
deserve? Robert Nozick argues that people do choose to develop some
of their natural assets as opposed to others. Moreover, if this choice results in the possession of more valuable assets, then some desert claim
to those assets derives from the act of choice.[12] This objection has force
to it: we do not want to view the final product of all development of our

abilities and personality traits as completely determined by causal chains we have no responsibility for.

I think Nozick's objection can be circumvented provided we make certain, perhaps overly strong, empirical assumptions. We might reply to Nozick that, although we deserve some credit for some actions that develop our natural assets, nevertheless we are still only developing potentialities constrained by the natural lottery. Whatever credit we deserve is only a thin overlay on a substantial base of arbitrary lottery results. Even our range of choice is limited by the lottery. I cannot effectively choose to develop natural assets I do not have. To the extent, then, that our marketable assets are significantly determined, even if not completely determined, by the natural lottery, they are not assets we have in any way earned or which we deserve. Notice, however, that this reply to Nozick on behalf of Rawls itself depends on an important and powerful empirical assumption, one which Nozick's objection also does not challenge. It assumes that our developed assets *are* in general largely determined by causal sequences that are rooted in biological and psychological causes beyond the individual's control. Just how much truth there is to this assumption cannot be determined here.

Part of the problem here comes from the fact that the same people who view the natural lottery as a morally arbitrary basis for the distribution of some social goods, like rewards, nevertheless still treat it as an acceptable basis for distributing other social goods, the jobs themselves. All the meritocrats I have been considering are committed to the view that job placement, though it depends on a morally arbitrary distribution of natural assets, is nevertheless morally acceptable. Rawls, for example, most vigorously pursues the charge that the distribution of natural assets is morally arbitrary and should not determine the distribution of other social rewards. Yet I believe his principles of justice are meritocratic. He explicitly shares with my other meritocrats provisions for fair equality of opportunity. And he implicitly shares with them the view that abilities which determine job performance should be the basis for placing people in jobs even though the distribution of these abilities is, at least significantly, dependent on the natural lottery. Let us take a closer look at Rawls' argument.

In Sections 12, 13 and 17 of *A Theory of Justice* Rawls offers an *intuitive* argument in favor of a preferred interpretation for the principle of justice that says inequalities should work to "everyone's advantage" and that offices should be "open to all." He argues that "open to all" should be defined by a principle of fair, not just formal, equality of opportunity. Fair, but not formal, equality of opportunity requires that basic institutions are arranged to compensate for inequities of social position. Such social contingencies, Rawls insists, are morally arbitrary and should not determine further distributions of social goods. But even if we modify a free market distributional system—presumably a model of the principle of efficiency—by incorporating fair equality of opportunity, and even if the resulting system works to perfection in eliminating the influence of social contingencies, it still permits the distribution of wealth and income to be determined by the natural distribution of abilities and talents. Within the limits allowed by the background arrangements, distributive shares are decided by the outcome of the natural lottery and this outcome is arbitrary from a moral perspective. There is no more reason to permit the distribution of income and wealth to be settled by the distribution of natural assets than by historical and social fortune.[13]

Accordingly, in order to avoid the moral arbitrariness present in a system in which "to everyone's advantage" is defined by the principle of efficiency, we should instead interpret "to everyone's advantage" as determined by the difference principle. The difference principle specifies that differences or inequalities in social goods are allowable only if they act to maximize the interests of the worst-off members of society.

It might seem tempting to infer, from the sequence of points in Rawls' intuitive argument, that the move from the principle of efficiency to the difference principle will avoid or *nullify* the moral arbitrariness involved in the natural lottery. But such an inference is clearly too strong. The natural lottery still determines, under conditions of fair opportunity, access to jobs. Though it is not explicit in Rawls, I believe he is committed to something like my Productivity Principle of efficient job placement. But since the difference principle is compatible with significant inequalities attaching to jobs,[14] the natural lottery will still play a role in determining access to a double payoff—or a double loss for natural losers—however much it is constrained by the interests of the worst off.

A better way to construe Rawls' argument is that the difference principle ameliorates or *moderates* as much as possible the effects of allowing morally arbitrary differences among people to determine access to other social rewards. Because the meritocratic principles still operate in a context of inequalities of reward, Rawls does not avoid tainting his system with the same kind of moral arbitrariness he found under the principle of efficiency. But there is less of a taint:

> The difference principle represents, in effect, an agreement to regard the distribution of natural talents as a common asset and to share in the benefits of this distribution whatever it turns out to be. Those who have been favored by nature, whoever they are, may gain from their good fortune only on terms that improve the situation of those who have lost out. . . . No one deserves his greater natural capacity nor merits a more favorable starting place in society. But it does not follow that one should eliminate these distinctions. There is another way to deal with them. The basic structure can be arranged so that these contingencies work for the good of the least fortunate.[15]

So Rawls' intuitive argument for the difference principle is based centrally on the contention that moral arbitrariness in the distribution of social goods should be reduced to an acceptable minimum. This intuitive argument, it should be noted,[16] is not an argument usable in the original position itself, where appeal to prior moral intuitions is ruled out.

Must We Avoid Morally Arbitrary Distributions?

Rawls' argument from the need to minimize moral arbitrariness in distributions to the selection of the difference principle over the principle of efficiency is not without challenge. Nozick, in Chapter 7 of *Anarchy, State and Utopia*, is very much interested in showing that there is no such obligation to avoid distributions of social goods that are in any significant way determined by the operation of the natural lottery. He wants to show that we are under no general moral obligation to *nullify* the effects of the natural lottery because an entitlement system like this, using a free market as a distribution mechanism, might well result over time in distributions of holdings causally influenced by the distribution of natural assets. It is not that Nozick wants to establish a distributional principle, "distribute according to the results of the lottery" or "distribute according to merit." He does not. Rather he wants to rebut the presumption he thinks is present in Rawls that we must nullify the effects of the lottery.

Unfortunately, I think Nozick's strategy to rebut the argument from moral arbitrariness cannot establish what he wants. His strategy seems to be to argue that there is no good argument Rawls has which both (a) shows that *nullification* of moral arbitrariness is desirable, and which (b) leaves Rawls' own principles of justice free of moral arbitrariness. But Nozick's argument turns completely on asserting that Rawls is committed to *nullifying* completely the effects of the lottery, not just to *moderating* its effects. If Rawls were committed (1) to eliminating all effects of the natural lottery, *and* (2) to allowing significant inequalities in reward, *and* (3) to meritocratic job placement, then he would be in the bind Nozick describes. But, as we have seen, Rawls is only committed to reducing as much as he can the effects of the morally arbitrary lottery. If Rawls is right that the difference principle accomplishes this moderation, then Nozick has not undercut Rawls' argument.[17]

Despite Nozick's objections, then, I think we are led to the view that it is morally desirable either to moderate or to nullify the effects of the natural lottery by not allowing them to be used as the basis for distributing other significant social rewards, even if they may be used as a basis for distributing jobs. Of course, accepting this conclusion depends on accepting the strong empirical assumptions I isolated earlier. Nevertheless, Type One meritocracies, those with reward schedules that allow significant inequalities unconstrained by a concern to redress inequalities in the natural lottery, are open to the objection that they ramify moral arbitrariness. Type Two, and if Rawls is right, Type Three meritocracies may avoid this special objection.

I think the merit of my earlier schema is now better revealed. It allows us to see that the type of merit claim I allowed to be derived from productivity considerations need not commit one to the charge of moral arbitrariness many have felt endemic to meritocracies. The price for avoiding the charge, however, is to insist on egalitarian—or fairly egalitarian—reward schedules. Unfortunately, most proponents of meritocracy have often hidden their infatuation for highly inegalitarian reward schedules behind their praise of meritocratic job placement, blurring the distinction I have insisted on between principles governing job placement and principles governing reward. The meritocrat who advocates meritocratic job placement as just reform may only be replacing one unjust arrangement with another if he fails to worry about the interaction of job placement and reward principles.

Notes

1. Cf. Michael Young, *Rise of the Meritocracy* (London: Thames and Hudson, 1958). I am not concerned with certain classical meritocracies, that is, with certain views of aristocracy according to which social class was thought to be constitutive of differences in merit and positions were conferred accordingly. Perhaps such meritocracies are just as much concerned with "productivity" as are modern meritocracies, only their social goals differ significantly.

2. Some meritocrats assume (cf. Richard Herrnstein, *IQ in the Meritocracy* [Boston: Atlantic, Little Brown, 1973]) that there is some one scale of capacity differences, usually taken to be IQ, which suffices to rank-order people for job eligibility across the whole spectrum of jobs. I do not think such a uniquely hierarchical view is presupposed by the meritocratic core principles I describe. For critical discussion of IQ as a basis for such a scale, see my "IQ, Heritability, and Human Nature," Proceedings PSA 1974 in *Boston Studies in the Philosophy of Science* XXXII (Dordrecht: Reidel, 1976), pp. 143-180; see also J. Cronin, N. Daniels et al., "Race, Class & Intelligence," *International Journal of Mental Health*, Vol. 3, No. 4 (1975), pp. 46-132; see also N. J. Block and G. Dworkin, *The IQ Controversy* (New York: Pantheon, 1976), and S. Bowles and H. Gintis, *Schooling in Capitalist America* (New York: Basic, 1976).

3. Strictly speaking, we do not know there is only one array that is most productive. Instead, we should assume there are a number of equally "most productive" arrays (technically, an "equivalence class" of maximally productive arrays). The Productivity Principle tells us to select any one from among those "most productive" arrays, though for the sake of simplicity of expression, I ignore this complication in the text.

4. John Troyer urged me to consider the implications of this case.

5. Yet another alternative, which I am not concerned to refute here, is that personal traits or achievements other than those related to job competency should be the basis for desert or merit claims for job placement.

6. One possibility is the view that such desert claims derive from a purported "right to self-fulfillment": Jill has a right to be maximally self-fulfilled and exercising her best abilities in a suitable job is necessary for such self-fulfillment. It is worth noting, however, the lack of any uniform connection between a person's sense of fulfillment and the exercise of his best abilities. I may be more fulfilled not doing what I am best at, even more fulfilled than someone better at doing the same job. Further discussion of self-fulfillment, or other ways of trying to rescue and found a stronger notion of desert, would take me too far afield.

7. My argument above does not take into account the role of expectations in actual situations. One could argue (cf. Alan Goldman, "Affirmative Action," *Philoso-*

phy and Public Affairs, Vol. 5, No. 2 [Winter, 1976], p. 191) that people who claim a right to a given job on the basis of their better qualifications are doing so because they have been led to form specific expectations about how society distributes social goods, like desirable positions. When institutions standardly lead to certain expectations, and indeed are expected to lead people to form them, and then society "changes the rules of the game," then some sort of compact or contract may be violated. But such an argument from expectations can become woefully conservative if it turns out that the principles governing those institutions and the expectations they generate are not acceptable principles of justice.

Two further objections are worth noting. First, suppose that Rawlsian contractors would agree (as I think they implicitly do) to adopt meritocratic job placement principles and would do so on the basis of productivity considerations. Then the productivity principle would give rise to entitlements even though it is based on such considerations. I have no quarrel with this objection provided the contractors lexically order the Productivity Principle *below* appropriate compensatory and retributive principles that may specify more important entitlement claims to jobs. Second, it might be argued that certain recipients of services or products, say students or patients, have a right to the highest quality service or product possible. This right might then correlate with a social duty to give the job to the most competent applicant. This duty then gives rise to entitlement claims by the most competent. If such an objection can be supported by a sound argument, it might well force important qualification of the Productivity Principle, perhaps even driving us to use the micro-principle instead.

8. John Rawls, *A Theory of Justice,* Harvard, 1971, p. 84.

9. Thomas Nagel makes a related point when he says,

> Certain abilities may be relevant to filling a job from the point of view of efficiency, but not from the point of view of justice, because they provide no indication that one deserves the rewards that go with holding that job. The qualities, experience, and attainments that make success in a certain position likely do not in themselves merit the rewards that happen to attach to occupancy of that position in a competitive economy.

Cf. "Equal Treatment and Compensatory Discrimination," *Philosophy and Public Affairs,* Vol. 2 No. 4 (Summer 1973), p. 352.

10. See note 2.

11. Three further objections might be raised here. John Troyer has suggested the first one: Why would someone who rejects productivity considerations in his reward schedule, adopting instead a strong desert-based reward schedule, subscribe to the Productivity Principle? The answer is, I think, that people might consistently want to know that their rewards will be based on, say, moral worthiness or industriousness and still believe that access to jobs should be determined by merit, as earlier defined, because it is important to secure proper job performance. A second objection is that not all the principles of reward I have described can be readily construed as governing a society's basic institutions or structure, as Rawls would have it. This objection has weight to it, but how much depends on how clear the notion of "basic structure" is. For worries about the clarity of the notion of structure, see Hugo Adam Bedau's "Social Justice and Social Institutions," Midwest Studies in Philosophy, Vol. III, Feb. 1978.

Finally, my analysis of meritocracy seems to allow too many types of theories in under that name. For example, Rawls explicitly argues that his Second Principle does not lead to a Young-type meritocracy because natural abilities are viewed as social, not just individual assets, and inequalities act to help the worst-off members of the society. But my saddling Rawls with the label "meritocrat" does not, on my schema, imply he is committed to any of the undesirable features of the meritocracy he attacked. At the same time, the label captures the fact that he shares with other meritocrats certain common principles.

12. R. Nozick, *Anarchy, State and Utopia* (New York: Basic, 1974), p. 214.

13. Rawls, *Theory,* pp. 73-74.

14. Rawls argues, however, that under conditions of fair equality of opportunity there will be a "tendency to equality" since talents will be more plentiful. Therefore, people will not be able to demand high levels of "incentives" (high transfer income and economic rent) before they would take certain jobs. Cf. Section 18.

15. Rawls, *Theory*, pp. 101-102.

16. Robert Nozick discusses this point in *Anarchy, State and Utopia*, p. 215.

17. Nozick reconstructs four possible arguments Rawls might have intended. Argument (C) is the one closest to what Rawls might have meant. But Rawls would agree only to a weaker premise (1) than the one Nozick attributes to him. Nozick's argument (G), couched in terms of entitlements rather than deserts, also fails to counter Rawls since its crucial premises (2) and (3) beg the question about whether we are entitled to whatever "flows from" our natural assets.

liberty and the market

The Market refers to the exchange of products, to the buying and selling of goods, between individual persons or enterprises. The market is the spiritual center of any laissez-faire economic system, since there is no overall social planning. Where the market is free, individual initiative and decision shape the content of production and the distribution of economic goods. Commerce is unregulated, and individuals exchange as they please without any government assistance or restriction. Libertarians, as we have seen, defend the pure capitalism of the laissez-faire model as an answer to the problem of distributive justice. This contention is the focus of the contributors to this section.

Defenders of the free market from Adam Smith to Milton Friedman have always pointed to the productive efficiency of capitalism. Not only does it have record accomplishments to its credit, they argue, but if it were really given full rein—if the market were truly unfettered by government restrictions —then its productive fruits would be even more bountiful. True, wealth is not distributed equally, but to a large extent this only reflects individual differences in taste, ambition, and perseverance. Moreover, not only do free-market initiative and enterprise produce abundance, but wealth will spread to all: profits are available to encourage the wealthy to invest in enterprises that are efficient and productive, thus benefiting the less well-off. Leaving the economic realm to the free choices of individuals provides incentive to innovation, development, and (thus) progress while still protecting liberty. All people are free to work on what or for whom they wish. Free enterprise also serves more responsively and flexibly the demands of consumers than can any rival system. Customers get what they want, and this economic democracy is matched by the general freedom promoted by a laissez-faire system.

The economic systems in the United States and other Western countries, as the defenders of laissez faire are first to point out, are a far cry from this free market ideal. The government actively intervenes in the marketplace: a minimum wage is set, individuals and companies are taxed, the interest rate is decreed, union monopolies are supported, profits are monitored, and corporate activities from hiring to marketing are policed and regulated. By a variety of economic devices like tax policy, the state attempts to direct economic growth, as well as to set its pace. Such efforts may be motivated in part by the political philosophy of contemporary liberalism, which has as an ideal the ensuring of the material well-being of the citizenry. But more importantly, government interference in the market results from a critique of laissez-faire economic theory, which in the last few decades has fallen from orthodoxy.

Critics of laissez faire make a variety of points, of which the following are among the more basic:

(1) The free market model is totally unrealistic. Consumers, far from being the rational satisfaction-maximizers required by the free market theory, display all sorts of economically irrational behavior (a tendency which, for example, advertising makes worse). Furthermore, the market system is not truly competitive; important industries and resources are fully or partially monopolized. This monopolization itself, left-wing critics add, naturally and inevitably develops in any capitalist system.

(2) The market mechanism cannot provide certain goods which are in everyone's interest—a decent urban environment, pollution-free air, public transportation, parks—goods which lack an attractive profit angle. And the goods which it does provide—think of television shows—tend toward mediocrity, since competition and the advantages of producing for the largest market possible encourage firms to cater to the common denominator of the population. The only culture is that of mass production.

(3) Finally, economists since John Maynard Keynes have argued that the laissez-faire market is not necessarily so efficient. Equilibrium in a free-market system, can, in fact, be reached at a less than optimal utilization of resources—at, for example, a high rate of unemployment. Consequently, the market cannot be relied upon to eliminate poverty. Government intervention is necessary to accomplish this and to smooth out the normally cyclical (boom-bust) functioning of the system.

While left-wing critics are skeptical of the government's (as well as the market's) ability to solve these and other problems of a capitalist economic system, defenders of laissez faire answer all these charges with a barrage of counterclaims. They deny that monopolies can grow out of the free market, that lack of restrictions promotes poverty, and that government interference can improve the operation of the system. We have, then, a welter of empirical issues about which there is widespread disagreement. Because of this factual controversy, a utilitarian would find it hard to advocate confidently a totally free market system as promoting the greatest total of happiness.

As a result, the strongest case for an unregulated market comes today from libertarians who defend it as a matter of principle, not necessarily as the most efficient vehicle for human happiness. Thus, Eric Mack argues in "Liberty and Justice" that market institutions must play a central role in any society in which one's Lockean rights—one's rights to be free from the interference of others—are taken seriously, and he rebuts the objection that libertarians enshrine liberty in the market, only to let it be thwarted in other ways by those very institutions. Only market-type associations and arrangements (whether they exist for strictly economic purposes or not) respect fully, he maintains, the choices of each individual. The free market successfully preserves liberty, and the requirements of justice are met when goods are distributed in accord with the uncoerced choices of individuals.

This priority on liberty in the negative sense of freedom from the coercion of others is challenged by Hugh LaFollette in "Why Libertarianism is Mistaken." One must, he asserts, be careful not to confuse two senses of "liberty": descriptive and normative (what I am free to do literally or physically and what I am free to do morally). Now libertarians themselves place substantial moral limits on my liberty to do as I please, since, for example, I am not free to invade the domain of another. But why, asks LaFollette, should my freedom be limited in just these ways and not others? Why should one suppose there are only rights of noninterference and not general positive rights and duties as well? The need to protect liberty, argues LaFollette, cannot justify libertarianism; nor can the theory be satisfactorily grounded on some other basis.

Likewise, Peter Singer argues in "Rights and the Market" that libertarians hold too narrow a conception of rights: there are positive rights to recipience as well as the negative rights to noninterference favored by libertarians. Singer's main argument, however, contends that the market is not a neutral operator. Its very existence in some cases can restrict the options available to individuals and even violate their rights. A comparison of systems of blood distribution illustrates this. Further examples are adduced to show that what may be economically rational from the point of view of an individual in the market can be irrational from a collective point of view. Unlike libertarianism, concludes Singer, any plausible moral theory must allow for social and economic planning.

ERIC MACK

Tulane University

Liberty and Justice

My thesis in this essay is that a coherent and attractive program for decentralization and participation on the one hand and for justice on the other hand can be found in the implementation of what I will call, alternatively, a Lockean or libertarian theory of rights. Since the central value expressed in such a theory of rights is respect for the liberty of persons, I shall be arguing that respect for liberty carries with it decentralization, participation, and justice. The emphasis in the first section on decentralization and participation serves to highlight the central role of free market institutions and transactions in any likely society in which persons' Lockean rights are respected. In such a society political institutions and practices will be replaced by forms of voluntary association. And market transactions and relationships are paradigmatically voluntary. Although I would argue that full implementation of persons' rights would require that the State itself be abolished, for present purposes we can image the State as continuing on the scene in nightwatchman form. That is, we shall image a State which is successfully restricted to protecting the Lockean rights of individuals.[1] In the following section, I defend the conception of liberty (and the conception of coercion) that has been employed in this essay and show the congruence between respect for liberty and respect for just holdings. In this section the value of liberty, specifically the wrongness of inflicting coercion upon people, is shown to underlie the entitlement conception of just holdings.

LOCKEAN RIGHTS AND MARKET RELATIONSHIPS

According to the Lockean or libertarian view of rights, each person possesses a natural moral right to life and liberty—i.e., a moral right to freedom from coercion of his person or of his activity. Each person possesses these rights against all other men and correlatively each person is under a natural moral obligation not to coerce any other person. Furthermore, persons may acquire property rights to various external objects—to fields, tools, and so on—by laboring upon or producing them or by acquiring them by voluntary transfer from parties who (until the transfer) respectively had rights to them. Whatever the philosophical difficulties connected with clarifying and defending these Lockean claims, their general import is clear enough. As Locke puts it, each man is by nature "absolute lord of his own person and possessions" (Second Treatise, para. 125).

We can imagine what could be called a premarket Lockean society. Trade and contractual rights and obligations do not exist. Each (surviving) person is propertied and self-sufficient. Here we have the epitome of economic and social decentralization. Each exercises his lordship over his own domain and does just as he sees fit with it, coordinating his actions with those of others only in the negative sense of not interfering with their comparable lordship. To enjoy liberty is not to enjoy everything or even everything worth enjoying. Rather, to enjoy liberty is to stand in a certain relationship to other persons. It is to be free of disruptions caused by other persons in the ongoing activities which constitute one's life.[2]

Although no one is obligated to do so, it is tremendously in persons' interests to move away from the type of social and economic isolation that would characterize a premarket society. Typically, there are many things within a person's domain—e.g., his labor or some of the products he has produced—which he would be eager to exchange for things within the domain of another who is himself eager for such an exchange. Most such exchanges lead to the possibility and desirability of additional exchanges. Similarly persons may agree, not so much to exchanges, but to engage in various joint activities, partying, church-going, etc. Voluntary agreements or permissions lower or relocate the initial fences between persons and do so on terms which are preferred over the status quo by all the parties involved. It would be tedious to list all the ways in which businesses, unions, fraternal societies, charitable organizations, and so on, might appear within the vast, multilayered web of associations which free agreement among individuals would produce—at least when individuals are secure in their domains and secure in their expectations that the rights generated by agreement, both simple and complex, will be respected.

Of course, two societies which were equally the product of such a complex of agreements and voluntary coordinations might be quite different—the differences being traceable to variations in culture and aesthetics, in technological levels and natural resources, and in the reflections of these and other factors in personal and individual preferences. But a central feature of any such contractual society would be the production of goods and services "for the market"—i.e., the production by firms, cooperatives, individuals or whatever of goods and services for the purpose of sale to other parties. Wanting what they can get in exchange for goods and services, producers will tend to provide those goods and services for which the demand is strongest and will tend to utilize in their production those resources which are least in demand. Hence the tendency toward efficiency in production for the market. Although the market will be central to all societies in which persons' Lockean rights are respected and persons do not live as self-supporting hermits, we should not think that all the associations and coordinations among individuals in such a society will be, in an interesting sense, economic.

With respect to decentralization, the Lockean market society seems to capture whatever is desirable about premarket decentralization, while including other dimensions of decentralization. Each individual remains free to maintain a premarket isolation, no matter how discomforting this is to him or how annoying it is to those who would have him engage in various social roles. Of course, it would be a rare person who, without having previously entered social relations, would have the skills and resources available for a commodious, isolated life. But what remains crucial is that no one is ever *coerced* into cooperation with others and each person retains throughout his life (complexities arising from long-term contractual relationships aside) the freedom to separate himself from the doings of others, i.e., a freedom to secede from some particular or all associations. All decisions about any single person's life and property are centered in that given person. Similarly, whenever a decision is made about the disposition of the lives, activities, or properties of more than one party—a decision about an exchange or some coordinated activity—the decision is centered in just those individuals whose persons or property are involved. Nobody whose life or property is not involved has any say whatsoever. Thus, decision-making is radically decentralized, not by any political decree, but rather by respecting the moral injunction: Do not cross the boundaries defined by persons' rights. Given the Lockean conception of rights, this injunction rules out participation in the sense of having a say in the doings of society at large.

Adherence to Lockean principles does not merely decentralize in the sense of limiting the number of parties involved in a given decision. It fosters genuine participation by requiring unanimity among all the parties to a given decision and, a fortiori, by requiring adjustments to each party's voiced or anticipated preferences which are sufficient to achieve this unanimity.[3] That the agreement of each must be obtained requires that each participate in the decision in the sense that the final terms must be adjusted to his desires at least to the extent that he prefers an exchange at those terms to the status quo. When joint activities of any sort occur in accordance with Lockean principles, each party involved must coordinate his activities and demands to those of the other parties involved. One's participation consists in making known and in having others accommodate themselves to one's own goals and desires in this way. For any party involved in any actual free exchange, the value of the accommodations made to him must outweigh, in his eyes, the disvalue of the accommodations he makes to others.

One must add, of course, that in an articulated market economy announced prices represent anticipated terms of accommodation. A seller would like more, a buyer would like to pay less. A price announced by a seller represents what he thinks he can get, given what the seller is willing to settle for. Like prices, various social norms, roles, conventions, and traditions represent anticipated terms of accommodation. And like prices, they are continually open to conscious or nonconscious re-negotiation or realignment as long as persons remain free to refuse agreement to those terms. If all of a person's exchanges and associations are based on mutual assent, as they are in free-market exchanges and asso-ciations, then that person enjoys liberty: His participation in any ex-change or association is based upon his evaluation of the congruence of that exchange or association with his purposes. Goals which are his, or which he makes his, guide his actions rather than his activity's being subordinated to the purposes of others.

The participation which characterizes freely entered joint activities should be contrasted with what passes for participation in political (e.g., majority rule) policy decisions. Imagine that a decision has to be reached about whether to use fundamentalist or progressive textbooks in public schools. Each side must seek, through getting out a majority referendum vote or through capturing the local school board, etc., to enforce its preference upon the other side. There is no strong reason for the more powerful side to accommodate itself to the other side (though the power-ful side may itself be a coalition built on certain accommodations among its members). The more powerful will be able to enforce its preference on all at no greater cost (except those, if any, arising from resentment) to itself than if it merely satisfied its own preference. For the losing side must continue to pay its taxes and support the programs which are being forced upon it. A real political coup would consist in one side's arranging to get its preference enforced and financed by some tax which happened to fall selectively on members of the other side. The losing side has, of course, no right to secede; and any putative participation it has in the decision is a sham. Only if each side is uncertain of victory will there be any accommodation. The best accommodation, i.e., decen-tralization—with people free to choose between fundamentalist and pro-gressive classrooms and competition between orientations for students—involves depoliticalization and the appearance of a protomarket. But as long as there is a single authoritative voice (the school board, the vote in a referendum, etc.) whose decision is the decision for all, any truce will be uneasy. For the mechanism whereby one group can insure the satisfaction of its preferences, but only by defeating the preferences of the other group, will still exist and stand as a threat to those who do not control and use it. This example nicely illustrates how the existence of political institutions can generate a Hobbesian war of all against all.

In trying to outline the sort of decentralization and participation which would exist for those persons whose intercourse was in accord with Lockean principles, I have so restricted my focus that it might be charged that I have dangerously ignored the general socioeconomic patterns which allegiance to these principles would release and, a fortiori, have ignored the centralizing and antiparticipatory features of these patterns. For example, many people believe the natural course of economic affairs under laissez faire to be toward greater and greater concentration (centralization) and oligarchy and toward the (relative, at least) impoverishment of large groups of individuals. If this complex of common claims and predictions about impoverishment and concentration were correct, then the type of decentralization, participation, and liberty I have outlined would have little attraction. For many people would have little domain over which to exercise their lordship. There would be few alternatives regarding those with whom these individuals could genuinely participate in interparty economic arrangements. And, although persons would enjoy liberty, there would be reasonable doubts about the worth of this liberty. But this conventional view is incorrect. Indeed, the removal of all restraints upon peaceful economic activity is the best formula for avoiding economic oligarchy and economic exploitation. But neither the case against the conventional view nor the case for this unconventional empirical-historical view can be made here.[4]

NEGATIVE LIBERTY AND ENTITLEMENT

A good deal of resistance to the thesis presented previously will stem from dissatisfaction with the conception of coercion and the correlative conception of (negative) liberty which I employ. There are also likely to be doubts about making the demand that coercion be eschewed, or, correlatively, that liberty be respected, the supreme social-political principle. In response to these dissatisfactions and doubts, I present, in a very abbreviated fashion, a two-stage argument. First I provide a more precise specification of coercion which shows that the acts which are impermissible turn out to be coercive (violations of liberty) and the acts which have been deemed permissible turn out to be noncoercive (nonviolations of liberty). Second, I argue that the demand for noncoercion as specified, i.e., respect for liberty, should be accepted as the supreme social principle.

Characteristic of dissatisfaction with the conceptions of coercion and liberty which I use is this argument offered by James Sterba. Comparing Social Security taxation of persons with cases of hiring for low wages, he writes:

> . . . how can requiring a person to pay $500.00 into a social security program under threat of greater financial loss infringe upon the person's liberty when requiring a person to take a job paying $500.00 less under

threat of greater financial loss does not infringe upon the person's liberty? Surely it would seem that if one requirement restricts a person's liberty, the other will also.[5]

The implications of such arguments are that liberty can be denied in more ways than are recognized by the libertarian and that it may be necessary and proper, even in the name of liberty itself, to limit the liberties held dear by libertarians in order to thwart the denial of liberties not recognized by them.

There is both a short and a long answer to Sterba's argument. The short answer is that in the first case what is threatened is the deprivation of something to which the threatened party has a right, while in the second case what is "threatened" (by whom?) is that no employer is around who will offer more of his money to the job-seeker than is currently being offered. This is why the Social Security case involves treating a person objectionably while the job-seeker case does not. But this short answer does not differentiate between the case in terms of liberty (or coercion). To get an answer in terms of coercion one must argue that to be deprived of, or to be threatened with the nonconsensual deprivation of, justly held possessions (the Social Security case) is to be coerced, is to suffer a violation of liberty, while not to be offered what are some other party's justly held possessions is not to be coerced, is not to suffer a violation of liberty. That is, one deepens the (short) property rights answer into an answer in terms of coercion (or liberty) by showing that person A can be so related to an object that to deprive him of it without his consent is to coerce him and that it is in virtue of being so related to an object that A is entitled to (has a right to) it. Hence, if A is entitled to an object, then his being nonconsensually deprived of it is coercive. This deepening of the property rights answer into the answer in terms of coercion will also show why the demand for noncoercion encompasses the demand that persons' just holdings (their entitlements) be respected.

In very brief form the argument runs as follows: The just acquisition of object O by person A involves an intentional investment by A of his time and effort which results in O's becoming an instrument of A's (ongoing though, perhaps, intermittent) purposes. Since coercion involves nonconsensual interference with/into an agent's purposeful activity, an agent's being nonconsensually deprived of what he has justly acquired is coercive. In contrast, failure to provide someone with some object, service, etc., does not involve such interference with/into his activity with that (possible) instrument of activity. It is one thing not to provide another with the means for certain activities and quite another thing to intervene into his (ongoing) activity. If A justly holds O, B can acquire O noncoercively only with A's consent. Otherwise B will acquire O by nonconsensually depriving another party (A) of what is already an instrument of that party's (ongoing) purposes. On this sort of basis I claim that failure to provide a person with some object never is coercive, never is a violation of liberty,[6] while depriving a person of what he has acquired as an instrument of his purposes (without depriving another of an acquired instrument of his purposes) is always coercive, is always a violation of liberty.

In Sterba's Social Security case a person is genuinely threatened with a coercive act, i.e., with an intervention into his purposeful activity or with a nonconsensual deprivation of something which he has (noncoercively) made an instrument of his purposeful activity. But in Sterba's job-seeker case no comparable intervention or disruption is "threatened." It is not as though the job-seeker has had an offer of a better-paying job his acceptance of which has been disrupted or blocked. The job-seeker's complaint is not that he has suffered some intervention but rather that he has not been offered a certain opportunity by, say, some employer.

The person who is required to participate in Social Security is coerced because he is threatened with a coercive act. That is, he is threatened with interference into his ongoing purposeful activity either in the form of an imposed loss in his capacity to move his body as and where he sees fit or an imposed loss in his capacity to utilize some other object which is an instrument of his purposes. We can say that he is threatened with being deprived of something to which he has a right (something to which he is morally entitled) because he is being threatened with a deprivation which would be coercive. It is the coerciveness of a person's loss of (capacity to use) an object which makes it wrongful for another to impose that loss. And it is because others are obligated not to impose that loss that the person who would suffer the coercive loss has a right to the object involved. An agent's right to any object rests on his being so related to it that nonconsensually depriving him of it constitutes coercion. Hence, it is the demand for noncoercion, for each person's liberty being respected, which underlies each person's moral titles (including each person's moral title to his own body, which can be seen as necessarily an instrument of his purposes). Insofar as justice is the condition of persons' possessing that to which they respectively are entitled, the call for liberty is also a call for justice.

On the entitlement view, each person is entitled to what he intentionally acquires from nature and from others in voluntary transfers or through voluntary mutual endeavors and which he has not abandoned or traded away. A person is entitled to whatever holdings result from economic activity in which he exercises his Lockean rights and violates no one's Lockean rights. If the holdings of each member of some group are the result of such a rights-respecting process, then the distribution of holdings within the group is just. If members of this group were to have engaged in different rights-respecting economic moves, e.g., different voluntary exchanges or different use of their resources, a different distribution of holdings would have been produced. And had that distribution, in fact, been produced by rights-respecting procedures, then it would have been just.[7] For, what distribution is just depends upon how persons, individually and cooperatively, have exercised their respective rights. But a just distribution can only arise when people are left free to exercise these rights. So the strategy for producing distributive justice must be the procedural strategy of leaving people free to engage in (any) rights-respecting economic activities. Although economically free persons might choose to be economic hermits (i.e., to remain in pre-market Lockean relationships) or might agree to economic communalism, it is likely that most individuals and communes will not choose to be communally related to others. Rather, they will opt for instances of economic interaction and association which will generate a complex market-centered society. Thus, the very social system which recommends itself to us in terms of decentralization and participation and in terms of liberty recommends itself to us in terms of justice.

This program of liberty and justice turns on the view that the only rights which individuals possess against one another—other than the special rights that are traceable to specific, concrete, and noncoerced agreements—are rights against interference. However, it is often asserted, e.g., in Peter Singer's "Rights and the Market," that in some way this conception of rights faultily ignores the fact that we are "social beings." [8] If we were but to attend to this fact a different moral perspective would be forthcoming. Now, if we take the claim that we are social beings as indicative of some sort of radical organicism, then it is clear that such a different moral perspective is called for. We are each really just parts of a greater, living, striving whole whose well-being is the morally relevant issue. And so on. But, short of this sort of organicism, what is the relevance, faultily missed by the libertarian, of the fact that we live in communities (some politically better than others), that we interact along all sorts of dimensions, that we often see ourselves through the eyes of others, or whatever? After all, the libertarian theorist himself focuses upon the manifold interactions among persons for the purpose of answering the normative question, Which are permissible and which are impermissible? As do competing theorists, he focuses upon all the claimed or recognized rights and obligations and offers a theory about which of them are well-founded.

The vagueness of the "social beings" gambit appears in Singer's own statement of its relevance.

> If we reject the idea of independent individuals and start with people living together in a community, it is by no means obvious that rights must be restricted to rights against interference. When people live together, they may be born into, grow up with, and live in, a web of rights and obligations which include obligations to help others in need, and rights to be helped oneself when in need.[9]

First, we might pause at the contrast between "independent individuals" and "people living together in a community." Second, we should note that one need not reject the idea of independent individuals and so on in order to realize that "it is by no means obvious that rights must be restricted to rights against interference." This libertarian thesis is not obvious—but that does not mean that it is false. Third, it indeed "may be" that when people live together there is a web of well-founded rights and obligations of a positive sort. Whether there is, of course, is a matter of philosophical debate. Furthermore, supposing that there are certain well-founded positive rights and obligations among individuals, the next question is, on what are they founded? For on the libertarian view such webs of rights and obligations among individuals do arise in the formation of voluntary social relationships. The challenge posed by libertarian theory to other theories is for them to indicate a plausible basis for positive rights and obligations other than (or in addition to) the contractual basis.[10] This challenge is not met by reminding us that people live together in communities.

But should liberty (and with it justice-as-entitlement) be accepted as the supreme social-political principle? In its demanding version this question requires nothing less than a full philosophical grounding for the natural right against coercion. It seems that such a grounding would focus on the need to recognize each person's status as a moral end-in-himself. It would see the obligation not to coerce as a moral side-constraint on our actions toward others which proceeds from the fact that all persons are morally on an equal footing as purposive beings whose lives have value, while there is no overarching value which can justify the subordination of one person's life or activity to the purposes of others. The general fact that for each person his life is a separate and ultimate value is recognized in human interaction by respect for liberty, i.e., by not subordinating anyone's life or any portion or aspect thereof to anyone else's ends.

In *Anarchy, State and Utopia*, Robert Nozick cites, as the notions and contentions that motivate the natural rights (against coercion) point of view, the "principle that individuals are ends and not merely means; they may not be sacrificed or used for the achieving of other ends without their consent," and the views that, "To use a person . . . does not sufficiently respect and take account of the fact that he is a separate person, that his is the only life he has," and "that there are different individuals with separate lives and so no one may be sacrificed for others. . . ."[11] And in characterizing the ideal of negative liberty, Isaiah Berlin says,

> To threaten a man with persecution unless he submits to a life in which he exercises no choices of his goals; to block before him every door but one, no matter how noble the prospect upon which it opens, or how benevolent the motives of those who arrange this, is *to sin against the truth that he is a man, a being with a life of his own to live.*[12]

But it cannot be the (mere) fact of the separateness of persons or the (mere) fact that each has only his own life that underlies persons' rights (i.e., the wrongfulness of coercing persons). For these facts might be seen as calling for a program of remaking and unifying all persons into one great social sponge. What underlies rights must, at least in part, be the value, desirability, or rightness of persons being separate beings, each having his own life and living it. One could only *sin* against a person's being a being with a life of his own to live if his having and living his own life is what ought to be.[13]

We should not forget that in choosing a supreme social-political principle we are choosing a principle which is to be backed by the police power of legal institutions. Awareness of the philosophical difficulty of establishing the existence of duties so fundamental that police power may properly be brought against individuals to further compliance should dispose us favorably to modest ascriptions of social-political duties. Similarly, a recognition of the disvalue of bringing police power to bear against individuals and of the disvalue of whatever contributes to a propensity to bring this power to bear should dispose us toward modest ascriptions of duty. It is, then, an attractive feature of the principle of negative liberty that it requires only that persons not coerce—that they leave their neighbors in peace. Justice-as-entitlement requires only that persons not deprive others of what they have noncoercively acquired. Yet, compliance with these modest requirements has the strong justice-like consequence that all parties to all exchanges and mutual endeavors benefit (at least in their own eyes). No one ever benefits by imposing a cost, in loss of freedom of movement or loss of legitimately acquired holdings, on anyone else. No one is ever required to suffer an invasion of his person, liberty, or property for the sake of that moment's version of vital social interests.

Finally, to endorse freedom from coercion (and, therefore, justice-as-entitlement) as the supreme social-political principle is not to forgo interest in the realization of other values. Rather, values such as efficiency, social and economic mobility, a relatively high correlation between deserts and rewards, and steady improvement in the general standard of living are among the values which libertarians see as *consequences* of liberty (and the justice involved in liberty). Indeed, no social goal (not to mention private goals) is precluded by the recognition of respect for negative liberty as the supreme principle. Persons remain free to pursue as ardently as they desire any social ideal whatsoever and are only constrained in the means which they may employ in these pursuits. Unlike alternative principles, the enshrinement of liberty does not impose upon any individual the goals of others. It merely envisions for each a respect for, and an immunity for, his own peaceful pursuits.

NOTES

1. For nineteenth century advocates of this view see: Herbert Spencer, *Social Statics* (London: Chapman, 1851), and Frederic Bastiat, *Essays in Political Economy* (New York: Putnam, 1877). For recent advocates see: John Hospers, *Libertarianism* (Los Angeles: Nash, 1971); T. R. Machan, *Human Rights and Human Liberties* (Chicago: Nelson-Hall, 1975); Ayn Rand, *Capitalism: The Unknown Ideal* (New York: New

American Library, 1966); and Robert Nozick, *Anarchy, State and Utopia* (New York: Basic Books, 1974).

Part I of Nozick's book attempts, unsuccessfully I think, to justify a Night-watchman state in the face of the moral objections against this coercive monopoly formulated by free market anarchists.

For the three most extensive recent expositions of market (non-State) generated systems of defense and law see: Morris and Linda Tannehill, *The Market for Liberty* (New York: Arno Press, 1972); Murray Rothbard, *For A New Liberty* (New York: MacMillan, 1973); and David Friedman, *The Machinery of Freedom* (New York: Harper and Row, 1973). For further discussion of the character of such a system see: Eric Mack, "Nozick's Anarchism," forthcoming in the NOMOS volume on anarchism.

2. Two recent valuable discussions of liberty are: William Parent, "Some Recent Work on the Concept of Liberty," *American Philosophical Quarterly* (July 1974), 149–167; and Hillel Steiner, "Individual Liberty," *Aristotelian Society Proceedings* (1974–1975), 33–50.

3. That unanimous consent is the only form of political decision that would be acceptable in the light of the worth of autonomy is a central point in R. P. Wolff's *In Defense of Anarchism* (New York: Harper & Row, 1970). Wolff recognizes, however, that unanimity in political decisions is impossible in practice. By depoliticizing decisions by turning each decision back to those specific parties whose domains are involved, satisfaction of the demand for unanimity becomes practical.

4. Against this conventional vision of laissez faire see (roughly from the theoretical to the historical): Murray Rothbard, *Man, Economy and State* (Los Angeles: Nash, 1970), Ch. 10; D. T. Armentano, *The Myths of Antitrust* (New Rochelle: Arlington House, 1972); John S. McGee, "Predatory Price Cutting: The Standard Oil (N.J.) Case," *The Journal of Law and Economics*, I (1958), 137–169; Gabriel Kolko, *Railroads and Regulation* (Princeton: Princeton University Press, 1965), and *The Triumph of Conservatism* (Chicago: Quadrangle Books, 1971); F. A. Hayek (ed.), *Capitalism and the Historians* (Chicago: University of Chicago Press, 1954).

5. James Sterba, "Neo-Libertarianism," read at a symposium on Libertarianism, American Philosophical Association Western Meeting, April 29, 1977, Chicago, Illinois. Part I of this paper is a descendant of part of a paper, "Decentralization, Participation and Individualist Anarchism," also read at that symposium at which the helpful commentators were David Luce and Edmund Pincoffs.

6. In some senses this claim is false with respect to the failures that violate *contractual* rights. In this paper I have been avoiding the complexities introduced by contractual rights and obligations. But for a discussion of these issues, see Eric Mack, "Natural and Contractual Rights," *Ethics* (January 1977), 153–159.

7. To avoid unprofitable complexity throughout this paper, I have omitted reference to rights-respecting acts of restitution, i.e., to acts which restore to persons what they have been coercively deprived of.

8. Peter Singer, "Rights and the Market" in this volume, pp. 207–221.

9. Singer, p. 210.

10. I would argue that (characteristically) parents have positive obligations to their children and that, rather than these being contractual, they are exemplifications of natural rights principles. But that is a complex side-issue.

11. Nozick, p. 30f.

12. Isaiah Berlin, *Four Essays on Liberty* (London: Oxford University Press, 1969), p. 127, emphasis added.

13. I have tried to develop this sort of argument elsewhere—most recently in "Egoism and Rights Revisited," *The Personalist* (July 1977), pp. 84–90.

HUGH LA FOLLETTE

East Tennessee State University

Why Libertarianism Is Mistaken

Taxing the income of some people to provide goods or services to others, even those with urgent needs, is unjust. It is a violation of the wage earner's rights, a restriction of his freedom. At least that is what the libertarian tells us. I disagree. Not all redistribution of income is unjust; or so I shall argue.

Libertarianism has experienced a noticeable re-emergence in the past few years. F. A. Hayek, Milton Friedman, and Robert Nozick have given new intellectual impetus to the movement [1] while a growing concern for personal autonomy has provided personal ground for the sowing of the idea. Yet even though this theory is prima facie plausible and demands serious reassessment of the concepts of liberty and property, it ultimately fails. Once we admit, as the libertarian does, that the state justifiably takes on certain functions, for example, police protection of persons and property, there is no rational basis for believing that the state is unjustified in redistributing tax revenue. We cannot stop, as the libertarian suggests, with the minimal state of classical liberal philosophy. I will not, in this paper, say exactly how far beyond the minimal state we should go. I only argue that libertarianism is not a moral option. On the surface this conclusion seems meager, yet its implications are far-reaching. By eliminating a previously plausible and popular conception of distributive justice, we will narrow the alternatives. By identifying a major flaw in libertarianism, we will secure direction in our search for an adequate theory.

After briefly describing libertarianism I will argue that the theory is guilty of internal incoherence: the theory falls prey to the very objection it offers against competing theories. Then I will consider four possible libertarian replies to my argument. Each, I will claim, fails to disarm my internal objection. After concluding my argument, I will speculate on the roles freedom and property should play in an adequate theory of distributive justice.

A Description of Libertarianism

Central to libertarianism is the claim that individuals should be free from the interference of others. Personal liberty is the supreme moral good. Hence, one's liberty can justifiably be restricted only if he consents to the restriction. Any other restriction, including taxing incomes for purposes of redistribution, is unjust. Or the libertarian may couch his theory in the language of rights: each individual has natural negative rights [2] to at least life, liberty, and property. No one can justifiably harm him, restrict his freedom, or take his property—that is, no one can violate his rights—without his consent. Moreover, these are general *(in rem)* rights; they apply, so to speak, against the whole world. And since rights invariably have correlative duties, all the people in the world have the duty not to interfere with the right holder's life, liberty, and property. Each person possesses these rights simply in virtue of his humanity—he does not have to *do* anything to obtain this moral protection. The possession of rights does not depend upon the consent of others. They are essential moral constituents of personhood.

However, we should note that these two ways of speaking seem to amount to the same thing for the libertarian. Libertarian theorists often move back and forth between talk of negative rights and talk of liberty. I suspect that is because they ultimately see rights and liberty as equivalent or because they hold a theory of rights which is grounded in personal liberty. That is, the libertarian might say, the *reason* we have all and only libertarian rights (absolute negative rights to life, liberty, property, etc.) is that these rights protect individual liberty. Hence, on both models liberty is fundamental.

Libertarianism also contends that in certain prescribed circumstances there can be positive *in personam* rights, that is, that individual X has a positive right to, say, $1,000 and someone else Y has a positive duty to give X that money. These positive rights, however, are not natural rights; they are not possessed by all persons just because they are persons. They can arise only consensually. For example, if A promises B that he will serve as a lifeguard at B's swimming pool, then B has a right against A and A has a duty to B—a duty to guard those in B's pool. But unless A so consents, he has no positive duties to B, or to anyone else for that matter. Consequently, for the libertarian, there are no general positive duties and no general positive rights. There are only *alleged* general positive rights; claims to such rights (or of such duties) are mistaken. For if there were positive general duties we would have to violate negative general rights to satisfy them. For example, suppose everyone had a positive general right to life; then everyone would have rights (entitlements) *to* those goods necessary to stay alive, e.g., food to eat. But food, or the money to buy it, doesn't grow on trees (or, if it does, the trees are owned). Those who own the food or the money have negative rights protecting their possession of these things. And negative general rights, for the libertarian, are absolute.[3] There are no circumstances in which these rights can be justifiably overridden, in which one's liberty can be justifiably limited without his consent. Hence, X's rights to property (or life or liberty) can never be overridden for the benefit of others (to satisfy the alleged positive rights of others). X can choose to charitably give his property to someone, or he can voluntarily give someone a positive right to his property. Nevertheless, morally he cannot be forced—either by legal sanctions or moral rules—to give up his life, liberty, or property. This moral/legal prohibition insures that an individual's liberty cannot be restricted in any way without his consent.

Thus we see two important features of libertarianism. First, the primary purpose of negative general rights is the protection of individual liberty, to insure that no one's life is restricted without his consent. Or as Nozick puts it: "Side constraints [which are equivalent to negative general rights] upon action reflect the underlying Kantian principle that individuals are ends and not merely means; they cannot be sacrificed or used for the achieving of other ends without their consent. . . . [These constraints] reflect the fact of our separate existences. They reflect the fact that no moral balancing act can take place among us." [4] Secondly, the libertarian holds that a sufficient reason to reject any alleged moral rule or principle of distributive justice is that that rule or principle restricts someone's freedom without his consent. Hayek, for example, argues that we should reject plans to expand governmental roles since such expansion necessarily undermines individual liberty.[5] And Nozick's primary objection to Rawls is that Rawls's two principles restrict individual liberty without consent.

Libertarianism, though morally austere, has a certain plausibility. Each of us wants to be able to live his own life, to be free from the unnecessary interference of others. We want, in Kant's words, to be ends in ourselves and not mere means for others.[6] But just because a theory is plausible does not mean that it is correct. Libertarianism, I think, can be shown to be mistaken. I will argue that negative general rights fail to protect individual liberty the way the libertarian suggests. Since the protection of liberty is the express purpose of these libertarian rights, the theory fails. My argument will also show that even the libertarian must hold that one should not reject a moral rule or principle of distributive justice simply because it permits (or requires) non-consensual limitations on freedom. Once this failure is exposed there appears to be no good reason for denying that there are at least some positive general duties and probably some positive general rights. How many and how extensive these duties or rights are is another question.

LIBERTARIANISM LIMITS LIBERTY

The problem with libertarianism can be seen once we recognize the limitations that negative rights (libertarian constraints) themselves place on individual liberty. Suppose, for example, that I am the biggest and strongest guy on the block. My size is a natural asset, a physical trait I inherited and then developed. But can I use my strength and size any way I please? No! At least not morally. Though I am physically capable of pummeling the peasants, pillaging property, and ravishing women, I am not morally justified in doing so. My freedom is restricted without my consent. I didn't make a contract with the property owners or the women; I didn't promise not to rap, rob, or rape. Just the same, morally I cannot perform these actions and others can justifiably prohibit me from performing them.

Consequently, everyone's life is not, given the presence of negative general rights and negative general duties, free from the interference of others. The "mere" presence of others imposes duties on each of us; it limits everyone's freedom. In fact, these restrictions are frequently extensive. For example, in the previously described case I could have all of the goods I wanted; I could take what I wanted, when I wanted. To say that such actions are morally or legally impermissible significantly limits my freedom, and my "happiness," without my consent. Of course I am not saying these restrictions are bad. Obviously they aren't. But it does show that the libertarian fails to achieve his major objective, namely, to insure that an individual's freedom cannot be limited without his consent. The libertarian's own moral constraints limit each person's freedom without consent.[7]

This is even more vividly seen when we look at an actual historical occurrence. In the nineteenth century American slaveholders were finally legally coerced into doing what they were already morally required to do: free their slaves. In many cases this led to the slave owners' financial and social ruin: they lost their farms, their money, and their power. Of course they didn't agree to their personal ruin; they didn't agree to this restriction on their freedom. Morally they didn't have to consent; it was a remedy long overdue. Even the libertarian would agree. The slaveholders' freedom was justifiably restricted by the presence of other people; the fact that there were other persons limited their acceptable alternatives. But that is exactly what the libertarian denies. Freedom, he claims, cannot be justifiably restricted without consent. In short, the difficulty in this: the libertarian talks as if there can be no legitimate non-consensual limitations on freedom, yet his very theory involves just such limitations. Not only does this appear to be blatantly inconsistent, but even if he could avoid this inconsistency, there appears to be no principled way in which he can justify only his theory's non-consensual limitations on freedom.

This theoretical difficulty is extremely important. First, the libertarian objections against redistribution programs (like those practiced in the welfare state) are weakened, if not totally disarmed. His ever-present objection to these programs has always been that they are unjust because they are non-consensual limitations on freedom. However, as I have shown, libertarian constraints themselves demand such limitations. Therefore, that cannot be a compelling reason for rejecting welfare statism unless it is also a compelling reason for rejecting libertarianism.

Secondly, once we see that justice demands certain non-consensual limitations on someone (X's) freedom, there seems to be no good reason for concluding (and good reason not to conclude) that X's freedom can be limited only by negative general duties. There seems to be no reason, for example, for concluding that X's freedom to make $1 million should not be restricted to aid other people, e.g., to give some workers enough funds to help them escape the de facto slavery in which they find themselves.

Think of it this way. Liberty, for the libertarian, is negative in nature. An individual's liberty is restricted whenever (and only if) his potential actions are restricted. This is essentially a Hobbesian view of liberty. So imagine with Hobbes and some libertarians that individuals are seen as initially being in a state of perfect freedom. In such a state, Hobbes claims, "nothing can be just. Right and wrong have there no place." [8] To introduce right and wrong of any sort is to put moral limitations on individual freedom. To that extent, everyone's freedom is restricted. Each person has an external impediment—a moral rule which can be coercively enforced—against doing some action A (and actions relevantly like A). Therefore, to introduce negative general rights and duties, as the libertarian does, is to admit that there are non-consensual limitations on freedom. And these limits—as I argued—are sometimes significant and far-reaching. They arise—and this is crucial—without consent; each person has them simply because he is a person. Now if one's freedom can be limited without consent by negative rights, then it is unreasonable to hold that these are the only limitations on freedom which can legitimately arise without consent. This is particularly apparent when we realize that in a number of cases the limitations on freedom imposed by negative duties are more—even much more—than limitations which would be imposed if some claims of positive rights or duties were recognized. For example, forcing a slaveholder to free his slaves would limit his freedom more than would a law forcing him to pay ten percent of his salary to educate and provide health care for his slaves. Or forcing Hitler to not take over the world (in other words, forcing him to recognize others' negative rights) would limit his freedom more extensively than would forcing him to support, by his taxes, some governmental welfare program. Yet the libertarian concludes that redistribution of income is unjust since it limits the taxed person's liberty without his consent. If redistribution is unjust for that reason, then so are libertarian constraints. Libertarian constraints also limit personal liberty without consent.

The libertarian might attempt to immediately avoid my conclusion by claiming that there is a principled difference between redistribution of income and libertarian constraints such that the former is *never* a justified restriction of liberty while the latter is always justified. For although both do limit personal liberty without consent, he might argue, libertarian constraints only restrict liberty in order to protect individual rights. And it is the protection of personal rights which justifies these, and only these, non-consensual restrictions on liberty.

However, this reply won't do. For as I have stated, any libertarian conception of rights is itself grounded in—justified by reference to—personal liberty. Or, as Eric Mack puts it, they are grounded in the right not to be coerced.[9] Hence, given my preceding argument, there is no principled way that concerns for personal liberty could generate *only* libertarian rights and duties, since negative rights restrict liberty as much as, or more than, would some positive rights or duties. Consequently, appeals to personal rights cannot provide the libertarian with a principled basis for distinguishing between types of non-consensual limitations on liberty.

We have uncovered a very telling incoherence. We have taken the main libertarian weapon against welfare statism and turned it on itself. The once-so-sharp sword is seen to have two sides. Instead of menacing the enemy, the sword only frustrates its wielder. As everyone knows, two-edged swords cut both ways. The libertarian is unable to support his conception of the minimal state. At least some redistribution of tax monies is justified.

Possible Libertarian Replies

"Liberty" Is Normative, not Descriptive

The libertarian might object to this argument by claiming that I have misunderstood his use of the word "liberty." "Liberty" is not, he might argue, a purely descriptive term. On a purely descriptive model of liberty, anything which restricts an individual's options would be a restriction of his liberty. Hence, negative rights would be a restriction of individual liberty. But not just any restriction of someone's option is a restriction of his liberty. Prohibitions of unjust actions are surely not limitations of freedom. For example, a person does not have the liberty to knife someone even though he physically might be able to do it. In short, individuals have liberty to do only those things which are just. Consequently, "liberty" should be seen as a normative term such that if A has the liberty to do X then not only is no one prohibiting him from doing it, but it is also morally permissible that he do it. "Therefore," the libertarian might conclude, "your objection fails since negative duties do not really limit individual liberty. It is not just that people kill each other, so prohibitions against killing are not limitations of freedom."

This linguistic proposal is intriguing since "liberty" clearly does have a positive emotive force which suggests ethical overtones. My own hunch, though, is that 'liberty' should be maintained as a descriptive term. That is, "liberty" is, and should be maintained as, a value-neutral term which merely states that there are limitations, without any judgment as to their propriety. For although we all have some tendencies to vacillate between the descriptive and normative senses of the term,[10] it seems clear that its basic sense is descriptive. It is only after we identify liberty descriptively that we are able to distinguish between just and unjust restrictions on it. For the purposes of this paper, however, I need not belabor the point. For even the acceptance of this linguistic proposal cannot patch up the libertarian's deflated case. For if "liberty" is a normative term in the way proposed, then we could not know if something is a restriction of liberty until we knew if the restrained action is just. For example, we would not know that taxing a millionaire's money and distributing it to the needy was a violation of the millionaire's liberty until we knew if it was just to so tax him. Hence, the claim that A has the liberty to do X (spend his millions any way he pleases) could not be a *reason* for believing that some action (taxing his millions) is unjust. The justificatory relationship on this model would be exactly opposite. We would have reason to believe that A had the liberty to do X only if we already knew that it was just that he do it. Consequently, the protection of individual liberty cannot be the purpose of (or consequence of) negative rights since the determination that someone had the liberty to do X depends upon the determination that he has the right to do it. For example, one would have the liberty to bequeath property P to Z only if he had the right of bequeathal. Yet the libertarian wants to ground such rights in personal liberty. Therefore, even if this linguistic proposal were acceptable, the libertarian's stated purpose of negative rights would be undermined. He would no longer be able to argue for stringent negative rights on the grounds that they protect individual liberties. Nor would he be able to reject other principles of distributive justice on grounds that they limited individual liberty without consent.

Liberty Should Be Maximized

The libertarian might attempt another tack. "Admittedly negative rights limit individual freedom. There has never been any doubt about that. What the libertarian demands is that everyone have maximum personal liberty with equal liberty consistent for all." However, this popular statement of libertarianism fails to soften my objection. The maximum amount of liberty with equal liberty for all is absolute liberty —a state in which there are no legal or moral prohibitions of any kind. (Notice that this is a Hobbesian state of nature.) In such a state there are no prohibitions and everyone is equally free from prohibitions. The libertarian, I suspect, would disagree. Although in such a state people would *ideally* have equal liberty, the libertarian would probably contend that because some people would take advantage of the situation and deprive others of their liberty, people so situated would not, in fact, have equal liberty. In other words, though liberty is ideally maximal, it would not be prudentially maximal.

There are three problems with this reply. First, on this view there would no longer be absolute prohibitions against restriction of liberty. Liberty could be justifiably restricted; it would not be an absolute good. True, it is only liberty which overrides liberty. Nevertheless, to say that one species of liberty overrides another is to say that there is something about one of them (liberty$_1$) which makes it morally more potent than the other (liberty$_2$). This something—e.g., good consequences following the action—which makes liberty$_1$ more potent, must be something other than liberty. Otherwise, there would be no rational basis for preferring liberty$_1$ over liberty$_2$. This implies that this other feature (e.g., good consequences) is more important than liberty or that liberty is morally good only when it has this (or some other) specific feature.[11] Thus, liberty would be neither absolute nor supreme.

Secondly, if the libertarian concern *is* with maximizing liberty, then there would no longer be absolute rights to liberty. Instead, liberty would be a goal, an end-state to be maximized. And, as Robert Nozick realizes (he makes his point in the language of rights), "This . . . would require us to violate someone's rights when doing so minimizes the total (weighted) amount of violations of rights in the society."[12] That is why he rejects such an option. An individual's liberty could be justifiably protected only if certain empirical statements (about whether the requisite action maximized liberty) were true. Hence, negative rights would be neither theoretically nor practically absolute. And to deny that they are absolute is to deny libertarianism.

Thirdly, if liberty must be *exactly* equal, as the rebuttal suggests, then we would have to have an extremely repressive government (a police state with constant electronic surveillance, etc.). Otherwise some people's (but not all people's) rights would be violated by murders, muggers, etc. Consequently, if the demand were on maximizing liberty, a Hobbesian state of liberty would be chosen; if the emphasis were on equality of liberty, then something like a police state would be chosen.

In other words, any reference to maximal or equal liberty indicates only a formal criterion of justice which fails to distinguish between alternative determinations of what counts as maximal or equal liberty.

Individuals Tacitly Consent to Libertarianism

The libertarian could attempt another reply by appealing to the notion of implied or tacit consent. "You have correctly identified my criterion for justifiably restricting personal freedom," he might say. "An individual must consent to any restriction. Consent, however, need not be explicitly offered. An individual can, merely by his action, tacitly consent to some limitations of his freedom."[13] The libertarian then might go on to conjecture that by seeking interaction with others, all individuals tacitly agree to respect others' liberty in certain specified ways, namely, those ways protected by negative general rights.

There are, however, several difficulties with this reply. Initially there is the difficult question of how to adequately describe some action(s) such that it does indicate tacit consent. And no matter how one describes such an action, undoubtedly someone in the world would fail to perform it— yet the libertarian would still assume that that person had a duty not to violate libertarian constraints. We could also note that the notion of tacit consent normally implies that such consent is like explicit consent, it is just that it is not verbally offered. That suggests that A cannot be said to have tacitly consented to X, if, when he is explicitly asked if he so consents, he (A) denies it. Yet surely there would be at least one person in the world who would vehemently deny that he had consented to the presence of all and only negative general rights. Hence, there would be no basis for claiming that A is morally or legally required to do X. Still the libertarian would want to contend that A could not justifiably kill others, steal their property, etc.

Secondly, it is highly implausible to think that all people would consent—explicitly or implicitly—to all and only libertarian constraints. Robert Nozick, for example, recognizes this when he emphatically rejects the principle of fairness.[14] If a rule of tacit consent could undergird negative general rights, then it could also justify at least some governmental redistribution programs. We don't, however, need to cite Nozick here; we can simply make the obvious claim that people would choose something other than libertarianism. They would at least opt for a system which also gave them sufficient goods (or the ready opportunity to obtain them) to stay alive. Finally, we could also note John Rawls's argument in *A Theory of Justice* [15] which shows that *if* one works from a consent model, a more-than-minimal state would emerge. The rebuttal fails.

Libertarianism Is Grounded in Immediate Intuition

Libertarianism is beginning to flounder. So the libertarian might attempt to salvage his theory by arguing that his view of morality, and its emphasis on negative general rights, is established by immediate intuition. "Rights are not grounded in liberty," he might say; "hence your arguments just miss the mark. I intuitively recognize that we have these and only these rights." Or he might offer a slightly more sophisticated intuitionist model: he claims to immediately intuit some fundamental moral "fact" which justifies all and only libertarian rights. For example, he might claim that he intuitively knows that people can *never* be used as a means for others' ends (à la Kant), and that this truth strictly implies his account of rights.

There are two questions to be raised about this proposal. First, even if the suggested intuition about the Kantian imperative were true, would it imply the truth of libertarianism? Secondly, are *any* intuitions singularly sufficient to ground particular moral principles? The answer to both, I will argue, is: "No."

Let us imagine for a moment that the proposed intuition is indubitably true: "(I)ndividuals are ends and not merely means; they cannot be sacrificed or used for the achieving of other ends without their consent." [16]

Why must we suppose, as this reply suggests, that the only way people are used as a means for others is if libertarian rights are violated? Why, for example, isn't a poor worker being used by a rich factory owner as a means for his making a million dollars? I, for one, think he clearly is.[17]

Besides, I could also point out, following my argument in the second section, that libertarian restraints themselves involve using some individuals as means for others. For example, the slaveholder is used against his will as a means for achieving the freedom of the slaves; he is forced to do something just to benefit others. In fact, all libertarian constraints use us to benefit others. They force us to do (or not do) certain actions as a means of allowing individuals to do other actions—actions which are deemed more important than the prohibited ones. The presence of other individuals uses each of us by limiting our range of permissible alternatives. Admittedly, we may sometimes not see ourselves as being used under these circumstances; but if we don't, I suspect it is because we don't desire (for the most part) to kill other people, enslave them, etc., or because we have been so ingrained with the view that such restrictions are morally required. But when the cost is significant, people often do, in fact, see this. The slaveholders, for example, argued that since they didn't agree to abolition, they shouldn't have to set their slaves free— to force them to was a non-consensual limitation of their freedom. And they're right: it was a violation of their descriptive liberty. It is just that it was a just violation. The libertarian, it seems, must agree. But, of course, that implies that there are no absolute prohibitions against using people.[18]

In fact, this argument helps focus on an underlying difficulty with libertarianism. Libertarians seem to desire a totally individualistic system in which one's interests never have to be weighed against anyone (or everyone) else's. But that is impossible. People's interests inevitably will conflict in any society in which there is limited space and resources. The purpose of law and morality is just to provide a rational procedure for settling such conflicts. For example, on this view X's enslaving someone to increase his (X's) income, is clearly a worse "using" than is prohibiting X from enslaving others. That is why we prohibit slavery. One person's interest (not to be enslaved) is weighed against another person's interest (to enslave) and the former is clearly superior. Surely this is a more plausible understanding of negative rights. Therefore, even if we grant the suggested intuition, the libertarian view of rights is not established.

However, there is still the general question concerning the role of intuition in moral argument. I would contend that intuitions *may* play some legitimate role in moral argument. But if they do, these intuitions must be revisable in the face of cogent argument; they must also be sensitive to opposing intuitions. Yet I have shown that there appears to be no principled basis for the absolute emphasis on negative general rights. So if the libertarian does found his theory only on intuitions, particularly when basic distinctions within the theory (the emphasis on libertarian constraints rather than positive duties) seem *ad hoc* and even counter-intuitive, then the theory crumbles in the sands of weak intuitions. In short, since the claim that there are no general positive duties or rights is unprincipled, we must reject it. Therefore, even *if* the suggested intuitions did strictly imply a libertarian conception of rights, libertarianism would still not be established since the intuitions themselves would be highly questionable.

CONCLUSION AND SPECULATION

My argument is completed. I have argued that libertarianism is untenable.[19] I have challenged four possible replies to my argument. I would like to end with some rather brief speculation on the direction an adequate theory of justice must go. My speculation emerges from the previous arguments. I have shown that neither property nor liberty (as defined by the libertarian) should be seen as the only social good; singling these out as the only social values is unreasonable. Instead, these should be seen as two values among many, all competing for recognition.

Property, as I have said, is important. But how important? Well, it should be apparent that an individual cannot be alive without some property, or at least some goods to use; neither can a person have any real options without goods to work on. In addition, there is some force to the Hegelian claim that individuals need property with which to "identify" themselves, and there is the Jeffersonian point that property seems to be necessary for the protection of civil liberty. These might suggest that everyone is entitled to some minimum of goods, and that that minimum is protected by negative rights. Beyond this minimum? That's a difficult question.

And what of liberty? Surely it is important. Just as surely it is not all-important. But in some societies, say, rather affluent ones, it (e.g., political and civil liberties) may be the highest (but even here not the only) value. The libertarian's claim that it is is mistaken.

NOTES

1. F. A. Hayek, *The Constitution of Liberty* (Chicago: Henry Regnery Company, 1960) and *Individualism and Economic Order* (Chicago: Henry Regnery Company, 1948); Milton Friedman, *Capitalism and Freedom* (Chicago: The University of Chicago Press, 1958); Robert Nozick, *Anarchy, State, and Utopia* (New York: Basic Books, Inc., 1974).

2. These rights are natural, inasmuch as they exist prior to the existence of the state and set limits within which the state can justifiably act. They are negative since they prohibit external, other-agent interference.

3. E.g., Nozick, particularly pp. 28–32.

4. Although Nozick equates liberties and negative rights, there are good reasons to separate the concepts. See, e.g., W. N. Hohfeld's analysis, *Some Fundamental Legal Conceptions as Applied in Judicial Reasoning* (New Haven, Conn.: Yale University

Press, 1953). Still, since Nozick does identify them—in fact, many theorists do—I will, in this paper, adhere to that identification.

5. Hayek, *The Road to Serfdom* (Chicago: The University of Chicago Press, 1944).

6. There is serious question whether Kant would want his "slogan" appropriated by libertarianism. Still, it is easy to understand why they gravitate toward Kant.

7. Some libertarians might object: Negative rights are not limitations of liberty. You have simply misunderstood, they might say, the very nature of libertarianism. One does not have the liberty to kill others. However, it seems to me that such rights are restrictions of liberty and hence my objections go through. Nonetheless, I will consider this suggestion in some detail in the next section.

8. Thomas Hobbes, *Leviathan*, ed. Michael Oakeshott (New York: Collier Books, 1973 edition), p. 101.

9. Eric Mack, "Natural and Contractural Rights," *Ethics*, vol. 87, no. 2 (1977), pp. 153ff.

10. Actually, I think it is the libertarian's vacillation in his use of this term that makes his case so initially compelling.

11. See Joel Feinberg, *Social Philosophy* (Englewood Cliffs, N.J.: Prentice-Hall, Inc., 1973), p. 19.

12. Nozick, p. 28.

13. For two discussions of tacit consent see R. P. Wolff's *In Defense of Anarchism* (New York: Harper & Row, 1970), and P. Singer's *Democracy and Disobedience* (Oxford: Oxford University Press, 1972).

14. Nozick, pp. 90–95.

15. John Rawls, *A Theory of Justice* (Cambridge, Mass.: Harvard University Press, 1971).

16. Nozick, p. 31.

17. It won't do for the libertarian to argue that this is a just "using" while violations of negative rights are unjust "usings." Such a distinction (between just and unjust "usings") presupposes that the Kantian ends/means principle is not the fundamental building block of libertarianism. Hence, such a response would undermine the very ground of this objection.

18. A similar argument could be developed against any libertarian attempt to use the act/omission distinction to undergird his theory of rights. Let me explain: occasionally the libertarian will claim that there is an unbridgeable moral gulf between actively harming someone and "merely" letting harm happen to him. Active harms are always wrong while omissions (failures to act) are never wrong. This explains why all general rights are only negative, the libertarian might say. Violations of negative rights are active harms while omissions never violate negative rights.

I have three comments about such a reply. First, though this distinction apparently has some service—there is, in many cases, some moral difference between omissions and commissions—it does not seem, even to most supporters of this distinction, that the moral difference is so vast that omissions are *never* wrong. Secondly, the libertarian has never tried, as far as I know, to defend his use of the distinction. Thirdly, and probably more to the point, my main argument first aired in the second section spells trouble for the distinction's utility as a grounding for the libertarian view of rights. Libertarian constraints themselves actively intrude into individuals' lives. They justify coercively prohibiting individuals from doing actions they may want to do and are able to do. So by his own account, active intrusions are not always wrong. The act/omission distinction cannot undergird the libertarian conception of rights. And it won't do for the libertarian to argue that active intrusions to stop active intrusions are permissible since there is no non-question-begging way in which such an analysis would support the libertarian view of rights. The slaveholder, for example, could claim that by enslaving others he was actively intruding to stop the state from actively intruding on him.

Therefore, I would again want to argue that the libertarian is overlooking the obvious reason why the slaveholder's activities are curtailed: an individual's interest in not being enslaved is more fundamental and more extensive than his (or anyone else's) interest in enslaving another. One need not resort to mysterious talk of either intrusions to stop intrusions or acts and omissions. In fact, I suspect that if the act/ omission distinction is morally significant it is because it describes part of our moral life—not because it proscribes that life.

19. There is one possible variety of libertarianism that I have not examined here. Someone might offer a distinctly consequentialist argument for libertarianism. They might argue, for example, that a society which recognized only negative general rights would be freer, happier, etc. However, this certainly does appear to violate the spirit as well as the letter of libertarianism. Libertarianism involves the claim that violations of negative general rights are always wrong, come what may, and it is difficult to envision how such a theory could be compatible with anything but a deontological justification.

Secondly, it is wildly implausible to think that any traditional consequentialist principle could generate libertarian claims—or even something closely approximating them. Classical utilitarianism, for example, would at least insure that each individual has the basic goods necessary for survival (given the truth of the principle of diminishing utility).

Still, I suppose someone might develop such a theory, and if he did, then further argument would be required to demonstrate its inadequacies.

PETER SINGER

Monash University

Rights and the Market

Introduction

How should goods and services be distributed? In theory there is a wide range of possible answers to this question: in accordance with need, utility, merit, effort, contribution to production, seniority, strict equality, competitive examinations, ancestry as determined by a free market, and so on. At some time each of these answers has been endorsed by some thinkers, and each has been put into practice as the basis of distribution of at least some goods and services in some societies. Within limited spheres, each is still used today. This use is often controversial. Should seniority be a ground for promotion, as it frequently is in areas of employment like teaching and the civil service? Should a person be able to inherit great wealth merely because he is the most direct living descendant of a miserly recluse who died without leaving a will? Should university places be allocated strictly in accordance with examination grades? Interesting as such issues are, they tend to be overshadowed by a more fundamental division of opinion: should distribution by and large be left to the workings of a free market, in which individuals trade voluntarily, or should society as a whole, through the agency of the government, seek to distribute goods and services in accordance with some criterion generally regarded as desirable? It is this issue which is at the center of the political division between right and left, and consequently is the subject of dispute between political parties, in most nations which have political parties, as well as between philosophers, who, like Robert Nozick, are clearly aligned with the free market advocates and those who, like John Rawls, support distribution in accordance with a favored criterion of justice.

This essay deals with only one aspect of this basic disagreement, though a central one. Those who favor leaving distribution to the market have used two distinct types of argument. One is utilitarian in character. It asserts that if we leave distribution to the market we shall end up with a better outcome than if we interfere with the market because the market will promote efficient methods of production and exchange, and hence will lead to more people getting what they want than any alternative means of distribution. I shall not discuss this type of argument here. It is obvious that, although difficult to test, the utilitarian argument rests on a factual claim and consequently would have to be given up if non-market modes of distribution could be shown to be compatible with as much or more efficiency in production and exchange as the market. This line of argument is not, therefore, a defense of the market in principle, but rather a defense of the market as a means to an end—the end of maximum satisfaction, or something similar.[1]

NOZICK'S VIEW

The second line of argument is less vulnerable to empirical criticism, for it does not defend the market as a means to an end. Nozick's position is an extreme instance of this. He rejects altogether the idea that institutions—or actions, for that matter—are ultimately to be judged by the ends they promote. That an institution maximizes happiness and minimizes pain would not, in Nozick's view, be a sufficient reason for recommending the institution. If the institution violates rights, then he would consider the institution unjustifiable, no matter how great its superiority in producing happiness or alleviating pain may be. Nor would other goals, like the maximization of freedom, or even the minimization of violations of rights, suffice to justify an institution which violates rights. Nozick's system takes absolute (or virtually absolute) "side constraints" as primary, and hence is structurally distinct from any "maximizing" view.[2]

Nozick therefore defends distribution through the market on the grounds that this method does not violate rights, whereas alternatives such as government distribution in accordance with, say, need do. For, Nozick would say, market distribution is distribution in accordance with the voluntary decisions of individuals to buy or sell goods and services, while government distribution in accordance with need will, in practice, involve the government in taking resources from some individuals, usually by taxation, to give to others, irrespective of whether those from whom the resources are taken wish to give to those in need. Nozick sees the voluntary nature of each of the many individual exchanges which together make up the market system as proof that the market does not violate rights, and the coercion by the government of those from whom resources are taken as proof that government distribution does violate rights.

Empirical investigation of how the market distributes goods and services will not refute this second type of defense of the market. Nozick acknowledges that any distribution at all can result from the market. Some may trade shrewdly and make great fortunes; others may gamble recklessly and lose everything. Even if everyone worked equally hard and traded equally wisely, fortune would favor some and ruin others. So far as justice is concerned this is all, in Nozick's view, irrelevant: any distribution, no matter how unequal, is just, if it has arisen from an originally just position through transfers which do not violate rights. This defense of the market is a philosophical argument. So far as its application to the real world is concerned it might be met by arguing—as Marxists have frequently argued—that the "free market" is a figment of the imagination of bourgeois economists, that all actual markets fall under the dominant influence of a few monopolists, and so do not allow consumers or producers to choose freely after all. Let us take Nozick's argument on a more theoretical level, however, and consider what philosophical objections can be brought against it. One strong philosophical objection is to the moral stance on which it is based. I have elsewhere suggested that the grounds Nozick offers for rejecting utilitarianism are inadequate, and that the utilitarian theory of distribution is preferable to Nozick's own view.[3] But it is also worth considering if such defenses of the market can be shown to be unsatisfactory even within the terms of a moral theory which takes the prohibition of violations of rights as prior to the maximization of utility, and on the assumption that a free market would not be distorted by monopolistic practices.

The first point to be made is that it is only if we accept a very narrow conception of the nature of rights that the market has any chance at all of being shown to be necessarily superior to other systems of distribution in avoiding violations of rights. To see this, consider, for instance, the right to life. It is commonly said that we have a right to life that comprises, not merely a right not to be killed by attackers, but also a right to food if we are starving while others have plenty, and a right to a minimal level of medical care if the society in which we live can afford to provide it. If a society allows people to die from starvation when there is more than enough food to go around, or to die from diseases because they are too poor or too ignorant to obtain a simple and inexpensive injection, we would not consider that society to be one in which the right to life is greatly respected. The right to life, in other words, is widely seen as a right of *recipience*, as well as a right against interference.[4] Another important and frequently claimed right of recipience is the right to education. Clearly, if there are such rights, the market will not necessarily protect them; if it does protect them at a particular time in a particular society, it does so only accidentally, since the market is not structured to produce any particular distribution. A planned distribution, financed by taxation, on the other hand, could aim directly at protecting such rights, and could thereby protect them more effectively.

Nozick recognizes that his position requires a narrow interpretation of rights. With reference to someone who argues, as he himself does, that the state should not interfere in distribution, he says that the position

> will be a consistent one if his conception of rights holds that your being *forced* to contribute to another's welfare violates your rights, whereas someone else's not providing you with things you need greatly, including things essential to the protection of your rights, does not *itself* violate your rights.[5]

Oddly, while Nozick is aware of the importance of this conception of rights to his general position, he provides no argument for it. Instead, he appears to take it as a natural consequence of his starting point, which is Locke's state of nature. If we start, as Hobbes, and following him Locke, do, with independent individuals in a state of nature, we may be led naturally enough to a conception of rights in which so long as each leaves the other alone, no rights are violated. This line of reasoning seems to go: "If I do not make you any worse off than you would have been if I had never come into contact with you, then I do not violate your rights, for I might quite properly have maintained my independent existence if I had wished to do so." But why should we start with such an unhistorical, abstract, and ultimately inexplicable idea as an independent individual? It is now well known that our ancestors were social beings long before they were human beings, and could not have become human beings, with the abilities and capacities of human beings, had they not been social beings first.

Admittedly, Nozick does not present his picture of the state of nature as an historical account of how the state actually arose. He says: "We learn much by seeing how the state could have arisen, even if it didn't arise that way." [6] But if we know that, human nature being what it is, the state could *not* have arisen that way, maybe we don't learn so much. On the mistakenly individualistic aspect of Locke's view of society, however, enough has been said by others and there is no need for repetition here. It is surprising that Nozick should ignore this extensive literature and accept Locke's starting point without providing any reply to these damaging criticisms.[7]

If we reject the idea of independent individuals and start with people living together in a community, it is by no means obvious that rights must be restricted to rights against interference. When people live together, they may be born into, grow up with, and live in, a web of rights and obligations which include obligations to help others in need, and rights to be helped oneself when in need.[8] It is reasonable to suppose that such altruistic practices are the very foundation of our moral concepts.

It is also worth noting that Nozick's conception of rights cannot be supported by appeal to the only other ethical tradition on which Nozick draws, that of Kant. Nozick defends his ethic of 'side constraints' rather than goals as a reflection of "the underlying Kantian principle that individuals are ends and not merely means; they may not be sacrificed or used for the achieving of other ends without their consent." [9]

The Kantian principle to which Nozick refers, however, cannot bear the gloss Nozick places on it. Any undergraduate who has studied Kant's famous (notorious?) four examples of the application of the categorical imperative knows that Kant thinks we have an obligation to help others in distress. Elsewhere he describes charity as "an act of duty imposed upon us by the rights of others and the debt we owe to them." Only if "none of us drew to himself a greater share of the world's wealth than his neighbour" would this debt and the consequent rights and duties not exist.[10]

It can, indeed, well be argued that rational beings have rights of recipience precisely *because* they are ends in themselves, and that to refuse a starving person the food he needs to survive is to fail to treat him with the respect due to a being that is an end in itself. Nor does it follow from the fact that people are autonomous, in the Kantian sense in which autonomy of the will is opposed to heteronomy of the will, that it is always wrong to force a person to do what he does not do voluntarily.[11]

AN EXAMPLE: A MARKET IN BLOOD

The distinction between "civil society" conceived as Locke and Nozick conceive it, as an association of fully-formed independent human beings, and the alternative conception of a community bound together by moral ties which affect the nature of the human beings who grow up in it, has been illustrated in a recent empirical study which is directly relevant to the choice between market and non-market modes of distributing goods: *The Gift Relationship* by R. M. Titmuss.[12] This work is worth examining in some detail, because it presents a rare opportunity to compare, not in theory but in the real world, the operation of market and non-market modes of distribution. Thereby it enables us to observe how rights and freedoms are affected by the two systems of distribution. We shall see that the question is a much more subtle and complex one than libertarian defenders of the market assume.

The good whose distribution Titmuss studied is blood. In Britain, human blood required for medical purposes is obtained by means far removed from the market. It is neither bought nor sold. It is given voluntarily, and without reward beyond a cup of tea and a biscuit. It is available to anyone who needs it without charge and without obligation. Donors gain no preference over non-donors; but since enough blood is available for all, they need no preference. Nor does the donor have any hope of a return favor from the recipient. Although the gift is in one way a very intimate one—the blood that now flows in the donor's veins will soon flow in those of the recipient—the donor will never know whom he or she has helped. It is a gift from one stranger to another. The system is as close to a perfect example of institutionalized generosity as can be imagined.

By contrast, in the United States, only about 7 percent of the blood obtained for medical purposes comes from similar voluntary donations. Around 40 percent is given to avoid having to pay for blood received, or to build up credit so that blood will be available without charge if needed. Approximately half of the blood and plasma obtained in America is bought and sold on a strictly commercial basis, like any other commodity.

Which of these contrasting systems of blood collection violates rights, and which does not? One obvious point is that if we accept that there is a right of recipience to a level of medical care consonant with the community's resources, then the British system provides for this right, while a pure market system would not. It is only the intervention of the state which can guarantee that everyone who needs blood will receive it. Under a market system those needing large quantities of blood have to be extremely wealthy to survive. Hemophiliacs, for example, may require treatment with large quantities of blood plasma twenty or thirty times a year. In the United States each such treatment costs around $2250. Not surprisingly, the private health insurance market considers hemophiliacs "bad risks" and will not insure them. In Britain hemophiliacs receive the blood they need free of charge.[13] If hemophiliacs have a right to life, which goes beyond the right not to be killed, the market cannot protect this right.

Titmuss's study also reveals some more subtle ways in which the market may violate rights, including rights which are not rights of recipience. It does this in two ways. First, it provides an example of how individual actions which appear harmless can contribute to the restriction of the freedom of others. Second, it shows that one cannot assume without a great deal of argument about the nature of rights, that the state acts neutrally when it allows people to trade without restriction. I shall take this second point first. Supporters of laissez faire overlook the extent to which one's conception of a "neutral" position is affected by one's view about what rights people have. If we ask: "Under which system does the individual have the right to choose whether to give or to sell his blood?" the answer must be that this right is recognized only when there is a commercial system as well as a voluntary one. This aspect of the situation is the basis of the claim made by many advocates of the market, that the market simply allows people to sell what is theirs if they so desire— providing they can find buyers—and thus grants a right to sell without in any way impairing the right of anyone else to give away his or her property if he or she prefers to do so.[14] Why, these supporters of the market ask, should we prohibit the selling of blood? Is it not a flagrant infringement of people's freedom to prevent them doing something which harms no one and is, literally, their own business?

This approach overlooks the fact that the existence of a market in goods or services changes the way in which these goods or services are perceived in the community. On the basis of statistical data, as well as the results of a questionnaire Titmuss carried out on blood donors in Britain, Titmuss has shown that the existence of a commercial system discourages voluntary donors.[15] This is not because those who would otherwise have made voluntary donations choose to sell their blood—donors and sellers come from, in the main, different sections of the population—but because the fact that blood is available as a commodity, to be bought and sold, affects the nature of the gift that is made when blood is given.

If blood is a commodity with a price, to give blood means merely to save someone money. Blood has a cash value of a certain number of dollars, and the importance of the gift will vary with the wealth of the recipient. If blood cannot be bought, however, the gift's value depends upon the need of the recipient. Often, it will be worth life itself. Under these circumstances blood becomes a very special kind of gift, and giving it means providing for strangers, without hope of reward, something they cannot buy and without which they may die. The gift relates strangers in a manner that is not possible when blood is a commodity.

This may sound like a philosopher's abstraction, far removed from the thoughts of ordinary people. On the contrary, it is an idea spontaneously expressed by British donors in response to Titmuss's questionnaire. As one woman, a machine operator, wrote in reply to the question why she first decided to become a blood donor:

> You can't get blood from supermarkets and chain stores. People themselves must come forward; sick people can't get out of bed to ask you for a pint to save their life, so I came forward in hopes to help somebody who needs blood.[16]

The implication of this answer, and others like it, is that even if the formal right to give blood can coexist with commercial blood banks, the respondent's action would have lost much of its significance to her, and the blood would probably not have been given at all. When blood is a commodity, and can be purchased if it is not given, altruism becomes unnecessary, and so loosens the bonds that can otherwise exist between strangers in a community. The existence of a market in blood does not threaten the formal right to give blood: but it does away with the right to give blood which cannot be bought, has no cash value, and must be given freely if it is to be obtained at all. If there is such a right, it is incompatible with the right to sell blood, and we cannot avoid violating one of these rights when we grant the other.

Is there really a right to give something that is outside the sphere of the market? Supporters of the market will no doubt deny the existence of any such right. They might argue against it on the grounds that any such right would be one that can be violated by two individuals trading, and trading seems to be a private act between consenting parties. (Compare Nozick's dictum: "The socialist society would have to forbid capitalist acts between consenting adults.") Acts which make commodities of things which were not previously commodities are not, however, purely private acts, for they have an impact on society as a whole.

If we do not now take the commercialization of a previously non-commercial process very seriously, it is because we have grown used to almost everything being commercialized. We are still, perhaps, vaguely uneasy when we see the few remaining non-commercial areas of our lives disappearing: when sport becomes a means of earning a living, instead of an activity entered into for its intrinsic qualities; when once-independent publishing houses, now swallowed by giant corporations, begin ruthlessly pruning the less profitable types of work from their lists; and when, as is now beginning to happen, a market develops in organs for transplantation.[17] But our unease is stilled by the belief that these developments are "inevitable" and that they bring gains as well as losses. The continuing commercialization of our lives is, however, no more inevitable than the American Supersonic Transport, and as Titmuss has convincingly shown in the case of blood, the alleged gains of commercialization are often illusory, and where not illusory, outweighed by the losses.[18]

Nozick's political theory itself represents the ultimate triumph of commercialization, for in his theory rights themselves become commodities with a price. Nozick often writes as if he holds that it is always wrong to violate someone's rights. In fact, however, he holds nothing of the kind: he holds that it is always wrong to violate someone's rights *unless* you compensate them for the violation. The distinction is crucial. If Nozick never allowed violations of rights with compensation, life in a world governed by his conception of rights would become impossible. One could not even move around without first obtaining the permission of the owners of the land one wished to cross—and one might well not be able to obtain this permission without moving on to the land first in order to locate the owner. Nozick recognizes the necessity of allowing violations of rights with compensation (Ch. 4, especially pp. 71–84) but he does not realize that implicit in allowing these violations is the assumption that rights have some monetary or at least barter value. For what can compensation be except money or the bartering of goods and services? But what if there is no monetary or other compensation that I am willing to accept in exchange for the violation of my rights? This is not an implausible assumption. Someone who has enough to feed and clothe himself may well prize solitude, quiet, or clean air above all compensation. So to violate rights, with an intention to compensate, may be an unconditional violation of rights—for in any given instance no adequate compensation may be possible. Hence Nozick's theory does not really protect rights at all. It can only be thought to do so if one assumes that every right has its price.

What must be borne in mind about the process of commercialization is that whether an act constitutes an interference in the lives of others cannot be decided independently of the nature of the society in which the act takes place, and the significance of existing social practices in the lives of the individuals who make up that society. Advocates of the market commonly claim, as Nozick does, that "the market is neutral between persons' desires" and merely "reflects and transmits widely scattered information via prices and coordinates persons' activities." [19] In fact, however, the market is not neutral. It affects the way in which goods and services are perceived, and it affects, as Titmuss has shown, how people act. If a prohibition on the buying and selling of a particular "commodity" interferes with those who wish to buy or sell it, the making of something into a commodity is also a form of interference with those for whom the fact that the good or service was not previously a commodity is significant. Whether we should recognize a right to buy and sell anything that is one's own, or whether, instead, we should recognize the conflicting rights of people to retain certain goods and services outside the influence of the commercial sphere is therefore not a question that can be decided by adhering to strictures about avoiding interference or remaining neutral between people's desires; it can properly be decided only if we take into consideration how recognition of these rights affects people, not only directly but also indirectly, through its effect on society as a whole.

These broader issues are entirely overlooked by most defenders of the market, who pay attention to the forms of freedom and ignore its substance. They regard every law extending the range of choices formally open to people as an increase in their freedom, and every law diminishing this range of choice as a decrease in their freedom; whether the choice is a real or attractive one is irrelevant. Nor is any consideration given to the long-range consequences of a large number of individual choices, each of which may be rational from the point of view of the interests of each individual at the time of making the choice, although the cumulative effects may be disastrous for everyone. Titmuss's study suggests that the decision to sell one's blood could be in this category.

Individual Rationality and Collective Irrationality

Other examples of this phenomenon of individual rationality and collective irrationality are now well known. If public transport is poor, it is in my interest to travel to work by car, for the car will get me there faster and more comfortably, and the marginal increase my additional vehicle makes to pollution, traffic jams and the depletion of oil reserves does not materially affect me. If everyone has this same choice of transportation and makes the same rationally self-interested decision, however, the result is a dangerous level of air pollution, choked roads and swift exhaustion of oil reserves, none of which anyone wants. It would therefore be in all our interests if steps were taken to improve public transport; but once a pattern of private transport has set in, public transport can only be economically viable if people are deterred from using their own vehicles. Hence restrictions on the use of cars may well be in everyone's interest.

Suppose that in the above situation a law is enacted prohibiting the use of private vehicles in a defined inner city area. In one sense the range of choice of transport open to people has been reduced; but on the other hand a new choice now opens up—the choice of using a fast and frequent public transport system at a moderate cost. Most reasonable people, given the choice between, say, an hour's crawl along congested, exhaust-filled roads and 20 minutes' comfortable ride on a bus or train, would have little hesitation in choosing the latter. Let us assume that for economic reasons the possibility of choosing the quick and comfortable ride on public transport would not have existed if private transport had not been restricted. Nevertheless, because the choice of driving oneself to work has been eliminated by a deliberate human act, the defenders of laissez faire will regard this restriction as an interference with freedom; and they will not accept that the nonexistence of the option of efficient public transport, if private transport is not restricted, is a comparable interference with freedom, the removal of which compensates for the restriction of private transport. They will argue that it is circumstances, not deliberate human acts, which preclude the coexistence of efficient public transport and the unrestricted use of private vehicles. In the view of laissez-faire theorists—and some other philosophers as well—freedom is not restricted, and rights are not infringed, by "circumstances," but only by deliberate human acts.[20] This position makes, in my view, an untenable moral distinction between an overt act and the omission of an act. If we can act to alter circumstances but decide not to do so, then we must take responsibility for our omission, just as we must take responsibility for our overt act.[21] Therefore circumstances which it is within our power to alter may limit our freedom as much as deliberate human acts.

Turning back now to the subject of a market in human blood we can see that here too profound social consequences, though of a more subtle kind, can arise from the cumulative effect of many seemingly insignificant decisions. We know that altruistic behavior by some can foster further altruistic acts in others.[22] Titmuss has suggested that a society which has and encourages institutions in which some members of society freely render important services to other members of the society, including others with whom they are not acquainted, whose identity they may never know, and from whom they can expect no reward, tends to differ in other important aspects from a society in which people are not expected or encouraged to perform services for strangers except for a direct, and usually monetary, reward. The difference is related to the different views of the state held by philosophers like Hobbes and Locke, on the one hand, and Rousseau, Hegel and Marx on the other. For Hobbes and Locke, as we have seen, the state is composed of people who join and remain in society for the advantage they get out of it. The state then becomes an association of self-interested individuals, which exists because, and as long as, all or most of its members find it useful and profitable. Rousseau and his successors, on the other hand, see the state more as a community which, in addition to merely providing opportunities for material gains, gives meaning to the individual's existence and inevitably has a formative influence on the nature of the people who grow up in it. Through this influence human beings become social beings, and see the interests of the community and of other members of it as a part of their own interests. While for Hobbes and Locke the state can do no more than paper over the ultimately irresolvable difference between the interests of its members, providing at best a superficial, temporary harmony which is always liable to break down, for Rousseau, Hegel and Marx a good society creates a genuine, deep-seated harmony because it actually resolves the differences between the interests of its members.[23]

The phenomenon of cumulative irrationality of individually rational choices, and the still more fundamental point that the nature of human beings is influenced by the institutions of the society in which they live, both point in the same direction: the need to recognize the rights of members of a society to act collectively to control their lives and to determine the nature of the society in which they live. Even if the distinction between laws which interfere with others (like laws prohibiting the sale of blood, or the driving of cars in a prescribed area) from laws which purportedly do not so interfere (like laws allowing people to sell their blood, or drive their cars to work) can be rescued from the objections I have offered, I would still argue that if a majority of the members of a society should decide that unless they interfere with the actions of others the lives of most members of society will become significantly worse—as in the examples we have been discussing—then the majority have a right to interfere. (This does not justify unlimited interference. The extent and nature of the interference that is permissible would vary with the seriousness of the harm that it is intended to avert; but this topic is too large to discuss here.[24])

It might be said that to allow the majority a right to interfere is dangerous, in that it sacrifices the individual to the collective, and leads straight to a totalitarian dictatorship of the majority. There is, however, no reason why the right I would allow the majority should lead to totalitarianism. It is quite compatible with many valid anti-totalitarian arguments, including utilitarian arguments against totalitarianism, and most of the arguments for individual liberty advanced by John Stuart Mill in *On Liberty*. These arguments are sufficient to rebut the claims of totalitarians. If, despite this, it is claimed that we need to uphold the absolute inviolability of individual rights because any other position, while not itself supporting totalitarianism, is always likely to be distorted by those seeking to establish a totalitarian state, then the appropriate reply is that it is fallacious to object to a principle because one objects to the actions of those who distort the principle for their own ends. If it is only through distortion that the principle lends support to totalitarianism, then it is to the distortion, and not to the principle itself, that objections should be made.[25]

In contrast to the dangers of granting a right to the majority to interfere with individual members of the society, which exist only if this
principle is distorted or added to in objectionable ways, the dangers of
the opposite position are real enough and are truly entailed by the
position itself. The effect of the doctrine that our freedom is not diminished and our rights are not violated by circumstances—including
the cumulative effect of individual choices, each of which would be
quite harmless on its own—is to tie our hands against effective action in
situations which threaten the survival of our species. Pollution, overpopulation, economic depression, the breakdown of social cohesion—all
of these may be brought about by millions of separate acts, each one
falling within what is normally perceived as the sphere of individual
rights.

Nozick and other defenders of individual rights may assert that the
moral status of rights does not depend on the consequences of not
violating them; but if they leave people with no legitimate means of
controlling the course their society is to take, with no legitimate means,
even, of steering away from looming disaster, then they have not suc-
ceeded in providing a plausible theory of rights.

Nozick might reply that what my argument shows is that these individual actions do violate rights after all, and his theory of rights can
therefore cope with them by the usual procedures for violations of rights,
namely prohibition or compensation. In the case of pollution, Nozick
does outline a scheme for enforcing the payment of compensation to
those whose *property* is damaged by pollution, but he concedes that his
discussion is incomplete in that it does not cover the pollution of unowned things like the sky or the sea.[26] Perhaps we can imagine how
Nozick would extend his view to handle those cases, but I at least cannot
see any way in which it could deal satisfactorily with, for instance, overpopulation. The claim that having children violates the rights of others
would be difficult to reconcile with other elements of Nozick's view of
rights. Yet by comparison with the problem of overpopulation, the
pollution problems Nozick thinks he can cope with are only symptoms,
not causes, of the real problem. Nozick might, I suppose, take a hard
line and say that when it comes to the crunch, evolutionary forces will
take care of the population problem, and only the fittest will survive.
Any moral theory that reaches this conclusion reveals its inadequacy
more convincingly than I could ever hope to do.

Conclusions

There are, then, three main conclusions which have emerged from
this discussion of the effects of markets on rights. First, the view that
the market necessarily respects rights, while government systems of distribution involving coercion do not, requires a peculiarly narrow conception of rights which lacks justification once its basis in an individualistic
theory of the "state of nature" is rejected. Second, it is incorrect to hold
that the state acts neutrally by allowing markets to operate without

restriction in any commodity. A market can interfere with people, and may reasonably be said to violate their rights. To draw a line between interference and non-interference is a far more complex task than advocates of the unrestricted market generally assume. Third, and finally, on any plausible theory of rights, some social and economic planning must be permissible. Individuals cannot have an absolute right to buy and sell without interference, any more than they can have an absolute right to pollute or to populate without interference. To grant individuals these rights is to make social planning impossible, and hence to deny to the "individuals" who make up that society the right to control their own lives.[27]

NOTES

1. I discuss the utilitarian argument for the market, in respect of the provision of health care, in "Freedoms and Utilities in the Distribution of Health Care" in R. Veatch and R. Branson (eds.), *Ethics and Health Policy* (Ballinger, Cambridge, Mass., 1976).

2. *Anarchy, State and Utopia*, pp. 28-33. My hesitation about the degree of absoluteness is prompted by the final paragraph of the footnote commencing on p. 29, in which Nozick refrains from stating whether his side-constraints may be violated to avoid catastrophic moral horror. If he were to say that they may be, he would need to show how this thin end of the utilitarian wedge can be accommodated while resistance to other utilitarian considerations is maintained. Since I cannot predict how Nozick would overcome this difficulty I shall henceforth ignore the possibility that his side-constraints may not be quite absolute.

3. See my review of *Anarchy, State and Utopia* in *The New York Review of Books*, March 6, 1975; and see also J. J. C. Smart's essay in this volume, pp. 103-115.

4. I take the term "right of recipience" from H. J. McCloskey, "Rights—Some Conceptual Issues," *Australasian Journal of Philosophy*, vol. 54 (1976), p. 103.

5. *Anarchy, State and Utopia*, p. 30.

6. *Ibid.*, p. 9.

7. The political philosophies of Hegel, Marx and their successors are built upon the rejection of Locke's individualist starting point. The classic, though characteristically obscure, reference in Hegel is Paragraph 258 of *The Philosophy of Right*. Marx makes the general point on several occasions. The following example is from the *Economic and Philosophical Manuscripts of 1844*:

> Above all we must avoid postulating "Society" again as an abstraction *vis-à-vis* the individual. The individual *is the social being*. (trans. Martin Milligan, International Publishers, New York, 1964, pp. 137-138).

A more recent and more fully argued philosophical critique of the individualism of Hobbes and Locke is to be found in C. B. Macpherson's *The Political Theory of Possessive Individualism* (Clarendon Press, Oxford, 1962). Further discussion of the literature on individualism can be found in Steven Lukes, *Individualism* (Blackwells, Oxford, 1973). For a dramatic introduction to the factual material bearing on the social nature of our ancestors, see Robert Ardrey, *The Social Contract* (Collins, London, 1970). Ardrey himself is unreliable, but his bibliography and references are useful.

8. It seems likely that our moral concepts have developed out of those altruistic practices. See, for instance, Edward O. Wilson *Sociobiology: The New Synthesis* (Belknap Press, Cambridge, Mass., 1975) and Richard Brandt, "The Psychology of Benevolence and Its Implications for Philosophy," *Journal of Philosophy*, LXXIII (1976), pp. 429-453.

9. *Anarchy, State and Utopia*, pp. 30-31.

10. See the *Groundwork of the Metaphysics of Morals*, trans. H. J. Paton under the title *The Moral Law* (Hutchinson, London, 1948), p. 86, and *Lectures on Ethics*, trans. L. Infield (Harper, New York, 1963), pp. 194, 236.

11. I am indebted to H. J. McCloskey for these points about Kant, although Alan H. Goldman makes a similar point in "The Entitlement Theory of Distributive Justice," *Journal of Philosophy*, LXXIII, pp. 823-835 (Dec. 2, 1976).

12. Allen & Unwin, London, 1970. The substance of the following paragraphs is taken from the article cited in Note 1, above, and also appeared in "Altruism and Commerce: A Defense of Titmuss against Arrow," *Philosophy and Public Affairs*, 2 (1973), pp. 312-320.

13. *The Gift Relationship*, pp. 206-207. The price quoted is a 1966 figure, and has no doubt risen considerably.

14. Cf. Kenneth Arrow, "Gifts and Exchanges," *Philosophy and Public Affairs*, 1 (1972), p. 350.

15. *The Gift Relationship, passim*. For a summary of the evidence see "Altruism and Commerce: A Defense of Titmuss against Arrow," pp. 314-315.

16. *The Gift Relationship*, p. 277. Spelling and punctuation have been corrected.

17. Amitai Etzioni, *Genetic Fix* (Harper & Row, New York, 1973), p. 137; *Wall Street Journal*, Dec. 16, 1975.

18. *The Gift Relationship*, especially chapters 8 & 9. Again, I am indebted to H. J. McCloskey for bringing the significance of Nozick's use of compensation to my attention.

19. *Anarchy, State and Utopia*, pp. 163-164.

20. For instance, F. A. Hayek: " 'Freedom' refers solely to a relation of men to other men, and the only infringement on it is coercion by men." (*The Constitution of Liberty*, Routledge & Kegan Paul, London, 1960, p. 12) and for a similar view, Isaiah Berlin, "Two Concepts of Liberty" in *Four Essays on Liberty*, p. 122. The discussion on pp. 237-238 of *Anarchy, State and Utopia* indicates that Nozick, though primarily concerned with rights rather than freedom, also holds that my rights are not infringed if the collective result of a series of legitimate individual actions by others is a drastic curtailment of my freedom of action. On this question see the discussion by Thomas Scanlon in "Nozick on Rights, Liberty and Property," *Philosophy and Public Affairs*, vol. 5, no. 1 (Fall, 1976), especially pp. 14-15. Scanlon writes:

> It is the connection with justification that makes plausible Nozick's restriction of attention to limitations on alternatives that are brought about by human action. Even though acts of nature may limit our alternatives, they are not subject to demands for justification. But individual human acts are not the only things subject to such demands; we are also concerned with social institutions that make it possible for agents to do what they do.

Scanlon is right to point out that social institutions need to be justified, but he lets Nozick off too lightly in respect to acts of nature. When acts of nature are preventable, the omission of human acts that would have prevented them may require justification.

21. See Michael Tooley, "Abortion and Infanticide," *Philosophy and Public Affairs*, 2 (1972), especially p. 50 ff; James Rachels, "Active and Passive Euthanasia," *New England Journal of Medicine*, 292 (1975), pp. 78-80.

22. Derek Wright, *The Psychology of Moral Behaviour* (Penguin, London, 1971), pp. 133-139.

23. One does not, of course, have to accept in their entirety the views of any of these philosophers in order to accept the central point that the structure of a society influences the nature of those who are members of it, and that given that this influ-

ence will occur, it is better that it be directed toward a community of interests than toward a conflict of interests.

24. I have touched upon it—though in a different context—in *Democracy and Disobedience* (Clarendon Press, Oxford, 1973), especially pp. 64-72.

25. Much of the argument against the positive concept of liberty in Berlin's "Two Concepts of Liberty" commits this fallacy.

26. *Anarchy, State and Utopia,* pp. 79-81.

27. H. J. McCloskey, J. J. C. Smart, C. L. Ten and Robert Young made useful criticisms of an earlier version of this article.

the socialist perspective

The Socialist Perspective

In the previous section the merits of an unregulated market society, as advocated by libertarians, were examined. To reject laissez faire, however, is not necessarily to reject capitalism. There are two options open to those dissatisfied with the libertarian position. First, one might opt for a restricted capitalist economy in which the profit motive and individual enterprise predominate, but where the influence of market forces is limited by government activity and where a social minimum is guaranteed. Alternatively, one might elect the socialist approach.

To many people socialism means welfarism, so that social services (like public health programs or pensions) and countries like Germany or England where there are extensive welfare services are considered "socialistic." But most socialists are concerned with more than social welfare measures or even measures for equalizing income. Socialism involves, rather, the collective ownership of the major means and resources of production and a planned economy in which production and distribution, instead of being left to private, individual control, are brought under some form of public direction. Socialists offer a variety of economic and moral criticisms of capitalism, whether regulated or not, but it is fair to note that a socialist society itself might use certain market mechanisms in carrying out its plan of distribution or in organizing production. What distinguishes socialism from capitalism, however, is social control of the economic realm as a whole, regardless of the specific techniques used.

Socialists have traditionally seen their demands as a call for the extension of democracy to the economic realm: the people should run the economy for their own benefit, instead of being run by it. This democratic control of society's overall production is to be matched by the greater say of persons over their immediate work environment, although socialists disagree about how these two goals are to be obtained simultaneously. Nonetheless, only the rational and humane regulation of production at both levels will, they contend, permit the solving of our major social problems (like poverty) and provide a springboard for true human emancipation.

Such progress, it is argued, is impossible in a class system resting upon exploitation. Exploitation designates the ability of some (usually those owning property) to "live off the labor of others," and socialists believe that justice requires the end of such systems, as soon as a society has the material capacity to dispense with them. While socialists advocate a more equal distribution of goods and services, their opinions vary as to the appropriate criterion or principle of distribution. Karl Marx, for example, held that under socialism people should be rewarded in accord with their labor. At the higher, communist stage of society, however, when (he believed) the selfish motivations of an earlier capitalist era will have withered away, distribution should follow the principle, "from each according to his or her ability, to each according to his or her need." Prior to the utopia of communism, socialists might well endorse some incentive system (perhaps as a result of following Rawls' Difference Principle), although generally they desire to move production, at least in the long run, away from such a "selfish" basis. In any event, socialists wish the economy restructured, not simply to promote economic justice, but in order to attain ideals of fraternity and freedom.

In this section Kai Nielsen and G. A. Cohen examine the Rawlsian and libertarian theories from the socialist perspective. In "Class and Justice" Nielsen outlines a socialist conception of justice and argues for a more egalitarian distribution of economic goods than Rawls would permit. The inequalities in economic power which a capitalist system, even of a Rawlsian sort, would allow, Nielsen contends, constitute a threat to liberty and may well affect negatively the moral autonomy of workers. Nielsen argues that Rawls has failed to take seriously the possibility of classlessness and that his own radically egalitarian conception of justice is more faithful to the very values with which Rawls is concerned.

In "Robert Nozick and Wilt Chamberlain: How Patterns Preserve Liberty," Cohen answers the major objection of Nozick and other libertarians to socialism. As illustrated by Nozick's famous Wilt Chamberlain parable, libertarians argue that a socialist (or any patterned) principle of justice must be rejected as incompatible with liberty. Cohen challenges Nozick's conception of justice, arguing that he has yet to prove his case against socialism. Further, Cohen denies that socialism is infeasible or that it would involve, as libertarians claim, an unacceptable interference with liberty. Socialists restrict (economic) liberties in order to expand our freedom generally. Libertarians cannot complain about this since capitalism itself erodes the liberty of a large class of people.

KAI NIELSEN

University of Calgary

Class and Justice

Liberty, without the commitment to equality . . . as the history of even the most wealthy capitalist societies reveals, never achieves genuine liberty for all, and threatens its destruction for each, because the people are deprived of real access to practicing liberty, to exercising their rights and assuming their responsibilities in directing their own social and personal affairs. Liberty becomes the power and privilege of the few, an instrument for the manipulation and exploitation of the many. As the mask for narrow self-interest destructive of community and mutuality of social responsibility, liberty divorced from equality discredits genuine liberty itself and places it in jeopardy to disillusion and cynicism.

Candid proponents of capitalism no longer make a pretense at honoring the equalitarian tradition. On the contrary, they fear it as the mortal enemy of capitalism.

The capitalist class disowned equality in the interests of exercising the liberty associated with their property rights, and tended to reduce liberty, in their elemental loyalties, to their own marketplace activity.

Martin J. Sklar

The Possibilities of Classlessness *

It has been argued, not implausibly, against those who would tax Rawls with reflecting a conservative/liberal ideological bias, that his

---

* I would like to thank John Arthur and William H. Shaw for their helpful comments on an earlier version of this essay. The errors that remain are, of course, mine.

account of egalitarian justice is the most egalitarian form of justice it is reasonable to defend.[1] I shall argue against this claim and attempt to articulate in skeletal form a socialist conception of justice, where liberty and equality are treated as indivisible, that is still more egalitarian and at least as reasonable as Rawls' form of egalitarianism.[2] Indeed, it is my belief that if it were to become a core conception guiding the design of our social institutions, it would guarantee more adequately than Rawls' own account the very values (so important to Rawls and indeed to any reflective human being) of equal self-respect, equal liberty and moral autonomy.

Rawls unreflectively, and without any supporting argument, makes certain problematic assumptions about classes and the possibilities of classlessness. Only if those assumptions are justified will it be the case that Rawls' account is as egalitarian as it is reasonable to be. My arguments shall be that these assumptions are not justified. Rawls has an inadequate conception of what classes are and what classlessness would be. When taken in conjunction with his theory of the primary social goods and the assumptions he makes about human nature, they lead him to adopt a theory of justice which has not been shown to be the uniquely rational one for contractors in the original position to adopt or for fully informed rational and moral agents to adopt after the veil of ignorance is lifted. It is not at all evident that his *difference* principle provides us with enough equality or, more surprisingly, that his two principles together afford sufficient effective liberty to provide the underlying structural rationale for a perfectly just society.

In this section I shall pose problems about the possibilities of classlessness and its relation to egalitarianism. In the next section I shall discuss, working with a paradigm, class and moral autonomy and Rawls' *difference* principle, while in the third section I shall discuss liberty and equality and probe the extent and nature of Rawls' commitment to egalitarianism. Finally in the last section I begin a direct argument for a more radical egalitarian conception of justice, requiring classlessness, and which sees equal liberty as being dependent on equality.

Even in societies that Rawls would regard as well-ordered, in which his two principles of justice were satisfied, there could be considerable differences in the life prospects between the advantaged strata of the society and the least well off. Indeed it may very well be that even in a society where the means of production are socially owned, differences in the whole life prospects of people will persist because of the differences in income, status and authority which remain even after capitalism has been abolished or died the death of a thousand unifying expansions. With differences in status, authority and income remaining, different groups, differently affected, may find that their whole life prospects are still very different indeed.

We plainly seem to require something very like an industrial society to feed, clothe, etc. our vast and, for the immediate future at least, growing world population. I speak now just of meeting subsistence needs. I do not speak of making the springs of social wealth flow freely and fully. That seems to require a division of labour and with that division of labour, divisions of people along class lines which deeply affect their life prospects. I grant that it is by no means certain that this is inevitable —particularly when the time comes when there is no longer any private ownership of the means of production—but it is, to put it conservatively, not unreasonable to believe that the division of labour is an inevitable feature of industrially developed societies. Yet it is also not unreasonable to believe that the division of labour could be reduced—that we could and should have far more versatile, many-sided human beings doing more varied work and standing in many different social roles and that we should and could, as well, develop various social devices to ameliorate the inequalities and inequities resulting from the division of labour. It is at least conceivable that a state of affairs could develop where there was a genuine social ownership of the means of production, with democratic control through workers' councils with the gradual transformation of state power into a governmental structure which, as Marx puts it, would come to have only simple administrative functions.[3] In that sense the State could wither away and exploitation of others could end, because there then would be no *structural* means of transferring to oneself the benefits of the powers of others. Thus, in that very important sense, there would be no classes, i.e. people who are at higher and lower levels, where the higher levels are the result of or the means to exploiting others, extracting from them surplus value. It is in this way and in this sense that class divisions and the existence of classes most deeply and pervasively affect us.[4] It is because of the existence of classes of this sort that the most appalling and extensive inequalities and injustices arise and persist in our social structures. It is vital to know whether in this sense class divisions are inevitable. If the assumption that they are can be successfully challenged, it makes room for the possibility of a more radically egalitarian form of justice than anything Rawls sanctions.

In seeking to articulate the principles of social justice and to attain an Archimedean point for appraising basic social structures, Rawls does not face the questions raised by the existence of social classes. I do not mean to suggest that he regards our actual class-divided societies as basically just or even well on their way to social justice. He eschews the making of such political judgements, but he does think that capitalist societies with their unavoidable class divisions can still be well-ordered societies which are plainly just societies and he would thus be committed to regarding societies in which class divisions and exploitation, in the sense characterized above, are inexpugnable features, as still societies which could be perfectly just societies.[5] Rawls takes the existence of classes to be an inevitable feature of social life and he, quite naturally, regards justice as something compatible with that unavoidable social condition.

In thinking about justice and class two general facts are very important. The first is that in capitalist societies there are deep class divisions and the second is that, barring some incredible catastrophe, the trend to complex industrial societies appears irreversible. This makes classlessness a problematic matter. Yet the very existence of exploiting classes as an integral part of a capitalist order poses evident problems for the attaining of social justice in capitalist societies. I shall argue that because of his unjustified assumptions about classes Rawls a) takes certain disparities in life conditions between different groups of people to be just which are not just or at least have not been shown to be just and appear at least to be very unjust and b) too easily accepts the belief that capitalism with its class relations can be just.

Capitalist societies are and must remain class-divided societies. Talk of 'people's capitalism' is at best fanciful. Rawls is right in seeing class divisions as an unavoidable feature of capitalist societies, but he is mistaken in uncritically accepting the conventional wisdom which maintains that all industrial societies must have class divisions. Rawls, unfortunately, does not examine classes or exploitation. But he does assume, as I remarked initially, the inevitability of classes at least in the sense to be specified in the next two paragraphs.

There is an important sense of 'class,' developed in the Marxist tradition, concerning which it is by no means evident that classes are inevitable. Rawls largely ignores that conception and generally talks about classes in the way most bourgeois social scientists do, where 'class' and 'strata' are roughly interchangeable terms. Indeed, Rawls is not clear about what he thinks classes are, but it is evident that he believes that institutionalized inequalities which affect the whole life prospects of human beings are inescapable in complex societies.

My counter is that it has not been shown that a society without classes (cohesive groups) which determine the broad life prospects of their members is an impossibility and that thus Rawls unnecessarily limits the scope of his egalitarian claims. Rawls seems principally to think of a class-divided society as a society with social strata in which there are differences in status, authority, income and prestige. He believes, plausibly enough, that some differences will persist in any society and thus assumes that classes are inevitable. But such a belief's evident persuasiveness is tied to the identification of class and strata. If, alternatively, we either think of classes, as a Marxist does, essentially in terms of the relationship to the means of production or as cohesive groups between which there are considerable differences in income, prestige or authority and because of these differences there are radically different life prospects, it is not so evident that we can safely assume, as Rawls does, that classes are inevitable.

It is not, however, clear that Rawls is committed to denying the possibility of a society without classes in the Marxist sense. After all, he admits that it is possible that societies can be both socialist and just. But he does take it to be an inescapable fact that there are and will continue to be classes in the sense that there are and will continue to be institutionally defined cohesive groups whose whole life prospects are importantly different. We cannot design and sustain a society where that will not obtain.

I shall argue that it has not been established that such class divisions are inevitable or that classes in the Marxist sense are inevitable. With these commonly assumed inevitabilities no longer secured, we are not justified, if we believe, as Rawls does, in the equal moral worth of all people, in qualifying egalitarianism and justifying inequalities in the way he does. But there are many challengeable propositions here that require establishment in a somewhat less conditional manner. It is to this that I now turn.

CLASS AND MORAL AUTONOMY

Rawls argues that for conditions of moderate scarcity, the principles of collective action that rational persons would accept in circumstances in which they were disinterested, uninfluenced by a knowledge of their own particular situation, their natural endowments, their individual life plans or aspirations but in which they did have *general* social science and psychological information about human nature and society are (in order of priority) the following: (1) "Each person is to have an equal right to the most extensive total system of equal basic liberties compatible with a similar liberty for all," and (2) "social and economic inequalities are to be arranged so that they are both (a) to the greatest benefit of the least advantaged, consistent with the just savings principle, and (b) attached to offices and positions open to all under conditions of fair equality of opportunity." [6] Now (a) above (the *difference* principle, i.e. the principle that inequalities to be just must benefit the least advantaged) has been thoroughly criticized, but it remains a distinctive and crucial element in Rawls' account.[7] I do not want to return to that dispute but to consider against the *difference* principle, in trying to sort out the issue of class and justice, a far less decisive, yet morally and politically more significant candidate counter-example. This example, I shall argue, exhibits how very intractable moral disputes can be and how knowledge and rationality are far less decisive in moral disputes than Rawls and a great many moral philosophers suppose.[8]

Rawls argues that in sufficiently favourable but still only moderately affluent circumstances, where his two principles of justice are taken to be rational ordering principles for the guidance of social relations, it could be the case that justice, and indeed a commitment to morality, would require the acceptance as just, and as through and through morally acceptable, of a not inconsiderable disparity in the total life prospects of the children of entrepreneurs and children of unskilled labourers, even when those children are equally talented, equally energetic and the like. A just society, he claims, could in such circumstances tolerate such disparities.

It seems to me that such a society could not be a just society, let alone a perfectly just society.[9] There might under certain circumstances be pragmatic reasons of expediency for grudgingly accepting such inequalities as unavoidable. In that way they could, in those circumstances, be *justified inequalities*. When people, whose only relevant difference is that one group had entrepreneurs as parents and the other had unskilled

labourers as parents, have, simply because of this difference, life prospects so different that one group's entire life prospects are considerably
better than the others, then that difference is unjust.[10] By contrast,
Rawls does not direct moral disapprobation toward a society or moral
scheme of things which accepts such disparities, not only grudgingly as
unfortunate expediencies necessary under certain distinctive circumstances to improve the lot of the most disadvantaged, but as disparities
which even a just, well-ordered society could accept. He believes that
such a society could still be a just society (perhaps even a perfectly just
society). For me, however, the witting acceptance of such disparities just
seems evil. It may be an evil that we might in certain circumstances have
to accept because we realize that under those circumstances the under-
mining of that state of affairs will bring about a still greater evil. But
it remains an evil all the same. The moral ideal embedded in a conception of a just and truly human society—a perfectly just society—must
be to eradicate such differences.

Rawls or a Rawlsian could reply that in making such judgements I am
being unnecessarily and mistakenly sentimental and perhaps a little
irrational, or at least confused, to boot. It is bad enough that such inequalities in life prospects must exist, but it is still worse by narrowing
them to make the children of the unskilled labourers even worse off.[11]
It is better and indeed more just to accept the considerable disparities
in life prospects and to apply the *difference* principle. Otherwise, in
absolute terms, these children of unskilled labourers will be still worse
off. It can never be right or just to knowingly bring about or allow that
state of affairs where it could be prevented. To achieve greater equality
at such a price is to do something which is itself morally indefensible.

Rawls is, in spite of himself, being too utilitarian here. Talk of in-
creasing the advantages of such a group with lower life prospects is not
the only thing which is morally relevant, even in those circumstances
where Rawls' principles of justice are to hold in their proper lexical
order.[12] Even when it is to their advantage, the working class people in
such a circumstance, who are or were children, have had, by the very
existence of this extensive disparity, their moral persons assaulted and
their self-respect damaged. This is true even if in terms of income and
wealth the inequality of opportunity will make them better off, and in
that sense, enhance their opportunities more than they otherwise would
be enhanced. That that is not just rhetoric, envy or resentment can be
seen from the fact that they suffer, among other things, with such a loss
of equality, the loss of effective equal citizenship.[13] Their continuing to
have these formal rights and liberties is cold comfort. Moreover, their
effective moral autonomy is undermined by such disparities in power, in
their inability to control their life conditions and in their inability
(situated as they are) to obtain meaningful work.[14] It is also important
to recognize that these disparities are inextricably linked to the different
life prospects of children of working class people and the children of
the capitalist class and the professional strata whose loyalties by and
large are to the capitalist class.

Rawls, it might be thought, could, in turn, respond that there is no actual conflict with his account even if this is so, for, if such conditions obtain, his equal liberty principle would be violated and his principles of justice would not be satisfied after all. For he does claim that "the basic structure is to be arranged to maximize the worth to the least advantaged of the complete scheme of equal liberty shared by all." [15]

However, that there is in reality no conflict with his theory is not so clear, for I had in mind the *effective* exercise of the rights of equal citizenship and the *effective* moral autonomy of people, while Rawls seems at least to be talking about something which is more *formal* and which could be satisfied in such a circumstance. By utilizing his putative distinction between liberty and the *worth* of liberty—a distinction effectively criticized by Daniels—Rawls tries to account for what I have been talking about under the rubric 'the worth of liberty' and not under the equal liberty principle. But, as Daniels' criticisms have brought to the fore, it is far from evident that anything like this can successfully be maintained.[16] Yet, Rawls might respond that in arguing as I have above, I have not given sufficient weight to a) his insistence that fair opportunity requires not only that no one be formally excluded from a position to which special benefits attach, but also that persons with like talents and inclinations should have like prospects of attaining these benefits "regardless of their initial place in the social system, that is, irrespective of the income class into which they were born," and b) I neglect that part of his second priority rule which lays it down that "fair opportunity is prior to the *difference* principle" and that any "inequality of opportunity must enhance the opportunities of those with lesser opportunity." [17] Rawls, with a fine moral sense and thorough integrity, seeks to make perspicuous a requirement "which treats everyone equally as a moral person." [18] Moreover, Rawls might add, I am failing to take into consideration his recognition that certain background institutions are necessary for distributive justice. In particular I am forgetting that we need institutions concerned with *transfer* and *distribution*. The institutions concerned with transfer will guarantee a social minimum to the most disadvantaged and will honor the claim to meet basic needs. Taxation will be used by this institution to prevent a concentration of wealth and power which would undermine political liberty and equality of opportunity. Rawls stresses that for principles of justice to be fully satisfied there would have to be a redistribution of income, a wide dispersal of property, and the long-run expectations of the least advantaged would have to be maximized (in a way compatible with the constraints of a fair equality of opportunity and with the constraints of equal liberty). To achieve these things we need institutions of transfer and distribution employing taxation and the like.

Yet right there, with the very conception that there will, in a well-ordered, perfectly just society, be a *social minimum*, there is the acceptance of class divisions as just, even though the life expectations of some groups are quite different than those of others. While Rawls has the welfare state ideals expressed in the previous paragraph, he also believes that there can be capitalist, and thus class-divided societies, which are well-ordered and in which his principles of justice are satisfied. Yet it is just such societies which have exploitative classes and which, as Rawls himself admits, have class differences which make for the substantial differences in life prospects that we noticed between the children of entrepreneurs and unskilled labourers. Rawls thinks such class differences are unavoidable and he thinks that his principles of justice can be satisfied even when they obtain. But then it is difficult to see how, in such a circumstance, fair equality of opportunity, on which he also insists, could possibly be realized. How (or even that) Rawls' theory can make a coherent whole here is not evident, but what is evident is that he is applying the *difference* principle and claiming an inequality is a just one when that claim is very questionable indeed and when it is not at all evident that a person committed, as Rawls is, to a belief in the equal moral worth of all persons, should not opt for a more radical form of egalitarianism.

There surely is merit in the claim, pressed by Dworkin, that Rawls seeks to translate into a working conception of distributive justice an egalitarian ideal that everyone be treated equally as moral persons. Yet there is also—and at least equally evidently—the stress in his theory that such disparities as I have discussed could be justified even in a just, well-ordered society.[19] Rawls' writings on this topic are reflectively self-conscious of objections and are often so qualified that it is difficult to make sure how the various parts go together. But there is in Rawls a line of argumentation—one which interprets the *difference* principle in terms of income rather than other primary goods—to which my counterexample addresses itself. What I have tried to do so far is to show how very much this line of argument conflicts with some tolerably deep sentiments (intuitions, considered judgements) about justice (including, as we have just seen, some of Rawls' other considered judgements).

However, without trying further to sort this out, I think that Rawls has available a still more fundamental reply, namely the reply that *such* class divisions are *inevitable* and that, since rational principles of justice, whatever they may be, must be compatible with the 'ought-implies-can maxim,' such disparities in life prospects must simply be accepted as something which is just there in the nature of things much in the same way as are differences in natural endowment. Indeed, Rawls suggests that inequalities may be to the benefit of the least advantaged in that they provide incentives to the better off members of society and thereby serve the interests of *all* members. We cannot reasonably complain about them as unjust when it is impossible to do anything about them. One might as well say that the cosmos is unjust.

There is an inclination within me to say that if those are the alternatives, then one should say that the cosmos is unjust. More seriously, and less tendentiously, one can reasonably follow C. B. Macpherson and Benjamin Barber in questioning whether Rawls has done anything more than uncritically and unhistorically to assume the inevitability of there being classes determining differences in whole life prospects.[20] There is,

as I remarked earlier, in spite of the length of Rawls' book, no supporting argument at all for this key assumption and yet it is a governing one
in his work and it is the basis for appealing to the ought-implies-can-
maxim in this context.

It may well be, as Rolf Dahrendorf argues, that a certain social stratification is inevitable—that there will be in any complex society some
differences in prestige, authority and income—but there is no good evidence that these differences must result from or result in institutionalized
differences in power—including ownership and control of the means of
production—which will serve as the basis of control and exploitation
such that the whole life prospects of people will be radically different.[21]
It is where such differences obtain that we have the reality of exploitative classes, but Rawls has done nothing at all to show that such class
differences are inevitable such that we would just have to accept—as not
unjust, since they are inevitable—the differences in life prospects between
the children of entrepreneurs and unskilled labourers.

Let us imagine a slight twist in the case I have been considering and
suppose that neither disputant believes there is much prospect of achieving classlessness but that one still takes the more egalitarian posture
I take and another the Rawlsian position. (Full equality, for the radical
egalitarian, now becomes a heuristic ideal to try to approximate.) Yet,
given those assumptions about classlessness, is not the Rawlsian position
more reasonable and more just? It is, of course, true that there are greater
inequalities if we reason in accordance with the *difference* principle, but
the *proletarian* or *lumpenproletarian* in such a circumstance is still in
a certain plain sense better off—at least in the sense that they have more
income. People in such a position also have, it is claimed, the chance,
given the way the primary social goods hang together, to achieve a greater
self-respect due to the fact that they will have larger incomes and—in
that way—more power than they would otherwise have.[22]

However, in another, and more crucial way, they would have less
power and not as great a realization of certain of the primary social
goods articulated by Rawls, including most fundamentally the good of
self-respect. That can be seen if we reflect on the following. In terms
of income and power (mostly buying power) that the income provides,
it is true that in the more egalitarian society the most disadvantaged
would be still worse off than they would be in the less egalitarian society
in which Rawls' *difference* principle is satisfied. But it is also true that
there would, in the greater equality that that society provides, still be
more in the way of effective equal citizenship and in that way a more
equal sharing of power and thus a greater basis for realizing the good
of self-respect and moral autonomy than in the Rawlsian well-ordered
society. In a society in such a circumstance, ordered on Rawls' principles, the least advantaged would have more power *in the sense of more
wealth* than they would have in the more egalitarian society, but, in the
more egalitarian society, they would have more power in the sense that
their equality, or at least their greater equality, would make it the case
that no one person would have power over another in virtue of his

greater wealth and greater consequent control of society. In determining how things are to be ordered, everyone, in a radically egalitarian society, stands in common positions of power or at least in more nearly equal positions of power.

I am not, of course, claiming that as a matter of fact the worst off will, even in the narrowest of economic terms, benefit by a regime of private ownership. Like other socialists, I do not think that, at this historical stage, capitalism benefits the most disadvantaged. Indeed I think it is plain that it does not. In fact I would go beyond that and argue that it hardly can benefit more than ten per cent of the people in societies such as ours. However, even if some trickle-down theory were correct and it could be shown that the worst off would have greater material benefits under the regime of private ownership of the means of production than in a socialist society, that still would not be sufficient to establish that the capitalist society would be the better or the juster society. In the previous paragraphs I attempted to give some of the reasons for believing that to be so. (I am, of course, speaking, as Rawls is as well, of societies in conditions of moderate scarcity.)

I suspect that, in reflecting on these two possible social orders, some would be more than willing to trade their equal power and consequent equal effective citizenship for greater wealth and some would not. But, particularly given Rawls' own moral methodology, there seem, at least, to be no grounds—no conclusive or even firmly reliable arguments—to push one in one way rather than in another. Reflective and knowledgeable people go in both directions such that it at least appears to be the case that what is the right and through and through just thing to do in such a situation cannot be objectively resolved. And this suggests, and partially confirms, the belief that justice is an essentially contested concept.[23] However, we shall examine in the next section whether this argument can be pushed a little further. Perhaps the disagreement about justice is not all that intractable.

Moreover, this belief could survive a clear recognition on the part of both parties to the dispute that it is unfair that such differences in life prospects exist because there are no morally relevant differences between the children of such entrepreneurs and the children of such unskilled labourers. But the Rawlsian, utilizing the *difference* principle and taking what is, in effect, a rather utilitarian turn, is committed to saying that this unfairness in such a circumstance does not, everything considered, create an overall injustice, for if the *difference* principle is not in effect, it will be the case that in such a society, still more harm and a still greater injustice will result for the least advantaged.

LIBERTY AND EQUALITY

Rawls' bedrock argument here is that the inequality in question is just if the equal liberty principle and the fair opportunity principle are not violated and the existence of such inequalities effecting the sons or daughters of unskilled labourers is to the advantage of the most disadvantaged stratum of society.

Suppose these children of unskilled labourers are part of that most disadvantaged stratum. Rawls, as we have seen, could argue that indeed their life prospects, given their situation, are already unfortunate enough and then rhetorically ask whether, given that situation, it is right or just or even humane to make them still worse off by narrowing the inequality? Isn't doing that adding insult to injury? This plainly utilitarian argument has considerable force. Yet one can still be inclined to say that such inequalities remain unfair, indeed even somehow grossly unjust. We have two children of equal talent and ability and yet in virtue of their distinct class backgrounds their whole life prospects are very different indeed. One can see the force of the utilitarian considerations which would lead the parents of such children or the children themselves to be resigned to the inequalities, to accept them as the best thing they could get under the circumstances, but why should we think they are *just* distributions? [24]

In a way parallel to the way Rawls himself argues against simply accepting a maximizing of average utility as the most just arrangement, it is possible to argue against Rawls here. Rawls says to the utilitarian that it is a requirement of fairness to consider the interests of everyone alike even when doing so will not produce the greatest utility. To fail to do that is to fail to be fair. I am inclined to respond to Rawls in a similar way by saying that we should—indeed morally speaking must— just reject such acute disparities in life prospects as unfair and unjust even though they do benefit the most disadvantaged. Are not both arguments equally good or equally bad? If we are justified in rejecting utilitarian reasoning in one case why are we not justified in rejecting it in the other?

It is not, as Rawls claims, envy that is operative here, for one can have the appropriate sense of injustice even if one is not a member of the oppressed and exploited class. One might even be a part of the ruling class—as Engels was—and still feel it. The point is that it offends one's sense of justice. Or perhaps, I should say, to give fewer hostages to fortune, it offends my sense of justice and I know it offends the sense of justice of some others as well. I am inclined to say that here Rawls' principles do not match with my considered judgements and the considered judgement of at least some others. Rawls might well counter that they would if we got them into reflective equilibrium. That is, Rawls might claim, if I considered all the facts, the alternative theories and the principles of rationality, my considered judgements would not be what they are now. It is irrational *not* to accept these inequalities as just or at least as justified.[25]

Such considerations push us back to some basic questions in moral methodology. If there is anything to the above parallelism and both arguments are equally good or equally bad, we still, of course, want to know which they are. Here our considered judgements come into play and, speaking for myself, even when I have utilized the devices linked with what Rawls calls 'reflective equilibrium,' it remains the case that they are not settled on this issue. I am drawn by the teleological 'utilitarian' considerations: why not, where we can, act in such a manner that we are likely to diminish as much as possible the occurrence of misery and maximize the attainment of happiness or at least (if that does not come to the same thing) the satisfaction of desire? What else, everything considered, could be the better, the more humane thing to do? But I am pulled in the other direction as well, for I also find myself asking: but are we to do this when this commits us to doing things which are plainly unfair, i.e. when we in effect, whatever our rhetoric, either ignore the interests of certain people, when considering their interests would not contribute toward maximization, or we simply accept as justified, as 'all right,' given how things are, vast disparities of life prospects between the children—often equally talented and equally intelligent—of entrepreneurs and unskilled labourers when the *difference* principle and an equal opportunity principle are satisfied?

Even on reflection with the facts and the consequences of both sets of strategems before me, vividly and fully, it still strikes me as grossly unfair so to treat the disadvantaged. Yet I can also see the humanity and indeed the rationality in 'utilitarian reasoning' here: why allow any more misery or unhappiness than necessary? If closing up the gap between the classes at some determinate point in history results in that, then do not close it. Still I am also inclined to come back, against such 'utilitarian reasoning' concerning such a case, with something (vague as it is) about fairness, human dignity and being in a better position to control one's own life (effective moral autonomy). Moreover, it is not clear that happiness should be so set in opposition to human dignity and a control of one's life as if being happy were independent of these things. But the concept of happiness also has its more familiar sides as well. Perhaps it too is an essentially contested concept.

I think that what is happening here is that very deeply embedded but, in this context, conflicting moral sentiments are being appealed to and our conflicting considered judgements are being matched with these conflicting sentiments.[26] On the side of a socialist conception of justice, more radically egalitarian than Rawls', we have a clearer recognition of and accounting for the danger to liberty of inequalities of economic power and the effects of concentrated wealth and power under capitalism (particularly modern monopoly capitalism) on the moral autonomy and sense of moral worth of such disadvantaged people. There is the recognition that, given the realities of social life, we are not justified in believing, as liberals do, that we can rightly treat as separate the political and economic spheres of life and still serve best each person's human flourishing or even, more prosaically, his welfare, by maximizing political freedoms while tolerating extensive economic disparities. Moral autonomy for all, the socialist believes, is simply not possible under such circumstances.

In circumstances of moderate scarcity, Rawls believes that we can and should act in accordance with the *difference* principle, while still acting in accordance with the equal liberty principle, i.e. the principle laying it down "that each person has an equal right to the most extensive scheme of equal basic liberties compatible with a similar scheme of liberties for all." [27] But talk of the priority of the equal liberty principle over the *difference* principle should not obscure the fact that in such circumstances reasoning in accordance with the *difference* principle, even when placed in its proper lexical order, will make for less moral autonomy—and in that crucial sense less liberty—than will reasoning in accordance with the more egalitarian socialist principles. That is so because the socialist always aims at diminishing morally irrelevant inequalities, inequalities in the primary social goods or in basic human goods. With fewer such inequalities, there would be less control of one group over another and thus there would be greater moral autonomy. By contrast, Rawls' *difference* principle has the unfortunate unintended effect of limiting the scope of his equal liberty principle.

This greater moral autonomy afforded by the socialist principles would most plainly be so if classlessness, or something far closer to classlessness than Rawls allows, were possible. Most crucially, that should be taken to mean the possibility of there being a complex society in which there are no radical differences in life prospects between different groups of people because some have far greater income, power, authority or prestige than others. Where there is such a class society there will be less moral autonomy than in a classless society where the more radically egalitarian socialist conceptions can be satisfied. Moreover, in spite of what Rawls may think, what we speak of here is not something which goes 'beyond justice,' for such considerations concern the fairness of distributions and relations between human beings. So some justification of Rawls' assumption that classlessness is not possible becomes crucial. However, if the division of classes is indeed inevitable, then, perhaps, for those who find a Nozickian trip neither very intellectually challenging nor morally acceptable, a Rawlsian egalitarianism is the best thing that can be had, if one cares about liberty (particularly equal liberty), equality and human well-being. But, given the choices, we ought to be tolerably certain that classlessness is impossible.

Would Rawls be justified in assuming that institutional inequalities rooted in class structures are inevitable? What Rawls must do, to establish that classlessness is impossible or unlikely, is to show that it is impossible or unlikely that a society can come into existence where there are only rather minimal differences in income and authority and where none of the differences that do exist result from or are the means to exploiting others. (Note, given its characterization, it is a conceptual impossibility that such an egalitarian society would be authoritarian.) That is, as Macpherson would put it, the society would be so organized that there would be no way to transfer "to oneself for one's own benefit some of the powers of others." [28]

Whatever we may want to say about the division of labour, it is plainly not necessary that there be private ownership of the means of production.

Yet it is the private ownership of the means of production which is the principal source of one human being's ability to extract for his own benefit some of the powers of others. Such exploitation is unavoidable in a capitalist organization of society, but there is nothing necessary, given our position in history, about the continued existence of a capitalist social order. Perhaps, as Dahrendorf believes, some social stratification is inevitable, but that is another matter. What we have no good grounds for taking to be a fixed feature of human life is the sorting of human beings into socio-economic classes in which one class will exploit the other. Unless it is a mistake to believe that it is these socio-economic class divisions (or something rather like them in statist societies) which make for such radical differences in life prospects, there is good reason to believe that a form of egalitarianism more radical than Rawls' is both feasible and morally desirable and that the principal human task will be to struggle to attain classlessness.[29]

RADICAL EGALITARIANISM

I want, at this juncture, to make a disclaimer. I do not claim for these views a support in Marx or the Marxist tradition, though I do hope that they are compatible with that tradition. What Marx's or Engels' views are on these matters is subject to considerable debate.[30] They do not systematically treat this subject and indeed they sometimes talk, when justice-talk is at issue, derisively of ideology or false consciousness.[31] To develop any kind of explicit Marxist theory here would require extensive injections of rather contestable interpretation. I will only remark that my radical socialist egalitarianism is in accord with Engels' claim, in a famous passage on the subject in his *Anti-Dühring*, that "the real content of the proletarian demand for equality is the demand for the *abolition* of classes." Significantly, he then goes on to remark that a "demand for equality which goes beyond that, of necessity passes into absurdity," thereby in effect rejecting what have become straw-men forms of 'radical egalitarianism' easily knocked about by philosophers.[32] Neither Marx nor Engels was a complete egalitarian in the sense that he thought all human beings should be treated exactly alike in every respect. No thoughtful person, egalitarian or otherwise, believes that everyone old and young, sick and well, introverted and extroverted, should be treated the same in every respect: as if all people had exactly the same interests, aspirations and needs.

I cannot here specify fully, let alone extensively defend, the form of 'social justice' or, as I would prefer to call it, 'radical egalitarianism' which I have argued is at least as reasonable as Rawls' account. In fact I would go further than that and contend that it is a superior conception, at least from someone who starts out with moral sentiments similar to those of Rawls, in that it squares better than Rawls' theory, both with what we know about the world (particularly with what we know about the need for meaningful work and the conditions of moral autonomy) and with some of Rawls' deepest insights—insights which led him to reject utilitarianism and to set out his conception of justice as fairness. Here I have in mind his Kantian conception of human beings as members of a kingdom of ends, the weight he gives to moral autonomy, self-respect, equal liberty and to moral community. My contention has been that such things are not achievable under even a liberal capitalist order with its resultant class divisions. Given the way political and economic phenomena interact, liberty and moral autonomy cannot but suffer when there are substantial differences in wealth.[33] It is not only, as is now becoming more generally recognized and apologized for (see the Trilateral Commission's Task Force report: *The Governability of Democracies*), that capitalism is incompatible with equality, it is also incompatible with equal liberty and moral autonomy for all humankind.[34] Equal liberty is impossible without people—all people of normal abilities—being masters of their own lives, but with the differences in power and control between classes within capitalism, this is impossible for most people.

Furthermore, given the control of the forces of production by one class and the consequent authoritarian allocation of work, meaningful work must be very limited under capitalism. Meaningful work, as Esheté well argues, must be autonomous, though this does not mean that it cannot be cooperative; it must, that is, bear the mark of our own making in the sense of our own planning, thought and our own decisions about what is worth doing, making and having.[35] But this is only possible where there is effective, cooperative, democratically controlled workers' social ownership of the means of production. For anyone who sees the plausibility of Rawls' 'Aristotelian principle' or thinks about the conditions of self-respect and thinks carefully about the role of work in life, it should be evident that under a capitalist organization of production these values and with them full moral autonomy are not achievable.

It is a very deep moral assumption of both Rawls' account and my own that all human beings have a right to equal respect and concern in the design of social (including political and economic) institutions. We must, that is, if our normative ethic is to be adequate, and our reactions as moral agents are to answer to that theory, treat all human beings with an equal moral respect. We must regard it as morally required that equal moral concern be given to everyone. What sort of principles of justice do we need to match with that underlying moral assumption and with the related conception that a good society will provide the basis for equal self-respect for all people? Rawls sees that it is true that in bourgeois societies, such as those in North America and Western Europe, relative wealth, to a very considerable degree, provides for most people the psychological basis for self-respect. (No claim need be made that these are the only societies so affected.) Given his belief that classlessness is unattainable and that important differences in wealth and power will remain and indeed are important in providing incentives for the accumulation of material wealth, which in turn will better everyone's circumstances, Rawls understandably tries to break the psychological connection between wealth and self-respect. I argued in the earlier sections that there is a tight link between wealth, power and autonomy and that equal moral autonomy cannot be sustained without something like a very near equality of wealth and power. It is a simple corollary of that to see that equal self-respect cannot be achieved without equal moral autonomy. If that is right, and Rawls is right in assuming that classlessness is impossible, one should draw some rather pessimistic conclusions about the very possibility of a moral order.[36] However, I have argued that we do not have good grounds for rejecting the empirical possibility of classlessness. Given the fundamental moral beliefs that Rawls and I share, I think that in looking for the basis for stabilizing—indeed making it something that could socially flourish—equal self-respect and equal moral autonomy, we should look again at a principle of justice which would stress the need for an equal division of wealth.

I want now to state my more radically egalitarian principle of justice. I shall do so in a somewhat Rawlsian manner for ease of comparison, though I am not particularly enamoured with its formulation and I am confident, if there is anything in it at all, that it will require all sorts of refinements, clarifications and (no doubt) modifications. Moreover, I do not offer it as a candidate eternal principle of justice, *sub Specie Aeternitatas*, but rather as a principle of social justice, for conditions of relative abundance (imagine present-day Sweden as the world). This still fits in the upper end of Rawls' situation of moderate scarcity, where considerations of distribution would still be important.[37] For conditions of full abundance, as Marx stressed, questions of distribution would be very secondary indeed.[38]

What I want to capture, in some rough initial way, with my radically egalitarian principle of justice, is a distributive principle committed to *equal division with adjustments for differences in need.* I am under no illusions about its being a magic formula, and much of its plausibility (if it has any) would depend on the reading given to its various constituent elements—a task not to be undertaken here.[39] But I hope the previous discussion has made evident the need to attempt an elucidation of the often cavalierly dismissed principle of radical equality. My formulation has two parts and is expressed as follows:

1. Each person is to have an equal right to the most extensive total system of equal basic liberties and opportunities (including equal opportunities for meaningful work, for self-determination and political participation), compatible with a similar treatment of all. (This principle gives expression to a commitment to attain and/or sustain equal moral autonomy and equal self-respect.)

2. After provisions are made for common social (community) values, for capital overhead to preserve the society's productive capacity and allowances are made for differing unmanipulated needs and preferences, the income and wealth (the common stock of means) is to be so divided that each person will have a right to an equal share.

I am making no claims about priority relations between 1 and 2. I am saying that in a perfectly just society, which is also a relatively abundant society, these two principles will be fully satisfied. It should be noted that such principles can only be so satisfied in a classless society where, in Marx's famous phrase, the free development of each is the condition of the free development of all. Furthermore, such principles require democracy for their realization, taken here to mean "the people's self-determination in political, economic and social affairs" and such a democracy, it is plain to see, requires socialism.[40]

Even in the circumstances where this principle can have a proper application, it is not the case that this is the conception of justice that any rational person would have to adopt who was constrained to reason impartially about what principles of action are collectively rational. I do not believe that my principle, or any other principle, including justice as fairness or average utility, can attain even such an atemporal rational Archimedean point.[41] I do not think that it can be established that there is a set of principles of collective action which are uniquely rational, even in a determinate historical epoch. *A Theory of Justice* is just the latest in a long line of distinguished failures to achieve such an Archimedean point.

What I think can be shown is that in the situation described, for persons with certain moral sentiments, a conception of justice of the type formulated above would be the rational choice. The sentiment I have in mind is the one that leads Rawls to what Ronald Dworkin regards as his deepest moral assumption underlying his commitment to justice as fairness, namely "the assumption of a natural right of all men and women to an equality of concern and respect, a right they possess not in virtue of birth or characteristic or merit or excellence but simply as human beings with the capacity to make plans and give justice." [42] I do not know how anyone could show this belief to be true or self-evident or in any way prove it or show that, if one is through and through rational, one must accept it.[43] I do not think a Nietzschean, a Benthamite or even an amoralist who rejects it can thereby be shown to be irrational or even, in any way necessarily, to be diminished in his reason. It is a moral belief that I am committed to and I believe Dworkin is right in claiming that Rawls is too. What I am claiming is that, in the circumstances I described, if one is so committed and one has the facts straight, reasons carefully and takes these reasons to heart, one will be led, not to utilitarianism or to justice as fairness or even to a form of pluralism, but to some such form of radical egalitarianism.[44]

NOTES

1. Ronald Dworkin, "The Original Position," *The University of Chicago Law Review*, Vol. 40, No. 3 (Spring, 1973), p. 533, and Thomas M. Scanlon, "Rawls' Theory of Justice," *The University of Pennsylvania Law Review*, Vol. 121 (1973), p. 1064.

2. It tries to capture in what is, I hope, clear argumentative discourse something

of what Marx had in mind with his conception of a classless society where the free development of each is the condition of the free development of all. An account, at core very close to my own but given a more political and historical expression, and closely related to the contemporary political scene, is given by Martin J. Sklar, "Liberty and Equality, and Socialism," *Socialist Revolution*, Vol. 7, No. 4 (July–August, 1977), pp. 92–104. Evan Simpson, "Socialist Justice," *Ethics*, Vol. 87, No. 1 (October, 1976) argues, much more abstractly, to similar conclusions, but I find his argumentation, as distinct from his conclusions and depiction of the liberal/socialist division, obscure.

3. Irving Fetcher, "Karl Marx on Human Nature," *Social Research*, Vol. 40, No. 3 (Autumn, 1973), p. 461.

4. I am here indebted to the work of C. B. Macpherson. His own important critical essays on Rawls have unfortunately been neglected. C. B. Macpherson, *Democratic Theory* (Oxford: Clarendon Press, 1973), Chapter IV, and "Rawls's Models of Man and Society," *Philosophy of the Social Sciences*, Vol. 3, No. 4 (December, 1973). I have in my own "On the Very Possibility of a Classless Society: Macpherson, Rawls and Revisionist Liberalism" (forthcoming) attempted to elucidate and critically assess the force of Macpherson's critique of Rawls. Elizabeth Rapaport, "Classical Liberalism and Rawlsian Revisionism" and Virginia McDonald, "Rawlsian Contractarianism: Liberal Equality or Inequality," both in *New Essays on Contract Theory*, Kai Nielsen and Roger Shiner (eds.), (Guelph, Ontario: Canadian Association for Publishing in Philosophy, 1977) have extended and developed, essentially along Macpherson's lines, a socialist critique of contractarianism.

5. Wesley Cooper has spotted some of the inadequacies in Rawls conception of a perfectly just society. Wesley E. Cooper, "The Perfectly Just Society," *Philosophy and Phenomenological Research*, forthcoming.

6. John Rawls, *A Theory of Justice* (Cambridge, Massachusetts: Harvard University Press, 1971), p. 302. That there is, or even can be, such general knowledge of society is challenged by P. H. Nowell-Smith, "A Theory of Justice?", *Philosophy of the Social Sciences*, Vol. 3, No. 4 (December, 1973), and Robert Paul Wolff, *Understanding Rawls* (Princeton, New Jersey: Princeton University Press, 1977), Chapter XIII. A powerful theoretical underpinning for the kind of claim made impressionistically by Nowell-Smith and Wolff is brilliantly articulated by Charles Taylor, "Interpretation and the Sciences of Man," *The Review of Metaphysics*, Vol. XXV, No. 1 (September, 1971).

7. Robert Paul Wolff, *op. cit.*, pp. 67–71, Brian Barry, *The Liberal Theory of Justice* (Oxford: Clarendon Press, 1973), pp. 50–51; David Copp, "Justice and the Difference Principle," *Canadian Journal of Philosophy*, Vol. 4, No. 2 (1974); and the essays by R. M. Hare, David Lyons and Benjamin Barber in *Reading Rawls*, Norman Daniels (ed.) (New York: Basic Books, Inc., 1975).

8. I have, in various ways, argued this against Rawls in several different contexts. Kai Nielsen, "The Choice between Perfectionism and Rawlsian Contractarianism," *Interpretation*, Vol. 6, No. 2 (May, 1977); "On Philosophic Method," *International Philosophical Quarterly*, Vol. XVI, No. 2 (September, 1976); "The Priority of Liberty Examined," *The Indian Political Science Review*, Vol. XI, No. 1 (January, 1977); and "Rawls and Classist Amoralism," *Mind*, Vol. LXXXVI, No. 341 (January, 1977). It has also been argued in various ways by Steven Lukes, "An Archimedean Point," *Observer* (June 4, 1972), and in his "Relativism: Cognitive and Moral," *Aristotelian Society Proceedings, Supplementary Volume*, XLVIII (1974); by Andreas Esheté, "Contractarianism and the Scope of Justice," *Ethics*, Vol. 85, No. 1 (October, 1974); and by William L. McBride, "Social Theory *sub Specie Aeternitatis*," *Yale Law Journal*, Vol. 81 (1972).

9. It is clear enough that Rawls would regard such a society, in conditions of moderate scarcity, as a well-ordered society, if certain conditions are met. Whether he would say it is a perfectly just society is less clear, though there is at least one passage (p. 102) that suggests that. Cooper, *op. cit.*, brings out very well the inadequacy of Rawls' conception of a perfectly just society.

10. Joel Feinberg expresses clearly the standard and, as far as I can see, a perfectly adequate rationale for such a belief as follows: "Let us consider why we all agree . . . in rejecting the view that differences in race, sex, IQ or social 'rank' are

the grounds of just differences in wealth or income. Part of the answer seems obvious. People cannot by their own voluntary choices determine what skin color, sex or IQ they shall have, or which hereditary caste they shall enter. To make such properties the basis of discrimination between individuals in the distribution of social benefits would be to treat people differently in ways that profoundly affect their lives because of differences for which they have no responsibility. Differences in a given respect are relevant for the aims of distributive justice, then, only if they are differences for which their possessors can be held responsible; properties can be the grounds of just discrimination between persons only if those persons had a *fair opportunity* to acquire or avoid them." Joel Feinberg, "Economic Justice," in Karsten J. Struhl and Paula Rothenberg Struhl (eds.), *Ethics in Perspective* (New York: Random House, 1975), p. 421.

11. Brian Barry, *op. cit.*, convincingly argues that there are good empirical reasons to doubt whether the narrowing of such inequalities would in fact have the effect of making the worst-off parties still worse off.

12. Yet it is clear enough that Rawls is not insensitive to these problems. John Rawls, *A Theory of Justice*, pp. 298–301.

13. Rawls makes far too much play with envy here. Besides envy and jealousy, the disadvantaged, as Rawls recognizes himself, could feel "resentment from a sense that they are unfairly treated." *Ibid.*, p. 540.

14. Andreas Esheté, "Contractarianism and the Scope of Justice," *Ethics*, Vol. 85, No. 1 (October, 1974).

15. John Rawls, *A Theory of Justice*, p. 205.

16. Norman Daniels, "Equal Liberty and Unequal Worth of Liberty," in Norman Daniels (ed.), *Reading Rawls* (New York: Basic Books, Inc., 1975).

17. John Rawls, *A Theory of Justice*, pp. 73-74, 275-79, and 512.

18. *Ibid.*, p. 75.

19. *Ibid.*, pp. 98–102, 511–12, 530–41 (most particularly 534, 536, 537 and 539). See also John Rawls, "Distributive Justice" in Peter Laslett and W. G. Runciman (eds.), *Philosophy, Politics and Society*, third series (Oxford: Basil Blackwell, Ltd., 1967), pp. 66–70. For a perceptive discussion of this see C. B. Macpherson, *Democratic Theory* (Oxford: Clarendon Press, 1973), pp. 88–92.

20. C. B. Macpherson, *op. cit.* and Benjamin Barber, *op. cit.*

21. Rolf Dahrendorf, *Essays in the Theory of Society* (Stanford, California: Stanford University Press, 1968), pp. 151–78.

22. Benjamin Barber powerfully probes whether they do so hang together. Barber, *op. cit.*

23. This leads us back to the literature cited in footnote 8.

24. Paul Taylor, "Utility and Justice," *Canadian Journal of Philosophy*, Vol. 1, No. 3 (March, 1972) has very forcefully argued, in a manner plainly influenced by Rawls' root conception of justice as fairness, how distinct questions of justice are from those of utility.

25. John Rawls, *A Theory of Justice*, p. 546. Rawls, as some have thought, seems to have confused 'just inequalities' with 'justified inequalities'. It may not be just to sanction such inequalities but it may still be justified on utilitarian grounds. It may be one of those cases, *pace* Rawls, where considerations of utility outweigh considerations of justice and where what we should do, through and through, is not identical with what justice requires. To claim this would require a rather considerable change in Rawls' system, but it would give him a rather more plausible justification for his *difference* principle.

26. I have discussed problems about matching and problems of Rawls' conception of reflective equilibrium in my "On Philosophic Method," *International Philosophical Quarterly*, Vol. XVI, No. 3 (1976), pp. 358–68.

27. John Rawls, "Some Reasons for the Maximin Criterion," *The American Economic Review*, Vol. 64 (1974), p. 142.

28. C. B. Macpherson, "Rawls's Models of Man and Society," *Philosophy of the Social Sciences*, Vol. 3, No. 4 (December, 1973), p. 341.

29. The conception I use of statist societies is clarified, applied and defended by

Svetozar Stojanović in his *Between Ideals and Reality* (New York: Oxford University Press, 1973), Chapter III.

30. William L. McBride, "The Concept of Justice in Marx, Engels, and Others," *Ethics*, Vol. 85, No. 3 (April, 1975); Lucien Goldmann, "Is There a Marxist Sociology?", *Radical Philosophy 1* (January, 1972); Derek Allen, "The Utilitarianism of Marx and Engels," *American Philosophical Quarterly*, Vol. 10, No. 3 (January, 1973); George Brenkert, "Marx and Utilitarianism," *Canadian Journal of Philosophy*, Vol. V, No. 3 (November, 1975); Derek Allen, "Reply to Brenkert's 'Marx and Utilitarianism'," *Canadian Journal of Philosophy*, Vol. VI, No. 3 (September, 1976); Robert Tucker, *The Marxian Revolutionary Idea* (New York: W. W. Norton & Co., 1969), Chapter 3; Allen Wood, "The Marxian Critique of Justice," *Philosophy and Public Affairs*, Vol. 1, No. 3 (Spring, 1972); Michael P. Lerner, "Marxism and Ethical Reasoning," *Social Praxis*, Vol. 2 (1974); Kai Nielsen, "Class Conflict, Marxism and the Good-Reasons Approach," *Social Praxis*, Vol. 2 (1974); Derek Allen, "Is Marxism a Philosophy?" and Marlene Gerber Fried, "Marxism and Justice," both in *The Journal of Philosophy*, Vol. LXXI, No. 17 (October 10, 1974); and Nancy Holmstrom, "Exploitation," *Canadian Journal of Philosophy*, Vol. VII, No. 2 (June, 1977).

31. We need in this context to face questions which arise about moral ideology. See here W. L. McBride, "The Concept of Justice in Marx, Engels, and Others," *Ethics*, Vol. 5, No. 3 (April, 1975); Andrew Collier, "Truth and Practice," *Radical Philosophy 5* (Summer, 1973), and "The Production of Moral Ideology," *Radical Philosophy 9* (Winter, 1974); Tony Skillen, "Marxism and Morality," *Radical Philosophy 8* (Summer, 1974); Peter Binns, "Anti-Moralism," *Radical Philosophy 10* (Spring, 1975); and Philip Corrigan and Derek Sayer, "Moral Relations, Political Economy and Class Struggle," *Radical Philosophy 12* (Winter, 1975).

32. F. Engels, *Anti-Dühring* (New York: International Publishers, 1939), pp. 117–18. For one recent such effort to refute egalitarianism, splendidly made into a straw man, see H. J. McCloskey, "A Right To Equality?", *Canadian Journal of Philosophy*, Vol. VI, No. 4 (December, 1976). Other such efforts include: Robert Nisbet, "The Pursuit of Equality," *Public Interest*, No. 33 (1974); Isaiah Berlin, "Equality," in *The Concept of Equality*, William Blackstone (ed.) (Minneapolis, Minnesota: Burgess Publishing Co., 1969); and Hugo Bedau, "Radical Egalitarianism," in Hugo A. Bedau (ed.), *Justice and Equality* (Englewood Cliffs, New Jersey: Prentice-Hall, Inc., 1971).

33. Evan Simpson, *op. cit.*, p. 2.

34. The provisions and ideological transformations of the concept of democracy are interesting to observe in the literature of the Trilateral Commission. See, for example, Samuel Huntington et al. (eds.), *The Governability of Democracies*, and the Trilateral Commission's publication *Trialogue*, particularly the Summer issue 1975, the Winter issue 1975-76 and the Spring issue 1976. Note particularly the writings of Huntington, Crozier, Watanuki, Dahrendorf and Carli. For trenchantly critical remarks about the Trilateral Commission see Noam Chomsky, "Trilateral's RX for Crisis: governability yes, democracy no," *Seven Days* (February 14, 1977), pp. 10–11.

35. Esheté's comments on work are particularly important here. See Andreas Esheté, *op. cit.*, pp. 41–44.

36. These conclusions are drawn about the attainment and sustaining of genuine moral relations in *class-divided societies*. See the references to Lerner and Nielsen in footnote 30 and to Collier, Skillen and Binns in footnote 31. The steadfast and probing recognition of this is captured in the deepest way in the work of Bertolt Brecht.

37. A rejection of a) the possibility of attaining such eternal principles and b) an argument that they are unnecessary for attaining a basis for rational social critique is made by William L. McBride, "Social Theory *sub Specie Aeternitatis*," *Yale Law Journal*, Vol. 31 (1972); Andreas Esheté, *op. cit.*; and Boris Frankel, "Review Symposium of *Anarchy, State and Utopia*," *Theory and Society*, Vol. 3 (1976), pp. 443–50.

38. See Marx's *Critique of the Gotha Programme*. For a perceptive discussion of issues arising from this and of Marx's slogan "From each according to his ability and to each according to his need," see Edward and Onora Nell, "On Justice Under Socialism," in Karsten J. Struhl and Paula Rothenberg Struhl (eds.), *Ethics in Perspective* (New York: Random House, 1976).

39. I turn to this task, among other things, in my "The Indivisibility of Liberty and Equality," forthcoming.

40. Martin J. Sklar, *op. cit.*, pp. 96 and 103. The arguments in the above paragraph, as well as Sklar's essay, should make it evident why my two principles require socialism. We cannot have industrial democracy of the type characterized or classlessness with any kind of capitalist organization of society. There simply will not be democracy in the workplace under capitalism. People will have to sell their labour and they will be controlled by others in their work.

41. My articles cited in footnote 8 were, in part, directed to establishing this point.

42. Ronald Dworkin, *op. cit.*, p. 532.

43. My "Scepticism and Human Rights," *The Monist,* Vol. 52, No. 4 (October, 1968) was meant to go some of the way toward establishing this. For two more general arguments which provide a theoretical underpinning for such type arguments, see my "Why There Is a Problem about Ethics: Reflections on the Is and the Ought," *Danish Yearbook of Philosophy* (1978) and "Principles of Rationality," *Philosophical Papers,* Vol. III, No. 2 (October, 1974).

44. In this last section I have peculated from, and turned to my own purposes, points often made in different contexts and for different purposes by Martin J. Sklar, *op. cit.*; Andreas Esheté, *op. cit.*; William L. McLride, *op. cit.*; Henry Shue, "Liberty and Self Respect," *Ethics,* Vol. 85 (April, 1975); Lawrence Crocker, "Equality, Solidarity and Rawls' Maximin," *Philosophy and Public Affairs,* Vol. 6, No. 3 (Spring, 1977); and Derek L. Phillips, "The Equality Debate: What Does Justice Require?", *Theory and Society,* Vol. 4 (1977), pp. 247–72.

G. A. COHEN

University College, London

Robert Nozick and Wilt Chamberlain: How Patterns Preserve Liberty

Let us now suppose that I have sold the product of my own labour for money, and have used the money to hire a labourer, i.e., I have bought somebody else's labour-power. Having taken advantage of this labour-power of another, I turn out to be the owner of value which is considerably higher than the value I spent on its purchase. This, *from one point of view,* is very just, because it has already been recognized, after all, that I can use what I have secured by exchange as is best and most advantageous to myself . . .[1]

Persons, who under a vicious order of things have obtained a competent share of social enjoyments, are never in want of arguments to justify to the eye of reason such a state of society; for what may not admit of apology when exhibited in but *one point of view?* If the same individuals were to-morrow required to cast anew the lots assigning them a place in society, they would find many things to object to.[2]

Robert Nozick occupies the point of view Plekhanov describes, and his *Anarchy, State and Utopia* is in large measure an ingenious elaboration of the argument for capitalism Plekhanov adumbrates. The capitalism Nozick advocates is more pure than the one we know today. It lacks taxation for social welfare, and it permits degrees of inequality far greater

An early version of this article appeared in *Erkenntnis* 11 (1977), 5-23. D. Reidel Publishing Company, Dordrecht-Holland. Reprinted by permission.

than most apologists for contemporary bourgeois society would now countenance.

This paper is only indirectly a critique of Nozick's defense of capitalism. Its immediate aim is to refute Nozick's major argument against a rival of capitalism, socialism. The refutation vindicates socialism against that argument, but no one opposed to socialism on other grounds should expect to be converted by this paper.

Nozick's case against socialism can be taken in two ways. He proposes a definition of justice in terms of liberty, and on that basis he argues that what socialists [3] consider just is not in fact just. But even if his definition of justice is wrong, so that the basis of his critique, taken in this first way, is faulty, he still has a claim against socialism, namely that, however *just* it may be, it is incompatible with *liberty*. Even if Nozick is mistaken about what justice it, he might still be right that the cost in loss of liberty imposed by what socialists regard as just is intolerably high. (Hence the title of the section of the book on which we shall focus: 'How Liberty Upsets Patterns'—patterns being distributions answering to, for example, a socialist principle of justice). So it is not enough, in defending socialism against Nozick, to prove that he has not shown it is unjust. It must also be proved that he has not shown that it is opposed to liberty.

A full definition of socialism is not required for our purposes. All we need suppose is that a socialist society upholds some principle of equality in the distribution of benefits enjoyed and burdens borne by its members. The principle need not be specified further, for Nozick's argument is against the institution of *any* such principle. Let us now imagine that such an egalitarian principle is instituted, and that it leads to a distribution of goods and bads which, following Nozick, we call D1. Then Nozick reasons by example that D1 can be maintained only at the price of tyranny and injustice. The example concerns the best basketball player in the imagined society.[4]

> . . . suppose that Wilt Chamberlain is greatly in demand by basketball teams, being a great gate attraction. . . He signs the following sort of contract with a team: In each home game, twenty-five cents from the price of each ticket of admission goes to him. . . . The season starts, and people cheerfully attend his team's games; they buy their tickets, each time dropping a separate twenty-five cents of their admission price into a special box with Chamberlain's name on it. They are excited about seeing him play; it is worth the total admission price to them. Let us suppose that in one season one million persons attend his home games, and Wilt Chamberlain winds up with $250,000, a much larger sum than the average income. . . . Is he entitled to this income? Is this new distribution D2, unjust? If so, why? There is *no* question about whether each of the people was entitled to the control over the resources they held in D1; because that was the distribution . . . that (for the purposes of argument) we assumed was acceptable. Each of these persons *chose* to give twenty-five cents of their money to Chamberlain. They could have spent it on going to the movies, or on candy bars, or on copies of *Dissent* magazine, or of *Monthy Review*. But they all, at least one million of them, converged on giving it to Wilt

Chamberlain in exchange for watching him play basketball. If D1 was a just distribution, and people voluntarily moved from it to D2, transferring parts of their shares they were given under D1 (what was it for if not to do something with?), isn't D2 also just? If the people were entitled to dispose of the resources to which they were entitled (under D1), didn't this include their being entitled to give it to, or exchange it with, Wilt Chamberlain? Can anyone else complain on grounds of justice? Each other person already has his legitimate share under D1. Under D1, there is nothing that anyone has that anyone else has a claim of justice against. After someone transfers something to Wilt Chamberlain, third parties *still* have their legitimate shares; *their* shares are not changed. By what process could such a transfer among two persons give rise to a legitimate claim of distributive justice on a portion of what was transferred, by a third party who had no claim of justice on any holding of the others *before* the transfer?

According to Nozick

(1) Whatever arises from a just situation by just steps is itself just. (p. 151)

Steps are just if they are free of injustice, and they are free of injustice if they are fully voluntary on the part of all legitimately concerned persons. Hence

(2) Whatever arises from a just situation as a result of fully voluntary transactions on the part of all legitimately concerned persons is itself just.

So convinced is Nozick that (2) is true that he thinks it must be accepted by people attached to a doctrine of justice which in other respects differs from his own. That is why he feels able to employ (2) in the Chamberlain parable, despite having granted, for the sake of argument, the justice of an initial situation patterned by an egalitarian principle.

Even if (2) is true, it does not follow that pattern D1 can be maintained only at the price of injustice, for people might simply *fail* to use their liberty in a pattern-subverting manner. But that is not an interesting possibility. A more interesting one is that they deliberately *refuse* to use their liberty subversively. Reasons for refusing will be adduced shortly. But is (2) true? Does liberty always preserve justice?

A standard way of testing the claim would be to look for states of affairs which would be accounted unjust but which might be generated by the route (2) approves. Perhaps, the strongest counterexample of this form would be slavery. We then say: voluntary self-enslavement is possible, slavery is unjust, therefore (2) is false. But whatever may be the merits of that argument, we know that Nozick is not moved by it. For he thinks there is no injustice in slavery to the extent that it arises out of the approved processes.

Though Nozick consistently endorses slavery of appropriate genesis, there is a restriction, derived from (2) itself, on the kind of slavery he accepts. (2) does not allow slave status to be inherited by offspring of the self-enslaved, for then a concerned party's situation would be decided for him, independently of his will. "Some things individuals may choose for themselves no one may choose for another" (p. 331). Let us remember this when we come to scrutinize the Wilt Chamberlain transaction, for widespread contracting of the kind which occurs in the parable might have the effect of seriously modifying, for the worse, the situation of members of future generations.

Should we say that in Nozick's conception of justice a slave society need be no less just than one where people are free? That would be a tendentious formulation. For Nozick can claim that rational persons in an initially just situation are unlikely to contract into slavery, except, indeed, where circumstances are so special that it would be wrong to forbid them to do so. This diminishes the danger that (2) can be used to stamp approval on morally repellent social arrangements.

I attribute some such response to Nozick on the basis, *inter alia* of this passage:

> . . . it must be granted that were people's reasons for transferring some of their holdings to others always irrational or arbitrary, we would find this *disturbing*. . . We feel more comfortable upholding the justice of an entitlement system if most of the transfers under it are done for reasons. This does not mean necessarily that all deserve what holdings they receive. It means only that there is a purpose or point to someone's transferring a holding to one person rather than to another; that usually we can see what the transferrer *thinks* he's gaining, what cause he *thinks* he's serving, what goals he *thinks* he's helping to achieve, and so forth. Since in a capitalist society people often transfer holdings to others in accordance with how much they *perceive* these others benefiting them, the fabric constituted by the individual transactions and transfers is largely reasonable and intelligible (p. 159, my emphases).

Accordingly, Nozick emphasizes the motives people have when they pay to watch Chamberlain, instead of stipulating that they do so freely and leaving us to guess why. The example would be less impressive if Chamberlain or his agent had induced in the fans an inordinate taste for basketball, by means which fell short of what Nozick would consider coercive or fraudulent, but which remained unattractive. It is important to the persuasive allure of the example that we should think what the fans are doing not only voluntary but sensible.

So transactions are disturbing (even though they are just? [5]) when we cannot see what the (or some of the) contracting parties think they are gaining by them. But we should surely also be disturbed if though we can see what the agent *thinks* he's gaining, we know that what he *will* gain is not that, but something he thinks less valuable; or that what results is not only the gain he expects but also unforeseen consequences which render negative the net value, according to his preferences and standards, of the transaction. We should not be content if what he *thinks* he is getting is good, but what he actually gets is bad, by his own lights. I shall assume that Nozick would accept this plausible extension of his concession. If he would not, so much the worse for his position.

Hence if we can show that Chamberlain's fans get not only the pleasure of watching him minus twenty-five cents, but also uncontemplated dis-benefits of a high order, then even if for Nozick the outcome remains just, it should, even to Nozick, be rather disturbing. We shall need to ask whether we do not find irrationality in the Chamberlain transaction, when we think through, as Nozick's fans do not, the *full* consequences of what they are doing.

But now we can go further. For, in the light of the considerations just reviewed, (2) appears very probably false. Nozick says a transaction is free of injustice if every concerned party agrees to it. Perhaps that is so. But transactional justice, so characterized, is supposed—given an initially just situation—to confer justice on what results from it. (That is why (2) follows from (1)). And that is questionable. Of each person who agrees to a transaction we may ask: *would he have agreed to it had he known what its outcome was to be?* Since the answer may be negative, it is far from evident that transactional justice, as described, transmits justice to its results. Perhaps the effect obtains when the answer is positive. Perhaps, in other words, (3) is true:

> (3) Whatever arises from a just situation as a result of fully voluntary transactions which all transagents would still have agreed to if they had known what the results of so transacting were to be is itself just.

(3) looks plausible, but its power to endorse market-generated states of affairs is, while not nil, very weak. Stronger principles may also be available,[6] but (2), Nozick's principle, is certainly too strong.

A Closer Look at Chamberlain

Let us now apply this critique of Nozick's principles to the parable which is supposed to secure (or reveal) our allegiance to them.

Before describing the Chamberlain transaction, Nozick says: "It is not clear how those holding alternative conceptions of distributive justice can reject the entitlement conception of justice in holdings" (p. 160). There follows the Chamberlain story, where we assume that D1 is just, and are then, supposedly, constrained to admit that D2, into which it is converted, must also be just; an admission, according to Nozick, which is tantamount to accepting the entitlement conception. But how much of it must we accept if we endose D2 as just? At most that there is *a* role for the entitlement principle. For what the transaction subverts is the original pattern, not the principle governing it, taken as a principle conjoinable with others to form a total theory of just or legitimate holdings. The example, even if successful, does not defeat the initial assumption that D1 is just. Rather, it exploits that assumption to argue that D2, though it breaks D1's pattern, is also just. The story, if sound, impugns not the original distribution, but the *exclusive* rightness of the principle determining it.

Now Nozick is certainly right to this extent, even if we reject the Chamberlain story: there must be *a* role for entitlement in determining acceptable holdings. For unless the just society forbids gifts, it must allow transfers which do not answer to a patterning principle. This is compatible with placing restraints on the scope of gift, and we shall shortly see why it may be justified in doing so. More generally, assigning a certain role to unregulated transactions in the determination of holdings is compatible with using an egalitarian principle to decide the major distribution of goods and to limit, for example by taxation, how much more or less than what he would get under that principle alone a person may come to have in virtue of transactions which escape its writ. I think socialists do well to concede that an egalitarian principle should not be the only guide to the justice of holdings, or, if it is, then justice should not be the only guide to the moral legitimacy of holdings.[7]

Among the reasons for limiting how much an individual may hold, regardless of how he came to hold it, is to prevent him from acquiring, through his holdings, an unacceptable amount of power over others.[8]

Is the Chamberlain transaction really beneficial (or at worst harmless) to everyone with an interest in it? I shall argue that it threatens to generate a situation in which some have unacceptable amounts of power over others.

The fans "are excited about seeing him play; it is worth the total admission price to them." The idea is that they see him play if and only if they pay, and seeing him play is worth more to them than anything else they can get for twenty-five cents. So it *may* be, but this fails to capture everything in the outcome which is relevant. For once Chamberlain has received the payments he is in a very special position of power in what was previously an egalitarian society. The fans' access to resources may now be prejudiced by the disproportionate access Chamberlain's wealth gives him, and the consequent power over others he now has. *For all Nozick says*, the socialist may claim that this is not a bargain informed people in an egalitarian society will be apt to make: they will refrain from so contracting as to upset the equality they prize. They will be especially averse to doing so because the resulting changes would profoundly affect their children. (This may seem an hysterical projection of the effect of the Chamberlain transaction, but I take it we have to consider the upshot of general performance of transactions of that kind, and then the projection is entirely realistic.)

It is easy to think carelessly about the example. How we feel about people like Chamberlain getting a lot of money *as things are* is a poor index of how people would feel in the imagined situation. Among us the ranks of the rich and the powerful exist, and it can be pleasing, given that they do, when a figure like Chamberlain joins them. Who better and more innocently deserves to be among them? But the case before us is a society of equality in danger of corruption. Reflective people would have to consider not only the joy of watching Chamberlain and its immediate money price but also the fact, which socialists say they would deplore, that their society would be set on the road to class division. In presenting the Chamberlain fable Nozick ignores the commitment people may have to living in a society of a particular kind, and the rhetorical power of the illustration depends on that omission. Later—see p. 254 below—Nozick takes up this point, but he says nothing interesting about it.

Nozick tacitly supposes that a person willing to pay twenty-five cents to watch Wilt play is *ipso facto* a person willing to pay *Wilt* twenty-five cents to watch him play. It is no doubt true that in our society people rarely care who gets the money they forgo to obtain goods. But the tacit supposition is false, and the common unconcern is irrational. Nozick exploits our familiarity with this unconcern. Yet a person might welcome a world in which he and a million others watch Wilt play, at a cost of twenty-five cents to each, and consistently disfavour one in which, in addition, Wilt receives a cool quarter million.

So if a citizen of the D1 society joins with others in paying twenty-five cents to Wilt to watch Wilt play, without thinking about the effect on Wilt's power, then the result may be deemed 'disturbing' in the sense of p. 159. Of course a single person's paying a quarter will make no appreciable difference if the rest are already going to do so. But a convention might evolve not to make such payments, or, more simply, there could be a democratically authorized taxation system which maintains wealth differentials within acceptable limits. Whether Wilt would then still play is a further question on which I shall not comment, except to say that anyone who thinks it obvious he would not misunderstands human nature, or basketball, or both.

In defending the justice of the Chamberlain transaction, Nozick glances at the position of persons not directly party to it: "After someone transfers something to Wilt Chamberlain, third parties *still* have their legitimate shares; *their* shares are not changed." This is false, in one relevant sense. For a person's effective share depends on what he can do with what he has, and that depends not only on how much he has but on what others have and on how what others have is distributed. If it is distributed equally among them he will often be better placed than if some have especially large shares. Third parties, including the as yet unborn, therefore have an interest against the contract, which is not catered for. It is roughly the same interest as the fans have in not making it.

Nozick addresses this issue in a footnote:

> Might not a transfer have instrumental effects on a third party, changing his feasible options? (But what if the two parties to a transfer independently had used their holdings in this fashion?) (p. 162)

He promises further treatment of the problem later, and though he does not say where, he presumably means his section on 'Voluntary Exchange,' which we shall examine at the end of this paper. Here I respond to his parenthetical rhetorical question.

First, there are some upshots of transfers of holdings, some effects on the options of the other parties, which will not occur as effects of the unconcerted use of dispersed holdings by individuals, because they could not, or because they would not use them in that way. The Chamberlain fans, acting independently, would probably be unable to buy a set of houses and leave them unoccupied, with speculative intent, but Chamberlain can. Sometimes, though, a set of fans, acting independently, could indeed bring about effects inimical to the legitimate interests of others, of just the kind one fears Chamberlain might cause. But whoever worries about Chamberlain doing so will probably also be concerned about the case where it results from the independent action of many. Nozick's rhetorical question does not provide those who ask the first one with a case where they need to agree with him.

As an argument about *justice* [9] the Chamberlain story is either question-begging or uncompelling. Nozick asks:

> If the people were entitled to dispose of the resources to which they were entitled (under D1), didn't this include their being entitled to give it to, or exchange it with, Wilt Chamberlain? (p. 161)

If this interrogative is intended as a vivid way of asserting the corresponding indicative, then Nozick is telling us that the rights in shares with which they were vested are violated unless they are allowed to contract as described. If so, he begs the question. For it will be clear that their rights are violated only if the entitlement they received was of the absolute Nozickian sort, and this cannot be assumed. Whatever principles underlie D1 will generate restrictions on the use of what is distributed in accordance with them.[10]

The other way of taking the quoted question is not as an assertion but as an appeal. Nozick is then asking us whether we do not agree that any restrictions which would forbid the Chamberlain transaction must be unjustified. So construed the argument is not question-begging, but it is inconclusive. For considerations which might justify restrictions are not canvassed, such as the fact that the contract may generate inordinate power. It is easy to think that what happens afterwards is that Chamberlain eats lots of chocolate, sees lots of movies and buys lots of subscriptions to expensive socialist journals. But, as I have insisted, we must remember the considerable power he can now exercise over others.[11] In general holdings are not only sources of enjoyment but in certain distributions sources of power. Transfers which look unexceptionable come to seem otherwise when we bring into relief the aspect neglected by bourgeois apologetic.

Turning from justice to *liberty*, is it true that a "socialist society would have to forbid capitalist acts between consenting adults" (p. 163)? Socialism perishes if there are too many such acts, but it does not follow that it must forbid them. In traditional socialist doctrine capitalist action wanes not primarily because it is illegal, but because the impulse behind it atrophies, or, less Utopianly, because other impulses become stronger, or because people believe that capitalistic exchange is unfair. *Such expectation rests on a conception of human nature, and so does its denial.* Nozick has a different conception, for which he does not argue, one that fits many 20th century Americans, which is no reason for concluding it is universally true. The people in his state of nature are intelligible only as well socialized products of a market society. In the contrary socialist conception human beings have and may develop further an unqualified (that is, non-'instrumental') desire for community, an unqualified relish of cooperation, and an unqualified aversion to being on either side of a master/servant relationship. No one should assume without argument, or take it on trust from the socialist tradition, that this conception is sound. But *if* it is sound, there will be no need for incessant invigilation against 'capitalist acts', and Nozick does not *argue* that it is unsound. Hence he has not shown that socialism conflicts with freedom, even if his unargued premise that its citizens will want to perform capitalist acts attracts the assent of the majority of his readers.

How much equality would conflict with liberty in given circumstances depends on how much people would value equality in those circumstances. If life in a co-operative commonwealth appeals to them, they do not have to sacrifice liberty to belong to it.

Is Socialism Morally Permissible?

This banal point relates to the first of Nozick's three 'unrealistic' presuppositions of the moral and practical feasibility of socialism:

(5) "that all will most want to maintain the [socialist] pattern"

(6) "that each can gather enough information about his own actions and the ongoing activities of others to discover which of his actions will upset the pattern"

(7) "that diverse and far-flung persons can coordinate their actions to dovetail into the pattern." (p. 163)

Something like the first presupposition is made by socialists in the light of the idea of human nature which informs their tradition. It is, of course, controversial, but its dismissal as 'unrealistic' contributes nothing to the controversy.

Only something *like* (5) is presupposed, because a socialist need think only that a great majority will have socialist sentiments, not all, especially not in the nascency of socialism. If (5) itself is unrealistic, three possibilities present themselves: very few would lack enthusiasm for socialism; very many would; some intermediate proportion would. What I mean by these magnitudes will emerge immediately.

Consider then the first possibility: there remain a few capitalistically minded persons, meaning by 'a few' that their capitalist acts would not undermine the basic socialist structure. No sane socialist should commit himself to the suppression of capitalist activity on the stated scale. (It might even be desirable to allocate to these capitalists a territory in which they can bargain with and hire one another.)

Suppose, though, that the disposition to perform capitalist acts is strong and widespread, so that 'socialism' [12] is possible only with tyranny. What socialist favours socialism in such circumstances? What socialist denies that there are such circumstances? Certainly Marx insisted it would be folly to attempt an institution of socialism except under the propitious conditions he was confident capitalism would create.[13] A socialist believes propitious conditions are accessible. He need not proclaim the superiority of socialism regardless of circumstances.

Could a socialist society contain an amount of inclination to capitalism of such a size that unless it were coercively checked socialism would be subverted, yet sufficiently small that in socialist judgment socialism, with the required coercion, would still be worthwhile? Marxian socialists believe so, and that does commit them to a prohibition on capitalist acts between consenting adults in certain circumstances, notably those which follow a successful revolution. But why should they flinch from imposing the prohibition? They can defend it by reference to the social good and widened freedom it promotes. Nozick will object that the prohibition violates moral 'side constraints': certain freedoms, for example of contract, ought never to be infringed, whatever the consequences of allowing their exercise may be. We shall look at side constraints in a moment.

But first we must treat presuppositions (6) and (7). Unlike (5), these are red herrings. At most, they are preconditions of realising socialist justice *perfectly*.[14] But justice is not the only virtue of social orders (and it is not even 'the first virtue' of socialism, for most socialists). Even if we identify justice with equality, as socialists, broadly speaking, do, we may tolerate deviations from equality consequent on differential capacity to enjoy the same things, or resulting from the random distribution that arises out of gift, etc. Considerations of privacy, acquired expectations, the moral and economic costs of surveillance, etc. declare against attempting a realization of justice in the high degree that would be possible if (6) and (7) were satisfied. We let justice remain rough, in deference to other values.

Accordingly, socialism tolerates gift-giving, and 'loving behaviour' is not 'forbidden' (p. 167). Gift is possible under a system which limits how much anyone may have and what he may do with it. Relatively well endowed persons will sometimes not be fit recipients of gifts, but we are assuming a socialist psychology whose natural tendency is not to give to him that hath. And the notion that the institutions we are contemplating fetter the expression of love is too multiply bizarre to require comment.

SIDE CONSTRAINTS

Any but the most utopian socialist must be willing under certain conditions to restrict the liberty of some for the sake of others. He thereby flouts what Nozick calls the "moral side constraints" on all human action. Nozick thinks we may never limit one man's freedom in order to enhance the welfare or freedom of very many others, or even of everyone, him included, where we know he will benefit as a result at a future time.[15]

If children are undernourished in our society, we are not allowed to tax millionaires in order to finance a subsidy on the price of milk to poor families, for we would be violating the rights, and the 'dignity' (p. 334) of the millionaires.[16] We cannot appeal that the effective liberty of the men the children will be would be greatly enhanced at little expense to the millionaires' freedom, for Nozick forbids any act which restricts freedom: he does not call for its maximization. (This means that if it were true that certain exercises of freedom would lead to totalitarianism, Nozick would still protect them. Market freedom itself would be sacrificed by Nozick if the only way to preserve it were by limiting it.[17])

If Nozick argues for this position, he does so in the section called 'Why Side Constraints?', which begins as follows:

> Isn't it *irrational* to accept a side constraint C, rather than a view that directs minimizing the violations of C? . . . If nonviolation of C is so important, shouldn't that be the goal? How can a concern for the nonviolation of C lead to the refusal to violate C even when this would prevent other more extensive violations of C? What is the rationale for placing the nonviolation of rights as a side constraint upon action instead of including it solely as a goal of one's actions? [18]
>
> Side constraints upon action reflect the underlying Kantian principle that individuals are ends and not merely means; they may not be sacrificed or used for the achieving of other ends without their consent. Individuals are inviolable. (pp. 30–31).

The second paragraph is lame as a response to the questions of the first, for they obviously reassert themselves: if such sacrifice and violation is so horrendous, why should we not be concerned to minimize its occurrence? There is more appearance of argument [19] at the end of the section:

> Side constraints express the inviolability of other persons. But why may not one violate persons for the greater social good? Individually, we each sometimes choose to undergo some pain or sacrifice for a greater benefit or to avoid a greater harm. . . Why not, *similarly,* hold that some persons have to bear some costs that benefit other persons more, for the sake of the overall social good? But there is no *social entity* with a good that under-

goes some sacrifice for its own good. There are only individual people, different individual people, with their own individual lives. Using one of these people for the benefit of others, uses him and benefits the others. Nothing more. What happens is that something is done to him for the sake of others. Talk of an overall social good covers this up . . . (pp. 32–33)

This passage is hard to construe. In one interpretation what it says is correct but irrelevant, in the other what it says is relevant but wrong, and anyone who is impressed has probably failed to spot the ambiguity. For it is unclear whether Nozick is only arguing *against* one who puts redistribution across lives on a moral par with a man's sacrificing something for his own greater benefit, or arguing *for* the moral impermissibility of redistribution. In other words, is Nozick simply rejecting argument *A*, or is he (also) propounding argument *B*?

A   Since Persons compose a social entity relevantly akin to the
             entity a single person is (*p*),
             redistribution across persons is morally permissible (*q*).
B   Since it is false that *p*, it is false that *q*.

If Nozick is just rejecting *A*, then I accept what he says, but the side constraints remain unjustified. Unless we take him as propounding *B*, there is no case to answer. And then the answer is that the truth of *p* is not a necessary condition of the truth of *q*. A redistributor does not have to believe in a social entity.[20]

Side constraints remain unjustified, and socialists need not apologise for being willing to restrict freedom in order to expand it.

Voluntary Exchange

We now examine Nozick's section on 'Voluntary Exchange,' which I presumed (see pp. 252-3) to be his more extended treatment of the problem of the effect of market transactions on persons not party to them, including the as yet unborn. He allows that agreed exchanges between *A* and *B* may reduce the options of an absent *C*, but he implies that they do not thereby reduce *C*'s freedom. He explicitly says that they do not render involuntary anything *C* does. And since what *C* is forced to do he does involuntarily, it follows that, for Nozick, the actions of *A* and *B*, though reducing *C*'s options, do not have the result that *C* is forced to do something he might not otherwise have done.

The last claim entails a denial of a thesis central to the socialist critique of capitalism, which may usefully be expressed in the terms of Nozick's doctrine of natural rights, without commitment to the truth of the latter.

For Nozick, every man has a natural right not to work for any other man. If one is a slave, then, unless one enslaved oneself (see pp. 248-9 above), one's rights were violated, as they are in slave states, which do not confer on every one as a matter of civil right the rights he enjoys naturally. And natural rights would remain violated if the law permitted slaves to choose for which master they shall labour, as long it forbade them to withhold their services from all masters whatsoever.

One difference between a capitalist state and a slave state is that the natural right not to be subordinate in the manner of a slave is a civil right in liberal capitalism. The law excludes formation of a set of persons legally obliged to work for other persons. That status being forbidden everyone is entitled to work for no one. But the power corresponding to this right [21] is differentially enjoyed. Some *can* live without subordinating themselves, but most cannot. The latter face a structure generated by a history of market transactions in which, it is reasonable to say, they are *forced* to work for some or other person or group. Their natural rights are not matched by corresponding effective powers.

This division between the powerful and the powerless with respect to the alienation of labour power is the heart of the socialist objection to capitalism. The rights Nozick says we have by nature we also have civilly under capitalism, but the corresponding power is widely lacking. The lack is softened in contemporary capitalism because of a hard-won institutionalization of a measure of working class power. In Nozick's capitalism that institutionalization, being coercive, would be forbidden, and the lack would be greater.

But Nozick, in the course of his full reply to the problem of 'third parties,' denies that even the most abject proletarian is forced to work for some capitalist or other. Addressing himself to "market exchanges between workers and owners of capital," he invites us to reflect on the situation of a certain *Z* (so-called because he is at the bottom of the heap in a twenty-six person economy) who is "faced with working [for a capitalist] or starving":

> . . . the choices and actions of all other persons do not add up to providing *Z* with some other option. (He may have various options about what job to take). Does *Z* choose to work voluntarily? . . . *Z* does choose voluntarily if the other individuals *A* through *Y* each acted voluntarily and within their rights. . . A person's choice among differing degrees of unpalatable alternatives is not rendered nonvoluntary by the fact that others voluntarily chose and acted within their rights in a way that did not provide him with a more palatable alternative. . . [Whether other people's option-closing action] makes one's resulting action non-voluntary depends on whether these others had the right to act as they did. (pp. 263–264, 262).

One might think that people of necessity lack the right so to act that someone ends up in *Z*'s position, a view we put forward later. But here we suppose, with Nozick, that all of *A* through *Y* acted as impeccably upright marketeers and therefore did nothing wrong. If so, says Nozick, *Z* is not *forced* to work for a capitalist. If he chooses to, the choice is voluntary.

Nozick is not saying that *Z*, though forced to work *or* starve, is not forced to *work*, since he may choose to starve. Rather he would deny that Z is forced to work or starve, even though Z has no other alternative, and would accept that Z is indeed forced to work, if contrary to what Nozick holds, he is forced to work or starve. For Nozick believes that if Z is forced to do A or B, and A is the only thing it would be reasonable to do, and Z does A for this reason, then Z is forced to do A.[22]

Nozick holds that (8) Z is forced to choose between working and starving only if human actions caused his alternatives to be restricted in this way, and (9) Z is forced so to choose only if the actions bringing about the restriction on his alternatives were illegitimate. Both claims are false, but we need not discuss (8) here.[23] For we are concerned with choice restriction which Nozick himself attributes to the actions of persons, *viz.*, some or all of A through Y. We need therefore only reject his claim that if someone is forced to do something, then someone acted illegitimately: we need refute statement (9) only. Again:

> Other people's actions may place limits on one's available opportunities. Whether this makes one's resulting action non-voluntary depends upon whether these others had the right to act as they did. (p. 262)

But there is no such dependence, as the following pair of examples show.

Suppose farmer F owns a tract of land across which villager V has a right of way. (To still objections Nozick might otherwise have to this statement, imagine that V has the right by virtue of a contract between F and himself). Then if F erects an insurmountable fence around the land, V is forced to use another route, as Nozick will agree, since F, in erecting the fence, acted illegitimately. Now consider farmer G, whose similar tract is regularly traversed by villager W, not as of right, but by dint of G's tolerant nature. But then G erects an insurmountable fence around his land for reasons which, all men of good will would agree, justify him in doing so. According to Nozick, W may not truly say that, like V, he is now forced to use another route. But the examples, though different, do not so contrast as to make that statement false. W is no less forced to change his route than V is. (9) is false even if— what I also deny—(8) is true, and the thesis that Z is forced to place his labour power at the disposal of some or other member of the capitalist class is resoundingly sustained.

CONCLUSION

Nozick's claim about Z is so implausible that it may seem puzzling, coming as it does from an extremely acute thinker.[24] Can it be that he is driven to it because it occupies a strategic place in his defense of libertarian capitalism? How is libertarian capitalism *libertarian* if it erodes the liberty of a large class of people?

Still, we can imagine Nozick granting that Z is forced to work for a capitalist, and attempting to recoup his position as follows: Z is indeed so forced, but since what brings it about that he is is a sequence of legitimate transactions, there is no moral case against his being so forced, no injustice in it. (Cf.(1) and (2), p. 248 above).

This would be less impressive than the original claim. Nozick is in a stronger position—could he but sustain it—when he holds that capitalism does not deprive workers of freedom than if he grants the worker is forced to subordinate himself yet insists that even so his situation, being justly generated, is, however regrettable, unexceptionable from the standpoint of justice. For the original claim, if true, entitles Nozick to say, given his other theses, that capitalism is not only a just but also a free society; while the revised claim makes him say that capitalism is just, but not entirely free. When Z is accurately described capitalism is less attractive, whatever we may say about it from the standpoint of justice.

Turning to that standpoint, and bearing Z in mind, what should we say about Nozick's important thesis (1)? It seems reasonable to add to the constraints on just acquisition a provision that no one may so acquire goods that others suffer severe loss of liberty as a result. We might, that is, *accept* thesis (1) but extend the conditions steps must meet to be just, and thus reject capitalism.[25]

Alternatively, we might grant, in concessive spirit, that there is no transactional injustice (no unjust step) in the generation of Z's position, but *reject* (1), and contend that the generative process must be regulated, at the cost of some injustice, to prevent it issuing in very unjust results. Nozick would invoke side constraints against that, but they lack authority (see pp. 256-7 above).

Whatever option we take—and there are others—it should now be clear that 'libertarian' capitalism sacrifices liberty to capitalism, a truth its advocates are able to deny only because they are prepared to abuse the language of freedom.[26]

NOTES

1. George Plekhanov, *The Development of the Monist View of History*, Moscow, 1956, pp. 94-95 (my emphasis). Plekhanov proceeds to associate himself with another point of view, one which is defended in this paper.

2. Jean-Baptiste Say, *A Treatise on Political Economy*, Philadelphia, 1834, p. liii (my emphasis).

3. And others, such as American liberals, but our concern is with the application of the argument to socialism.

4. *Anarchy, State and Utopia*, New York, 1974, pp. 161-162. All future references to Nozick, except the one in Note 22, are to this book.

5. Nozick does not say that what *disturbs* us undermines the *justice* of the transaction.

6. Some might say this is one of them, but I would disagree:

(4) Whatever arises from a just situation as a result of fully voluntary transactions whose transagents know in advance the probabilities of all significantly different possible outcomes is itself just.

7. I prefer the second formulation, being persuaded that justice, very roughly, *is* equality. (See Christopher Ake, "Justice as Equality," *Philosophy and Public Affairs,* November, 1975).

8. My near-exclusive emphasis on this consideration in the sequel does not mean I think there are no other important ones.

9. Recall the two ways of taking Nozick, distinguished on p. 247 above.

10. Thomas Nagel diagnoses Nozick as above, and this is his rebuttal of Nozick, so diagnosed. See "Libertarianism Without Foundations," *Yale Law Journal,* November, 1975.

11. Once again—see p. 251 above—this assessment will seem hysterical only if we fail to take the Chamberlain transaction as we must for it to pose a serious challenge, namely as an example of something which occurs regularly, or will occur regularly in the future.

12. I add scare-quotes because socialism, properly defined, is incompatible with tyranny; but, contrary to what some socialists seem to think, that is no argument against those who say that the form of economy socialists favour requires tyranny.

13. According to Marx, no socialist revolution will succeed unless "capitalist production has already developed the productive forces of labour in general to a sufficiently high level" (*Theories of Surplus Value,* Volume II, Moscow, 1968, p. 580), failing which "all the old filthy business would necessarily be reproduced" (*German Ideology,* Moscow, 1964, p. 46) in the aftermath of revolution. See sections (6) and (7) of Chapter VII of my forthcoming *Karl Marx's Theory of History,* Oxford and Princeton, 1978.

14. I say "at most" because even this is probably false. Given the truth of (5), people could form a Pattern Maintenance Association and appoint experts to watch over and correct the pattern. With popular willingness to do what the experts said, and a properly sophisticated technology for detecting deviations, (6) and (7) would be unnecessary to pattern maintenance without coercion (unless doing what the experts say counts as a way of coordinating action, in which case (7) is required in the above fantasy, but it is easily satisfied).

15. Qualifications imposed on this statement by the "Lockean Proviso" (pp. 174-183) are not relevant here.

16. " 'But isn't justice to be tempered with compassion?' Not by the guns of the state. When private persons choose to transfer resources to help others, this fits within the entitlement conception of justice" (p. 348). "Fits within" is evasive. The choice "fits" because it is a choice, not because of its content. For Nozick there is no more justice in a millionaire's giving a five dollar bill to a starving child than in his using it to light his cigar.

For subtle comments on Nozick's falsely exclusive and exhaustive distinction between compulsory and voluntary donation, see Nagel, *op. cit.,* pp. 145-146.

17. The hypothesised contingency has been actualised. Market freedom is less than it was, partly because, had the bourgeois state not imposed restrictions on it, its survival would have been jeopardized.

18. *Tertium datur,* but let that pass.

19. Note, though, that what Nozick initially contends against is *violating rights to reduce the violation of rights,* whereas in what follows his target is *violating rights to expand social welfare.* He is unconvincing on both counts, but one who agrees with him about "overall social good" could still press the opening questions of the section.

20. For elaboration, see Nagel (*op. cit.,* pp. 142-143), who takes Nozick to be propounding *B*.

21. The concept of a *power which corresponds to a right* is explicated briefly in my "On Some Criticisms of Historical Materialism," *Proceedings of the Aristotelian Society,* Supp. Vol., 1970, pp. 133-135, and at length in Chapter VIII of the book mentioned in Note 13 above. The basic idea: power *p* corresponds to right *r* if and only if what *X* is *de jure* able to do when he has *r* is what he is *de facto* able to do when he has *p*.

22. See Nozick, "Coercion," in *Philosophy, Science and Method: Essays in*

Honour of Ernest Nagel, New York, 1969, p. 446. I derive the claim formulated above from principle (7) of the "Coercion" essay on the basis of Nozick's commitment to: Z is forced to do A if and only if there is a person P who forces Z to do A. Nozick thinks principle (7) is perhaps only roughly true, but rough truth will do for present purposes.

23. For criticism of (8), see H. Frankfurt, "Coercion and Moral Responsibility," in Honderich (ed.), *Essays on Freedom of Action,* London, 1973, pp. 83-84.

24. Those who have read Nozick will know that this description is not ironical.

25. It is immaterial if this yields what Nozick would call a "gimmicky" reading of (1) (p. 157).

26. I thank Gerald Dworkin, Ted Honderich and Michael Slote for useful comments on a draft of this paper.